EUROPEAN
MASTERPIECES

EUROPEAN
MASTERPIECES

SIX CENTURIES OF PAINTINGS FROM THE NATIONAL GALLERY OF VICTORIA, AUSTRALIA

National Gallery of Victoria

THIS EXHIBITION IS SUPPORTED BY A UNITED STATES GOVERNMENT INDEMNITY

THIS PAGE: *Detail from* Jan Davidsz de Heem (Dutch, 1606–1683/84), *Still Life with Fruit*, *c*.1640–50, oil on canvas, 67.3 x 79.8 cm (26 1/2 x 31 1/2 in.). Felton Bequest 1935. (cat. no. 22)

Published by the National Gallery of Victoria
PO Box 7259
Melbourne VIC 8004
Australia

Printed in Australia

National Library of Australia Cataloguing-in-Publication data

European masterpieces: six centuries of paintings from the National Gallery of Victoria, Australia.

ISBN 0 7241 0206 X

ISBN 0 7241 0205 1 (pbk)

1. National Gallery of Victoria – Exhibitions. 2. Painting, European – Exhibitions. I. National Gallery of Victoria.

759.94

Editing: Dana Rowan
Design: Des Konstantinidis
Word processing: Judy Shelverton
Photography: Helen Skuse and Garry Sommerfeld
Colour separations and printing: The Craftsman Press Pty Ltd

COVER: *Detail from* Pompeo Batoni (Italian, 1708–1787), *Sir Sampson Gideon and an Unidentified Companion*, 1767, oil on canvas, 275.6 x 189.0 cm (108 1/2 x 74 1/2 in.). National Gallery of Victoria; Everard Studley Miller Bequest 1963. (cat. no. 49)

FRONTISPIECE: *Detail from* Edward Haytley (English, active 1740–1761), *The Brockman Family at Beachborough: Temple Pond with Temple in Right Foreground*, *c*.1744–46, oil on canvas, 52.7 x 65.0 cm (20 3/4 x 25 1/2 in.). Everard Studley Miller Bequest 1963. (cat. no. 35)

CONTRIBUTORS

Lisa Beaven	Margaret Legge
Laurie Benson	Jennifer Long
Jane Clark	Mark McDonald
Isobel Crombie	Christopher Marshall
Sonia Dean	David Marshall
Dagmar Eichberger	John Payne
Robert W. Gaston	Ruth Pullin
Vivien Gaston	Susan Russell
Ted Gott	Jason Smith
Frank I. Heckes	Rosemary Stone
Ursula Hoff	Peter Tomory
Alison Inglis	Gerard Vaughan
Jennifer Jones-O'Neill	Carl Villis
Tracey Judd	Kenneth Wach
Cathy Leahy	Irena Zdanowicz

EXHIBITION VENUES AND DATES

Cincinnati Art Museum
27 October 2000 – 14 January 2001

Kimbell Art Museum, Fort Worth
18 March – 26 May 2001

Denver Art Museum
23 June – 9 September 2001

Portland Art Museum
6 October 2001 – 6 January 2002

Air freight sponsored by EVERGREEN AVIATION

CONTENTS

MESSAGES

FROM THE PREMIER OF VICTORIA,
THE HON. STEVE BRACKS

The National Gallery of Victoria is a jewel in the thriving artistic and cultural life of not only Melbourne but also Australia itself. The Victorian Government recognizes this and supports the NGV in many ways. A magnificent new gallery for the NGV's collections of Australian art, The Ian Potter Centre NGV: Australian Art, is being constructed in the heart of the city of Melbourne.

At the same time there is a major redevelopment program being conducted at the NGV's existing premises, with only a short walk along St Kilda Road separating this building from the new gallery of Australian art. These projects are major Government undertakings, and testament to the significance of the NGV to the people of Victoria. The redevelopment has necessitated the temporary closure of the NGV, thus enabling this historic exhibition to take place.

The important old master and modern European paintings in this exhibition are treasured by the Australian public and this is the first time they have travelled as such a large collection from their home in Melbourne. The State of Victoria is privileged to have these significant collections and we are delighted that they are to tour the United States, where they will reach a wide audience and raise awareness of the NGV and of cultural life in Melbourne.

I am sure that the enjoyment these works bring the people of Victoria will be shared by the American public. We will look forward to showing the rest of our collections, and Victoria's rich cultural heritage, to those Americans who visit Australia. You will all be very welcome.

FROM THE PRESIDENT OF THE NGV COUNCIL OF TRUSTEES,
STEVE VIZARD

When the opportunity arose to tour works from the collection of the National Gallery of Victoria to the United States, it was quickly decided that major pictures from the Gallery's holdings of European old masters would have a strong impact on American audiences. When this proposal was first mooted, the interest from American museums was immediate and enthusiastic. On behalf of my fellow Trustees I thank the participating institutions and their sponsors for their cooperation and enthusiasm for this logistically complex and challenging project.

This is the first time that an exhibition of such extraordinary magnitude has left the NGV. The exhibition represents a selection of the most significant European paintings from the oldest and most important collection of old masters in the southern hemisphere. Included are works by major artists from the fourteenth to the twentieth century, including Tintoretto, Claude, Rembrandt, Canaletto, Bonnard, Magritte, Picasso, Balthus and Hockney.

The catalogue for this exhibition draws on the expertise of eminent scholars from Australia and Europe who have lived and worked in Australia and have intimate knowledge of our collection. The Trustees appreciate the work of the Director, Dr Gerard Vaughan, and his staff, and congratulate them on producing this splendid exhibition of the treasures from the European painting collection of the National Gallery of Victoria.

DIRECTORS' FOREWORD

The collections of the National Gallery of Victoria have long been known and admired by scholars and art lovers as the finest holdings of western art in the southern hemisphere. With the support of a generous endowment, the Felton Bequest of 1904, the Melbourne art gallery was for many years able to collect outstanding old and modern master paintings, as well as a broad array of decorative arts, at a level of quality and importance equal to that of the works being acquired by the major American and European museums. It is therefore a great pleasure and privilege to be able to present the finest paintings from this collection in their first major loan exhibition outside Australia. This is likely to be the only time that a wide American audience will have the opportunity to enjoy first-hand one of the great painting collections of the world.

For their generosity in making this exhibition possible we express our appreciation to Dr Gerard Vaughan, Director of the National Gallery of Victoria, and to the Gallery's Trustees. A special word of thanks is also due to Gordon Morrison and his staff, who have coordinated this tour amid the many challenges of a major renovation to the NGV and the reinstallation of its collections.

The transport of an exhibition of this scale across the Pacific is a major undertaking. We are extremely grateful to Evergreen Aviation for its support in shipping these masterpieces to America.

Timothy Rub
Director, Cincinnati Art Museum

Lewis I. Sharp
Director, Denver Art Museum

Timothy Potts
Director, Kimbell Art Museum

John E. Buchanan, Jr
Director, Portland Art Museum

INTRODUCTION

GERARD VAUGHAN

DIRECTOR, NATIONAL GALLERY OF VICTORIA

American visitors to *European Masterpieces: Six Centuries of Paintings from the National Gallery of Victoria, Australia* may be surprised to learn that the National Gallery of Victoria was founded in the then self-governing colony of Victoria in 1861, a decade earlier than the major public art museums established in quick succession in Boston, New York and Philadelphia. The great European masterpieces that belong to the National Gallery in Melbourne represent nearly a century and a half of collecting.[1]

To understand the development of the NGV's collections it is helpful to reflect upon the social, cultural and economic milieu of Melbourne in the nineteenth century. At the end of the century, the city was known throughout the world as 'Marvellous Melbourne'. Certainly (perhaps in common with Chicago, Toronto, or Birmingham in Britain), the almost instant creation of a rich and thriving metropolis, where only decades before there had been nothing more than a tiny frontier settlement, represents one of the great urban phenomena of the century.

The earliest European settlement on the banks of the river Yarra occurred in 1834. Within fifty years, as the result of the discovery of enormously rich goldfields in central Victoria in the early 1850s, a city of more than half a million people had emerged – a city characterized by wide streets and magnificent public and commercial buildings (for a brief moment in 1888, Melbourne boasted one of the tallest buildings in the world: the APA or Australia Building, which, with its twelve storeys and cutting-edge elevator technology, established new standards rivalled only in New York and Chicago).[2] Melbourne's wealthiest inhabitants built for themselves grand Italianate mansions and lived like English gentry. One of the great cities of the British Empire, Melbourne hosted International Exhibitions in 1880 and again in 1888, bringing the attention of the world; these exhibitions, emulating those of London and Paris, came chronologically between Philadelphia's Centennial Exhibition of 1876 and Chicago's great Columbian Exhibition of 1893.[3] The wealth brought by gold produced an astonishing confidence within the fledgling colony, and Melbourne today, despite significant architectural losses, remains one of the world's great Victorian cities.[4]

Melbourne was always intensely cosmopolitan, and its cosmopolitan flavour continues to be one of the city's most attractive characteristics. The discovery of gold in Victoria in the early 1850s coincided with the Californian gold rush, and as a result there was a good deal of traffic across the Pacific Ocean, with diggers from Victoria going on to try their luck in California. It is interesting to recall that one of Melbourne's leading nineteenth-century citizens, Thomas Welton Stanford, was the brother of Leland Stanford, the founder of Stanford University in Palo Alto, California.

The 1850s saw the creation of a government-funded Public Library and University. It is not surprising that very quickly the Trustees of the Public Library (inspired by their energetic and visionary chairman, the Irish-born lawyer Sir Redmond Barry (1813–1880), a Justice of the Supreme Court of Victoria)[5] felt it was essential to create a Museum of Art, which was duly founded in 1861 and renamed the National Gallery of Victoria in 1869. The first collection was predictable, consisting of plaster casts, mainly from the antique; medals, coins and gems; photographs of architectural interest; and many facsimiles of other examples of fine and applied art. Gradually, a small collection of original pictures, almost exclusively contemporary British, was formed.

The documents relating to the creation and development of the National Gallery of Victoria are almost identical in spirit and outlook to those that governed the creation of the new public art museums in New York, Boston and Philadelphia. What all of these museums had in common was a conscious desire to emulate the excitement of London's Great Exhibition of 1851 and the establishment of what was then known as the South Kensington Museum (now the Victoria and Albert Museum), with the collections seen, above all, as an educational resource, and most particularly as an aid to contemporary artisans and manufacturers, with a view to improving the design quality of industrial products. It was

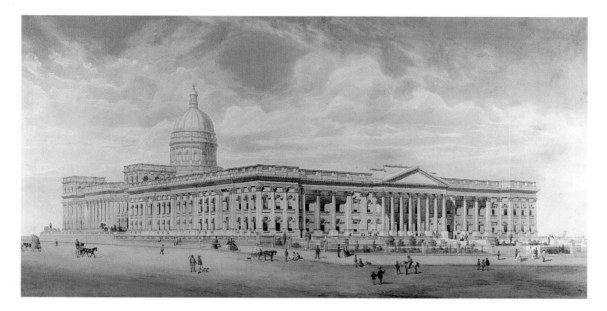

Nicholas Chevalier (Swiss-Russian (active in Australia and England), 1828–1902), *Public Library, Melbourne*, 1860, watercolour, 59.4 x 119.3 cm (23 1/2 x 47 in.). La Trobe Picture Collection, State Library of Victoria. Ideal view of the original home of the NGV; the rear section of the building was not completed as depicted.

only in later decades that these institutions became outstanding fine art galleries, actively collecting old and modern masters. Right at the beginning, the NGV was fortunate to secure the advice of the then Director of the National Gallery, London, Sir Charles Eastlake (1793–1865), who as early as 1864 sent out to Melbourne an interesting group of contemporary pictures.[6]

A crucial development, which continues to affect the collecting policy of the NGV even to this day, was the founding of its own school of art in 1870, and it is true to say that since then – at least until relatively recently – many of the painters and sculptors who have made a significant contribution to the development of Australian art have been graduates of that school. As a result, the NGV has always assumed a responsibility to collect contemporary Australian art, and in this area we possess the best and most comprehensive representation in the country. Indeed, a major new building, The Ian Potter Centre NGV: Australian Art, has been designed to house these collections and will open in late 2001. The present exhibition, however, is dedicated solely to our European pictures.

The Trustees of the National Gallery of Victoria continued to concentrate on acquiring contemporary British art until the turn of the century, and one of the best of these pictures is J. W. Waterhouse's remarkable *Ulysses and the Sirens*, purchased in 1891 (cat. no. 77). But then disaster struck. In the early 1890s the bubble burst and Melbourne entered a decade of severe economic depression. In this context, the outlook for the NGV appeared unpromising.

It is sometimes the case that the most profound events governing the ability of art museums to acquire great works of art are unplanned and come without notice. After a decade of cutbacks and necessarily cautious management, the NGV suddenly encountered a magnificent change of fortune. In his lifetime, the well-known Melbourne man of business Alfred Felton (1831–1904) had enjoyed a modest reputation as a collector of contemporary British and Australian art but his taste was conventional and unremarkable. When he died in 1904, however, Alfred Felton left the sum of £383,000 to be invested as a charitable trust, the income from which was to be divided equally, by the Felton Bequests' Committee, between nominated charitable causes and the NGV 'for the purchase of works of art ancient or modern or antiquities or other works or objects which the said committee may from time to time … select'.[7] Thus, Alfred Felton established the mechanism for the creation of one of the great public picture collections of the twentieth

Charles Nettleton (Australian, 1826–1902), *Interior View of the 1869 Art Exhibition*, 1869, gelatin silver photograph.
La Trobe Picture Collection, State Library of Victoria.

century, and it should be noted that the majority of the pictures in the current exhibition have come to us through the Felton Bequest. Alfred Felton's will is notable for its lack of proscription and for the very broad discretion it allows his Trustees. Of the eighty-eight pictures on display in this exhibition, sixty-one have been provided through the Felton Bequest, with only Waterhouse's *Ulysses and the Sirens* representing the earlier phase of collecting.

In 1905, the NGV's energetic young Director, Bernard Hall, himself a distinguished painter, visited Europe, armed with the first year's income from the Felton Bequest. While his purchases included, for example, a rather conventional mid-nineteenth-century genre scene by Eugène Isabey, he made what was, for Melbourne, an astonishing and radical choice: Camille Pissarro's definitive *Boulevard Montmartre*, 1897 (cat. no. 73), unquestionably one of the artist's most significant works. Ironically, Hall made the purchase not in Paris but in London, from the Grafton Gallery, which had taken a significant exhibition of Impressionist pictures from the Parisian dealer Durand-Ruel. We know from his diaries that Hall made numerous visits to what must have been a sensational event, and one cannot help wishing that he had had more funds at his disposal in that year.

However, the Felton Bequest continued, in the decades to come, to provide highly important French Impressionist and post-Impressionist pictures for Melbourne, including our two Monets – *Vétheuil* of 1879 (acquired in 1937) and *Rough Weather at Étretat* of 1883 (acquired in 1913) – Sisley's *Haystacks at Moret* of 1891 (acquired in 1913), Manet's *The House at Rueil* of 1882 (acquired in 1926) and Cézanne's *The Uphill Road* of 1881 (acquired in 1938) (cat. nos 69, 70, 76, 66, 71).

Throughout the early decades of the twentieth century the NGV, through the Felton Bequest, continued to purchase overtly modern works, both French and British, but also took advantage of the reaction, after the First World War, against Pre-Raphaelite and academic painting of the latter part of the nineteenth century, and the subsequent drop in the value of such works on the international market. Thus, in 1919 Edward Burne-Jones's late Pre-Raphaelite masterpiece *The Garden of Pan*, c.1886–87 (cat. no. 74), was acquired, and Sir John Millais's dramatic and deeply moving *The Rescue*, 1855 (cat. no. 63), followed in 1924. In 1928 the Felton Bequest acquired (the by then unfashionable) Jules Bastien-Lepage's

John Longstaff (Australian, 1862–1941), *Alfred Felton*, *c*.1932, oil on canvas, 136.5 x 92.7 cm (53 3/4 x 36 1/2 in.). National Gallery of Victoria; Felton Bequest 1932.

Potato Gatherers of 1878 (cat. no. 68). Bastien-Lepage had been one of the heroes of the 1880s and his realist/plein-air naturalist style had inspired generations of young artists throughout the world, including students of the Gallery School in Melbourne and of course American artists too.

The early twentieth century also brought with it a revival of interest in seventeenth-, eighteenth- and early-nineteenth-century British art, and the taste of Joseph Duveen (whose art dealing efforts contributed to many great American collections, most notably those formed by Henry Clay Frick, Samuel H. Kress, Andrew Mellon and Henry E. Huntington) was reflected in the acquisition of major portraits by van Dyck (cat. nos 14 and 15), Gainsborough (cat. no. 51), Reynolds (cat. nos 47 and 48), Romney (cat. no. 50) and Ramsay (cat. no. 45); similarly the British romantic landscape was magnificently represented through key pictures by Turner (cat. nos 55 and 56) and Constable (cat. no. 59), which are among the most important and engaging works in the current show.

Above all, however, the Felton Bequest for the first time enabled a major Australian art museum seriously to collect European old masters. The arrival in Melbourne of three Rembrandts (the *Self-Portrait* acquired in 1933 from the collection of the Duke of Portland has recently been deattributed) defined a new seriousness, and works by artists of the Dutch school were complemented by a group of major Italian pictures. Indeed, Melbourne is remarkable not only for its representation of Italian fourteenth- and fifteenth-century paintings (note, in particular, the Sassetta (cat. no. 2) and the Paolo Veneziano (cat. no. 1) in the current exhibition), but also for the depth in which it represents the sixteenth century. Thus, the exhibition contains major works by Perino del Vaga, Prospero Fontana, Tintoretto, and Veronese and his studio (cat. nos 6, 7, 9, 10). The seventeenth century is represented in the collection by major works such as the small but exquisite Claude Lorrain, *River Landscape with Tiburtine Temple at Tivoli*, *c*.1635 (cat. no. 16), and one of Nicolas Poussin's undisputed masterpieces, *The Crossing of the Red Sea*, *c*.1634; the Poussin, the pair to the London National Gallery's *Adoration of the Golden Calf*, regrettably cannot travel, due to its fragile condition.

The NGV is notable for the fact that its collections represent every aspect of European painting, sculpture, drawing, printmaking and decorative art in considerable depth. Our Print Room's holdings

Giambattista Tiepolo (Italian, 1696–1770), *The Banquet of Cleopatra*, c.1743–44, oil on canvas, 248.2 x 357.8 cm (97 3/4 x 141 in.). National Gallery of Victoria; Felton Bequest 1933.

of the work of, for example, Dürer and Rembrandt, are extraordinarily rich, and we have what is arguably the best collection of the watercolours of William Blake after that of the Tate in London. Our greatest European masterpiece is without doubt Tiepolo's *Banquet of Cleopatra*, c.1743–44, acquired in 1765 by Catherine the Great from the collection of the Elector of Saxony but sold from the Hermitage by the Soviet authorities in 1932, at the same time that American collectors such as Andrew Mellon and Joseph E. Widener were making major acquisitions (now in the National Gallery of Art in Washington DC) from the same source. Sadly, due to its size and the fragile condition of its surface, the Tiepolo cannot travel. The eighteenth century in Italy is, however, strongly represented in the current exhibition by significant pictures by Amigoni, Canaletto, Bellotto and Batoni (cat. nos 40, 33, 34, 49).

The Felton Bequest remains active to this day and is still the source through which the NGV acquires its most important works.[8] Although the current exhibition consists only of paintings, the NGV's collections of old master prints and drawings, antiquities, decorative arts and Asian arts, not to mention our Australian collections, including contemporary Aboriginal art, have also found their definitive character through the Felton Bequest. Indeed, Alfred Felton emerges as one of the great art philanthropists of the twentieth century, and the current tour of the United States provides for us an important opportunity to honour his memory. Recognizing the geographical remoteness of Melbourne from Europe, Alfred Felton also empowered the Felton Trustees to retain in Europe a distinguished adviser or advisers, to recommend potential acquisitions to the Trustees and to the Director of the NGV, and to be on hand to negotiate purchases. Sir Kenneth Clark, for example, was an adviser to the Felton Trustees for several years in the 1940s.

It is true to say that the income provided by the Felton Bequest enabled the NGV to collect confidently through much of the twentieth century. Today, however, this income can no longer keep pace with inflation in the international art market, and to compensate we have created an independent NGV Foundation, the endowment of which we work hard to increase. There have been other important bequests too. In 1956 we received the Everard Studley Miller Bequest, which is now spent out but which enabled us over several decades to respond to the wish of the donor that we buy 'portraits of persons of merit in history painted, sculpted or engraved by 1800'.[9] It is for this reason that visitors to the exhibition will see an important group of major portraits, ranging from Nicolas de Largillierre's *Crown Prince Frederick Augustus of Saxony* of 1714–15 to Pompeo Batoni's *Sir Sampson Gideon and an Unidentified Companion* of 1767, and from François-Hubert Drouais's *Madame Sophie de France* of 1763 to Johan Zoffany's *Elizabeth Farren as Hermione* of *c*.1780 (cat. nos 32, 49, 46, 43). Indeed, portraiture is one of the particular strengths of the NGV's collection.

Notwithstanding a certain bias in favour of what might be loosely termed old masters, the NGV worked hard in the second half of the twentieth century to collect contemporary European art. Thus, just a few years after its execution, Balthus's highly important *Nude with Cat* of 1949 (cat. no. 87) entered the collection through the Felton Bequest. Francis Bacon's *Study from the Human Body* (cat. no. 86), from the same year, arrived in 1953. David Hockney's *The Second Marriage* of 1963 (cat. no. 88), acquired through the Contemporary Art Society of London, arrived in 1965. The NGV has always been anxious to represent modern masters of the first half of the twentieth century and thus important works by Magritte, Robert Delaunay, Bonnard and Modigliani (cat. nos 83, 81, 79, 82) were acquired in the 1940s, 1950s, 1960s and 1970s. More recently, Picasso's *Weeping Woman* of 1937 (cat. no. 84) was acquired (in 1986), but the NGV, not surprisingly, is acutely aware of other lacunae in its representation of the modern movement and will continue to work hard to fill them. In the last few decades significant works by, among others, Kiefer, Richter, Clemente and Paladino, have entered the collection, and twentieth-century American painting is represented by Rothko, Frankenthaler, Guston, Krasner, Motherwell and Warhol, whose large *Self-Portrait* of 1986 was acquired in 1987. Jackson Pollock and Jasper Johns are, regrettably, unrepresented, and it is unlikely that funds will permit this gap to be filled.

In late 2001 we will occupy our new building dedicated exclusively to the Australian collections. At the end of 2002 we will return to our refurbished principal building, with the collections displayed in an interior magnificently rebuilt and redesigned by Mario Bellini of Milan. We invite everyone who enjoys the current exhibition to consider a visit to Melbourne, where they will find a fascinating, cosmopolitan city with a rich cultural heritage. The NGV has an ambitious exhibitions program planned for the coming years, and anyone with an interest in Victorian taste and Victorian cities will, we know, enjoy the *Marvellous Melbourne* exhibition, which is scheduled for mid 2004 and will be one of the most ambitious shows we have ever undertaken. To keep abreast of all developments at the National Gallery of Victoria, please visit us at www.ngv.vic.gov.au

Any exhibition on the scale of *European Masterpieces* requires effort and planning. Firstly, I would like to thank the Directors and staff of the four American art museums that are displaying our collection. Their enthusiasm for this show has been a huge encouragement. I would also like to take this opportunity to offer special thanks to those of my colleagues who have worked so hard in conceiving, developing, producing and marketing *European Masterpieces*, in particular: Tony Ellwood, Gordon Morrison, Sonia Dean and Tracey Judd. Thanks must also go to the many individuals at the NGV who, as always, worked to ensure an excellent result: the publications team – Philip Jago, Laurie Benson, Jennie Moloney, Judy Shelverton and Dana Rowan (catalogue editor); Des Konstantinidis in Graphic Design (catalogue designer); Fiona Bennie and Donna Noble in Exhibitions Management; Janine Bofill and her team in Registration; Tom Dixon, John Payne, Catherine Earley, Carl Villis, Eamon O'Toole and Gervais Battour in the Conservation Department; Sue Coffey and Kylie Huang in Public Relations; and Ruth Davidson and her colleagues in the Marketing Division.

I would also like to thank George Wachter, Executive Vice President & Director of Old Master Paintings; Christopher Apostle, Senior Vice President, Old Master Paintings; and Charles Moffett, Executive Vice President of Impressionist & Modern Art, all of Sotheby's, New York, for their generous assistance.

NOTES

1 For the history and development of the National Gallery of Victoria, see L. B. Cox, *The National Gallery of Victoria 1861 to 1968: A Search for a Collection*, Melbourne, 1970; U. Hoff, *The National Gallery of Victoria*, London, 1973; U. Hoff, *European Paintings before 1800 in the National Gallery of Victoria*, 4th edn, Melbourne, 1995; A. Galbally, *The Collections of the National Gallery of Victoria*, Melbourne, 1987; A. Galbally & A. Inglis, *The First Collections: The Public Library and the National Gallery of Victoria in the 1850s and 1860s* (exh. cat.), University of Melbourne Museum of Art, Melbourne, 1992.

2 See P. Goad, *Melbourne Architecture*, Sydney, 1999, p. 54. For the history of the boom style in Marvellous Melbourne, see J. Grant & G. Serle, *The Melbourne Scene 1803–1956*, Melbourne, 1978; G. Davison, *The Rise and Fall of Marvellous Melbourne*, Melbourne, 1978. For the best contemporary source, see the highly detailed A. Sutherland, *Victoria and Its Metropolis: Past and Present*, 2 vols, Melbourne, 1888.

3 For the history of the International Exhibitions held in Melbourne, and the Royal Exhibition Building, see D. Dunstan, *Victorian Icon: The Royal Exhibition Building, Melbourne*, Melbourne, 1996.

4 See A. Briggs, *Victorian Cities*, rev. edn, Harmondsworth, Middlesex, 1968, esp. ch. 7.

5 For Sir Redmond Barry, see Galbally, pp. 9, 14–19, 22–3.

6 See A. Galbally, 'The Painting Collection to 1870', in Galbally & Inglis, pp. 40–61.

7 Alfred Felton, will dated 20 August 1900, cited in D. Lindsay (ed.), *The Felton Bequest: An Historical Record 1904–1959*, Melbourne, 1963, p. 19; see also U. Hoff, *The Felton Bequest, National Gallery of Victoria*, Booklets on the Collection, Melbourne, 1983.

8 Recent acquisitions through the Felton Bequest include: Anselm Kiefer, *Evil Flowers*, 1985–91, acquired 1992; an Egyptian mortuary head covering, 1st–2nd century AD, acquired 1995; *Figure of an Athlete*, *c.*1st century BC, acquired 1997; Jean-Baptiste Regnault, *The Toilet of Venus*, 1815, acquired 1999.

9 For Everard Studley Miller and the history of his bequest, see U. Hoff, 'Portraits Acquired under the Everard Studley Miller Bequest', *Art Bulletin of the National Gallery of Victoria*, vol. II, 1960, pp. 15–20; P. Paffen, 'Everard Studley Miller and His Bequest to the National Gallery of Victoria', *Art Bulletin of Victoria*, no. 35, 1994, pp. 35–44.

NOTE TO THE READER

Measurements are provided in both centimetres and inches, with height preceding width.

Numbers within parentheses, following acquisition details, are National Gallery of Victoria inventory numbers.

Details recorded under *Provenance* represent a summary of the provenance data published in recent NGV collection catalogues (U. Hoff, *European Paintings before 1800 in the National Gallery of Victoria*, 4th edn, Melbourne, 1995; and S. Dean, *European Paintings of the 19th and Early 20th Centuries in the National Gallery of Victoria*, Melbourne, 1995), together with new NGV research. Dates following the identification of an earlier owner of a work are the different dates (e.g. date of inheritance, date recorded in contemporary inventory or other source, or date of exhibition) at which the work has been ascertained to be in that owner's possession.

Apparent discrepancies between the date of purchase by the Felton Bequest or the Everard Studley Miller Bequest recorded under *Provenance*, and the acquisition details recorded with the general details of a work, are due to the fact that the date of purchase often occurs in the year preceding the entry of the work into the NGV collection.

Selected Exhibitions includes significant local and international exhibitions of the past two decades.

No attempt has been made to standardize the orthography or punctuation of quotations from early documents, and the use of *sic* has been avoided.

FOURTEENTH CENTURY TO SIXTEENTH CENTURY

1. PAOLO VENEZIANO
Venetian, active 1333–58, d. *c*.1358–62

The Crucifixion

Unsigned, undated; painted *c*.1349
Tempera and oil on wood panel (arched top)
96.8 x 67.7 cm (38 x 26 3/4 in.)
Felton Bequest 1949 (1966–4)

PROVENANCE

William Graham (1817–1885),
Glasgow, 1884; Baroness Muir
MacKenzie (née Amelia Graham),
London, 1885; Kenneth Augustin
Muir MacKenzie, 1st Baron Muir
MacKenzie of Delvine (1845–1930),
London, 1912, 1930; Mrs Mark
Hambourg (née Dorothea Muir
MacKenzie), 1948; from whom
purchased by Agnew's, London,
1948; from whom acquired by the
Felton Bequest, for the National
Gallery of Victoria, 1948.

SELECTED EXHIBITIONS

San Marco and Venice, National
Gallery of Victoria, Melbourne, 1997,
cat. no. 60.

Paolo Veneziano, arguably the most important and influential Venetian panel painter of the early fourteenth century, introduced to Venetian painting a new impulse towards Byzantinism, which he combined with Western Gothic innovations.[1] While in the Muir-Mackenzie collection, the Melbourne *Crucifixion* was ascribed to Nicoletto Semitecolo (active 1353–70). Van Marle in 1925 rejected this attribution and ascribed the picture to the fourteenth-century Venetian school.[2] When the panel was shown in London in 1930, Fry pointed out the strongly Byzantine features of the composition.[3] Sandberg Vavalà saw the relation of the picture to the *Crucifixion* in the polyptych, dated 1349, in the Oratory of S. Martino, Chioggia,[4] and attributed the panel, together with related compositions, to Master Paolo and his workshop.[5] Variants quoted by Sandberg Vavalà are: the Chioggia *Crucifixion*;[6] the *Crucifixion* in a polyptych formerly at Veglia (now Museo Civico, Trieste);[7] the altarpiece in the Cathedral of Sv. Marija at Arbe, Dalmatia;[8] and the *Crucifixion* panel in a triptych at the Galleria Nazionale, Parma.[9] Fiocco in 1931 stressed in particular the relation of the Melbourne panel to the *Crucifixion* (attributed to Paolo and his workshop) in the polyptych in the Cathedral of Pirano, Istria.[10] He grouped the Pirano *Crucifixion* with other works by Master Paolo of a distinctly Byzantine style, including the altarpiece in the Cathedral of Dignano, Istria, which work he dated to 1323.[11]

Iconographically, the picture in Melbourne indeed shows strongly Byzantine elements. The Virgin fainting in the arms of supporting women, for example – a motif held by some earlier scholars to be of Italian origin[12] – was noted by Lasareff in two Armenian miniatures of the thirteenth century, whence 'it must have passed not only into Byzantium but also into Italy'.[13] The Armenian illuminations also show the crenellated wall in the background, the lamenting angels above the arms of the cross, the hillock, and the cave that are to be seen in the present work.

The round arch above the cross suggests that the Melbourne picture may have formed part of the middle panel of a triptych; this suggestion has also been made in the case of the *Crucifixion* at the National Gallery of Art, Washington DC, by analogy with other triptychs by Paolo.[14] A large *Crucifixion*, generally accepted as by Master Paolo, in the Lee Collection at the Courtauld Institute of Art, London – a work that is 'framed under an arch' and is close to the *Crucifixion* in the central panel of the triptych at Parma – is also assumed to have been part of a triptych.[15]

Sandberg Vavalà's dating of the Chioggia *Crucifixion* to 1349,[16] and her description of the Melbourne picture as 'an elaboration of the Chioggia composition',[17] have provided the basis for the dating given here.

Ursula Hoff

2. SASSETTA

(Stefano di Giovanni di Consolo) Sienese, c.1400–1450

The Burning of a Heretic

Unsigned, undated; painted between 1423 and 1425/26
Tempera and gold leaf on wood panel
24.6 x 38.7 cm (9 3/4 x 15 1/4 in.)
Purchased with the assistance of the Government of Victoria 1976 (E2–1976)

Art history's love affair with 'Sassetta' was stimulated by the mid-nineteenth-century research of Gaetano Milanesi and by the prescient collecting of an American consul in Italy, James Jackson Jarves.[1] Sassetta was almost certainly apprenticed in a Sienese workshop.[2] His first documented commission was an altarpiece contracted by Siena's wool merchants' guild (the Arte della Lana) shortly after July 1423. His large altarpiece *Madonna of the Snow* (Palazzo Pitti, Florence), executed in 1432 for the chapel of S. Bonifacio in Siena cathedral, reveals the impact of the contemporary Florentine masters Masaccio, Fra Angelico and Paolo Uccello. A mature work, the altarpiece commissioned in 1437 for the church of S. Francesco in Borgo Sansepolcro, had the *Virgin and Child Surrounded by Angels* (Musée du Louvre, Paris) as its central panel, and included the exquisite *St Francis in Glory* (Villa i Tatti, Florence) and the captivating *Mystic Marriage of St Francis* (Musée Condé, Chantilly). Critics since Jarves have marvelled at Sassetta's subtlety of emotion and at his poetic sensibility. Pope-Hennessy, not given to exaggeration, credited him with 'a speculative intelligence of an extraordinary kind'.[3]

The Melbourne panel is one of seven predella pictures from the Sassetta altarpiece commissioned by the Arte della Lana in 1423, probably for S. Maria del Carmine,[4] and perhaps completed before June 1425.[5] The pictorial ensemble was to enhance the city's ritual of the feast of Corpus Christi, when the wool guild's members led a procession to S. Maria del Carmine, where mass was celebrated at their altar.[6] Sassetta displays the coat of arms of the guild on the shields and banners held by the soldiers in the Melbourne panel.

Regarding the execution victim's identity, Scapecchi suggests Jan Hus, the Bohemian heretic burned alive before clergy and troops at Konstanz in July 1415. The Carmelites sought to combat Hus's denial of the transubstantiation of the Host,[7] and Hus, and the English reformer John Wycliffe, were condemned again at a Church Council in Siena in 1423–24, with the clergy being 'urged to suppress [the heretics'] disciples'. Perhaps the Arte della Lana perceived a role for itself in this process. Christiansen argues for identifying the victim in this picture as Francesco di Pietro Porcari, burned as a heretic outside Siena's Camollia gate in 1421.[8] Gilbert favours Jerome of Prague, executed in 1415.[9]

The fire is readied by a hunched executioner wearing clogs. The victim, dressed in a dark religious habit, displays composure in his terrible suffering, his lips sealed and his eyes elevated to the heavens. Such atrocities as this public burning were justified in canon law, and orthodox viewers would have taken pleasure in the man's cruel, deserved fate.[10] To the right stands an altar with a decorated frontal, at which a priest elevates the host before the rapturous gaze of a crowd, one member of whom is a cardinal, another a Carmelite monk.[11] The strict unity of the gazes of this congregation contrasts with the lively disunity among the lay and military witnesses to the execution, where a ripple of movement and the natural variety of attention create an impression of realism. The landscape is sombre, suggesting twilight on the outskirts of an unidentified city. A tiny devil(?) figure who hovers on the horizon, approximately above the dying heretic, may be there to receive the man's soul, on account of his unrepented transgressions.

Robert W. Gaston

PROVENANCE

Commissioned by the Arte della Lana, Siena, c.1423, for an altarpiece; altarpiece dismantled c.1777; private collection; from which purchased by a dealer; from whom purchased by Agnew's, London; from whom acquired by the National Gallery of Victoria with the assistance of the Government of Victoria, 1976.

SELECTED EXHIBITIONS

Painting in Renaissance Siena 1420–1500, Metropolitan Museum of Art, New York, 1988–89, cat. no. 1e.

3. SIMON MARMION?
French, *c*.1425–1489

The Virgin and Child

Unsigned, undated; painted *c*.1465–75
Oil on wood panel
38.1 x 28.0 cm (15 x 11 in.)[1]
Felton Bequest 1954 (3079–4)

This solemn depiction of the Virgin and Child within an open loggia is a fine example of the type of Marian painting favoured in the Burgundian Netherlands during the second half of the fifteenth century. Mary is depicted as a beautiful, yet humble, young woman with idealized facial features. She wears a dark blue dress with fur lining, and a matching cloak. Mary has offered the breast to her child for nourishment, a highly symbolic gesture that refers to her role as the most important intercessor for humankind. The white veil that frames her head suggests female chastity or modesty, as it is employed to conceal her open dress. Mary's head is tilted slightly to her left: she has cast down her eyes to gaze at the dainty child who is wrapped in white cloth and rests on her forearms. While looking in this pensive mode at the Christ Child, the Virgin has clasped her hands in prayer, thus paying homage to the divine nature of her son. The agile Christ Child is not, however, concentrating to the same degree on his mother. Instead, his head has turned to the right. He is looking towards another point of reference outside the pictorial space.

In the second half of the fifteenth century, devotional images of the Virgin and Child were frequently produced for the art market as stock images. On request, such paintings could easily be complemented by a custom-made portrait panel.[2] It can be assumed that the present painting was once combined with such a panel, which in all likelihood portrayed a man or a woman in prayer. While the Virgin Mary's face and upper body are depicted frontally, her lower body and the green velvet cushion under her arms have been shifted to the right, thus reorienting her towards the patron's portrait.

A widespread diptych formula, the 'devotional half-length portrait diptych' was already developed by the beginning of the fifteenth century. There exists a second, almost identical, version of the Melbourne painting. This second panel (present whereabouts unknown),[3] reproduces the Melbourne composition with only one major difference: Mary is depicted in front of a cloth of honour, made from expensive gold brocade.[4] The pictures were probably produced in the same workshop but by different hands.

Rogier van der Weyden (*c*.1399–1464) and his workshop were instrumental in popularizing this image of Virgin and Child, which occurs in numerous variations (for example, those at the Musée des Beaux-Arts, Caen,[5] and the Musée des Beaux-Arts, Tournai[6]). Later artists such as Dieric Bouts copied van der Weyden's formula. Hans Memling and the Master of the St Ursula Legend enriched van der Weyden's basic design by introducing a contemporary interior or a landscape as a narrative backdrop to the mother-and-child scene. The artist responsible for the Melbourne panel followed this trend by placing the Virgin within a modern loggia with deep red marble columns and a finely moulded stone parapet. The luminous background is filled with a mountainous landscape, several cityscapes, and meandering waterways that lead the eye of the beholder into the far distance. The colouring and the miniaturistic style of the background architecture recall contemporary book illuminations.[7]

In the case of the Melbourne panel, the artist not only embellished the background of his painting but also added to the furnishing of the interior space. In addition to including the green velvet cushion, he has attempted to ennoble his heavenly vision of the Virgin and Christ Child by including, to the left and the right of the central group, two crystal poles with ornate brass fittings.

Dagmar Eichberger

4. HANS MEMLING
Flemish, *c*.1430–40 – 1494

The Man of Sorrows in the Arms of the Virgin

Unsigned, dated u.l.: *1475*; painted 1475 or 1479[1]
Oil and gold leaf on wood panel
27.4 x 19.9 cm (10 3/4 x 7 3/4 in.)
Felton Bequest 1924 (1335–3)

This small panel painting by Hans Memling confronts the viewer with a devotional image that is both complex and compelling in nature. The picture is dominated by half-length depictions of the sorrowful Virgin and Christ bearing the wounds of the Crucifixion. Mary, who is dressed in the gown of a widow, has wrapped a linen sheet around the tortured body of her son and gently supports him with her arms. Mary's emotionally charged response to the death of Christ calls for compassion, and appeals directly to the beholder.

The artist who invented this composition – whether Memling or a predecessor – has borrowed from several distinct pictorial traditions, merging them into a new and powerful devotional image.

The rendition of the mourning Virgin calls to mind the iconography of the Pietà, a scene in which Mary sits in front of the cross, holding the body of the dead Christ on her knees. The motif of presenting the body of the crucified Christ to the viewer has been borrowed from an early-fifteenth-century image, the so-called Angel Pietà, where Christ is supported by an angel instead of the Virgin. The Melbourne painting, however, does not intend to reproduce the biblical narrative of the Passion of Christ in realistic terms, but aims for a high degree of symbolism and abstraction. Instead of mourning the dead Christ on Mount Golgotha, Mary is placed in a timeless environment, characterized by a sacred gold background. She presents us with an iconic image of her son. The Man of Sorrows bears the marks of the Crucifixion but is nevertheless depicted alive. In a devotional climate that concentrated in particular on the Passion, the Man of Sorrows became one of the most popular icons of the late Middle Ages. This image was connected with a special prayer and with papal indulgences. Drawing on a further iconographic tradition, Memling adds to the central group of figures the instruments of the Passion: the column, the whip, the cross, the purple gown, the nails, the hammer, the lance and the sponge. The various heads and gesturing hands to the left and right of the central scene can be understood as a kind of pictogram referring to additional episodes from the Passion of Christ. These symbols frequently appear in medieval images of the Mass of St Gregory, a popular Eucharistic image that is closely related to the iconography of the Man of Sorrows.

From early-sixteenth-century inventories we learn that a very similar painting, with wings, was kept in a noble residence in the city of Mechelen. Archduchess Margaret of Austria displayed the triptych in her ornate bedroom, together with further depictions of Christ's Passion. In one of these inventories, of 1516, Rogier van der Weyden is named as the author of the central image of the triptych, whereas Hans Memling is associated with the execution of the two angels on the attached wings.[2] Two painted wings by Memling, one showing an angel holding an olive branch and the other depicting an angel holding a sword, have recently been identified as part of this triptych. As these two panels do not match the Melbourne painting in size, it is unlikely that it was the central panel of Margaret of Austria's triptych.[3] It is, however, possible that Memling based his composition on an earlier work by Rogier van der Weyden. There exist several versions of the specific image of the Man of Sorrows found in the Melbourne panel, which is by far the finest surviving example. The panel in the Capilla Real, Museo de los Reyes Catolicos, Granada,[4] and the panel at Darmstadt, have reversed the positioning of the right and the left hand and have added an aureole of clouds at the bottom of the image.

Dagmar Eichberger

PROVENANCE

With a Caen dealer; from whom purchased by Théodore Grivau, Conneré, Sarthe; with Agnew's, London, 1924; from whom acquired by the Felton Bequest, for the National Gallery of Victoria, 1924.

SELECTED EXHIBITIONS

Hans Memling: Vijf eeuwen werkelijkheid en fictie, Groeningemuseum, Bruges, 1994, cat. no. 8.

5.   ITALIAN (FLORENTINE)

Profile Portrait of a Lady

Unsigned, undated
Tempera and oil on wood panel
42.9 x 29.6 cm (17 x 11 3/4 in.)[1]
Felton Bequest 1946 (1541–4)

Facing left, the sitter in this portrait is shown in half-length profile against a dark green background. The woman wears a yellow mitre headdress trimmed with pearls, which is tied over her ears with white bands. Her dress is of a rich red and gold cloth, the neckline lined with fine pearls. She wears several pieces of jewellery, including a narrow gold necklace decorated with pearls, an elaborate brooch of rubies and pearls crowned by a winged cherub, and a smaller brooch, pinned to her headdress.

Simons has argued that the portrait can be dated to the late fifteenth century, on the basis of the jewellery.[2] The brooch pinned to the woman's dress closely resembles one shown in the niche in Domenico Ghirlandaio's portrait of 1488 of Giovanna Tornabuoni, in the Museo Thyssen-Bornemisza, Madrid.[3] The figurative elements in both brooches – the winged cherub in one, a dragon in the other – are indicative of a level of skill not displayed by goldsmiths before the 1470s. Related jewellery is found in paintings by Botticelli (for example, the Graces in his *Primavera*, c.1484 (Galleria degli Uffizi, Florence), wear brooches and pendants composed of enamelled gold leaves set with pearls and precious stones) and in works by the Pollaiuolo brothers. The sculptural quality of the brooch in the Melbourne portrait is like that of the jewellery in Antonio Pollaiuolo's profile portrait of 1475 at the Uffizi,[4] while the shimmering, luminous pearls on the headdress and at the neckline are similar to the jewels in Piero Pollaiuolo's profile portrait of a young woman at the Metropolitan Museum of Art, New York.[5] The mitre headdress, on the other hand, was fashionable around 1430–50. Simons argues that the outmoded hairstyle may have been intended to suggest the woman's 'rich, exceptional status', or else the panel was painted some years after her marriage, and the artist deliberately represented her with a hairstyle fashionable at that earlier time.[6]

Simons is concerned with establishing the links between Florentine female profile portraits and contemporary marriage practices. She argues that the rich costumes and precious jewellery depicted would have formed part of the sitters' dowries, since weddings were occasions when women were allowed some freedom from strict sumptuary laws, and that such portraits were painted either at the time of a woman's marriage or shortly after.[7] The profile portrait was well suited to the display of women as static, decorative possessions, exposed to the male gaze, so that the female sitter became 'a framed object of palatial display'.[8]

Yet in one of the few cases where the sitter can be securely identified, Ghirlandaio's portrait of Giovanna Tornabuoni, an inscription within the work indicates that the portrait was executed posthumously, probably in the year Giovanna died, 1488, four years after her wedding. Hatfield, in his study of earlier fifteenth-century male profile portraits, found a number to be posthumous, among them Botticelli's portrait of Giuliano de' Medici, 1478 (National Gallery of Art, Washington DC), which exists in a number of versions and includes a turtle dove, a symbol of bereavement.[9] On the basis of these examples, Hatfield suggested that the profile format was sometimes used as a schema for representing the deceased.[10] It is possible, therefore, that the Melbourne portrait was made posthumously, in which case the cherub of the brooch setting may allude to the death of the sitter.[11] This hypothesis might explain the greater maturity of this woman compared with other such sitters, as well as her old-fashioned hairstyle.

A range of attributions have been suggested for the portrait,[12] among them Francesco di Giorgio, Piero Pollaiuolo, and the school of Verrocchio (the last on the basis of the depiction of the hair).[13] Although Ettlinger in his study of the Pollaiulo brothers rejected the attribution to them of a number of female profile portraits,[14] the jewellery in the Melbourne painting perhaps suggests an artist associated with them.

Lisa Beaven

PROVENANCE

Alexander Barker, 1858; Sir Francis Cook (1817–1901), Doughty House, Richmond, Surrey, 1873; Sir Frederick Cook, 1902; Sir Herbert Cook (1868–1939), Doughty House, 1928; with Agnew's, London, 1946; from whom acquired by the Felton Bequest, for the National Gallery of Victoria, 1946.

6. PERINO DEL VAGA
(Pietro di Giovanni Buonaccorsi)
Florentine (active in Rome and Genoa), 1501–1547

The Holy Family

Unsigned, undated; painted *c*.1545–46
Oil on wood panel
101.0 x 74.4 cm (39 3/4 x 29 1/4 in.)
Felton Bequest 1966 (1666–5)

According to Vasari, Perino, whose mother died of plague when he was two months old, was placed with the Florentine candle painter Andrea di Piero di Antonio del Piccino, but acquired good drawing skills from Domenico Ghirlandaio's son Ridolfo (1483–1561).[1] Perino drew from Michelangelo's cartoon for the *Battle of Cascina*, and subsequently accompanied the painter 'il Vaga' (whose name he adopted) to Rome, there studying classical and contemporary art. Joining Raphael's workshop *c*.1518, Perino assisted with the Vatican Logge decoration for Leo X. Perino's most significant later commissions were his frescos in the Palazzo Doria, Genoa (which were begun in 1528, after the sack of Rome),[2] his decorations for the Sala Regia in the Vatican Palace (1542–45)[3] and those for the Sala Paolina in the apartment of Paul III at Castel Sant'Angelo, Rome (1545–47).[4]

The *Holy Family* exhibits the hallmarks of Perino's mature style: a refined, classicizing and graceful elegance inherited from Raphael and his collaborators, blended with a taste for difficulty derived from Michelangelo. The shallow space, generating in the devout observer an impression of intimate proximity to the sacred figures, is characteristic of the small devotional picture: a close-up that replaces but still recalls the full narrative setting of a New Testament scene.

Signs of pouncing (dusting charcoal through pinpricks in a cartoon, so as to mark on the prepared ground the outlines of the composition) and underdrawing are clearly visible. Infrared examination has revealed astonishingly detailed pouncing on the gesso ground.[5] Virtually every nuance of line, fold and shadow in the figures, costumes and background drapery is mapped out to guide the painter.

The Madonna's drapery is a formidable structure, ranging from complex folds in the upper parts to broader passages in the foreground. Her gown's left sleeve is articulated in the exquisite detail that Raphael bestowed on the left sleeves in his Roman portraits, in response to quattrocento initiatives. The sleeve becomes a masterly demonstration of draughtsmanship and modelling, a technical problem solved with bravura. A robust Michelangelesque Christ Child stretches his arm towards his mother's neck, where his thumb and forefinger press against her flesh the diaphanous veil suspended from her hair. The child's slightly parted lips mirror those of the Madonna, whose emotional state hovers between maternal pleasure and foreknowledge of grief. The mood is tender, challenged only by the Christ Child's dynamism, an irruption of infantile energy gently contained by the Madonna's large, sure hands. Her inward gaze just evades that of her child, her iris obscured by the long, dark eyelashes that complete her Venus-like elegance. Her coiffure, neat but with a hint of disorder, signifies the 'careless beauty' that Roman lyric poets attributed to Venus. An adoring Joseph hovers in the background, as befits his marginal role as parent. His artisan's hands, strong nose and balding cranium are selectively highlighted, contrasting with the deep shadows that mask his eyes.

Estimates of the dating for this panel, a contemporary copy of which survives at the Palazzo Spada, Rome,[6] range from *c*.1534 to *c*.1545–46.[7] Comparable paintings by Perino or his workshop (at the Musée Condé, Chantilly,[8] and in the Collections of the Prince of Liechtenstein, Vaduz[9]) have been dated *c*.1539–40 and 1541 respectively; the late Roman years seem preferable for the Melbourne picture.[10]

Robert W. Gaston

PROVENANCE

With Hazlitt Gallery, London, 1966; from whom acquired by the Felton Bequest, for the National Gallery of Victoria, 1966.

SELECTED EXHIBITIONS

Rubens and the Italian Renaissance, Australian National Gallery, Canberra, National Gallery of Victoria, Melbourne, 1992, cat. no. 7.

7. PROSPERO FONTANA
(Prospero di Silvio Fontana) Bolognese, 1509/10–1597

Holy Family with St Jerome, a Female Martyr and the Infant St John

Signed l.r.: *PROSPER. FO[NT]ANEUS.*, undated; painted *c*.1552–55
Oil on wood panel
102.2 x 82.8 cm (40 1/4 x 32 1/2 in.)
Felton Bequest 1961 (839–5)

Vasari had little to say about Prospero Fontana,[1] whose high standing in Bologna was established by the seventeenth-century scholar Malvasia.[2] Prospero taught Lodovico and Agostino Carracci, but suffered the neglect accorded to artists whose students surpass them. He studied with the Raphaelesque painter Innocenzo da Imola, assisted Perino del Vaga on the frescos of the Palazzo Doria, Genoa, in 1528[3] and worked with Taddeo Zuccaro on the fresco cycle at the Villa Giulia (of Pope Julius III) at Rome between 1553 and 1555, under Vasari's direction.[4] Fontana also worked with Francesco Primaticcio at Fontainebleau *c*.1560, and with Vasari on the decorations for the wedding of Francesco de' Medici in Florence in 1565; in the same year Fontana was admitted to Florence's Accademia del Disegno. Vasari, an unconfessed eclectic, acquired some of Fontana's style through their prolonged association.[5]

This picture is a vibrant *sacra conversazione*, an imaginative vision of the Holy Family and three additional saints attending the Christ Child, who – in keeping with Mannerist taste for the difficult pose – reclines precariously on the Madonna's lap. The setting suggests a throne room, but beyond the green curtain at the upper left, and the martyr peeking in at the top right, a landscape extends the picture's space. The Madonna's sewing basket in the foreground, on which the infant St John the Baptist leans his reed cross, links the image with medieval legends of the Holy Family's life in Egypt, where Mary worked as a seamstress and Joseph as a carpenter.[6] Albrecht Dürer's woodcut *The Holy Family in Egypt*, *c*.1502,[7] disseminated via Marcantonio Raimondi's copy,[8] inspired Correggio, whose *Madonna of the Basket*, 1525 (National Gallery, London),[9] directly influenced Fontana. Correggio's *Madonna of St Jerome* (Galleria Nazionale, Parma)[10] also determined the placement of the vigorous St Jerome at the left of Fontana's picture. But the motif of his hand emerging from his cloak to steady the crucifix held before his eyes derives from works by Vasari and Parmigianino.

Responding to an iconographic tradition stemming from Leonardo and Raphael, and mediated through Correggio and Parmigianino, the figures exhibit in their faces and gestures subtle physical and psychological pleasure – an attentive religious desire satisfied by proximity to the sacred bodies of Mary and her son.[11] Fontana exquisitely represents the textures and colours of hair: from brown, silver and white, in the beards of Joseph and Jerome, to the palest gold of the hair of St John. St John is a pale-skinned, gentle little creature reminiscent of Raphael's child Baptists; he has full lips, with an underbite, his face an elegant curve from his hairline to the tip of his nose. To counteract the strong diagonal of the Christ Child's body, reasserted in St John's reed cross and the shears, Fontana suspends a translucent veil alongside the Madonna's face, aligning this veil with the golden cloth that spills from under Christ's body. Infrared imaging of the panel reveals 'firm and economical' underdrawing on the gesso ground, and the rather thickly applied brilliant glazes in the draperies endow the picture with a remarkable luminosity.[12]

The pairing of elderly men, of women and of children in this painting evokes issues of gender roles and the sociology of the family that may disclose contemporary assumptions about the proper division of child-rearing.

Robert W. Gaston

PROVENANCE

Earl of Feversham, Duncombe Park, Helmsley, Yorkshire, 1812; Earl of Feversham, 1879; with Colnaghi, London, 1960; from whom purchased by W. R. H. Jeudwine, London; from whom acquired by the Felton Bequest, for the National Gallery of Victoria, 1961.

SELECTED EXHIBITIONS

Rubens and the Italian Renaissance, Australian National Gallery, Canberra, National Gallery of Victoria, Melbourne, 1992, cat. no. 9.

PROSPER.FONTANEVS.

31

8. ANTONIS MOR
(Antonio Moro) Dutch, *c*.1516–20 – *c*.1576

Portrait of a Lady

Unsigned, undated; painted between 1555 and 1560
Oil on wood panel
107.0 x 72.1 cm (42 1/4 x 28 1/2 in.)
Felton Bequest 1948 (1823–4)

Antonis Mor's reputation as an artist rests solely on his portraits. Because of his facility as a painter, evident in the *Portrait of a Lady*, Mor enjoyed a highly successful career from the mid to the late sixteenth century.[1] He developed his inimitable manner of portraiture by tailoring his Dutch training and Italian influences to suit the taste of his Spanish patrons, who were his strongest supporters.[2] Understanding the pre-eminence of Mor's Spanish patrons is critical to understanding his style of portraiture. Although Mor spent only a little time in Spain (*c*.1550–53), he is commonly regarded as a painter of the Spanish court. This is because the Spanish Hapsburgs ruled almost everywhere he worked. Mor's principal patron was Philip II, and Mor was still called 'Philip's painter' in 1573, long after he had left Spain, as he continued to produce portraits of the Hapsburgs.[3]

The *Portrait of a Lady* provides an ideal opportunity to appreciate Mor's skill and aims as a portraitist. The woman stands in three-quarter profile, looking directly at the viewer. Her face and hands are highlighted and in her right hand she supports a gold chain belt tied around her waist.[4] Set against a carefully modulated neutral background, which underscores her attentive seriousness, she appears immovable. Mor deploys his technical skill to great effect in defining the status of the sitter through the elegance of her dress but does not draw attention to the painting process. His approach to painting might be considered 'subversive', because he allows his skill to carry the portrait to an extraordinary level of realism while rendering invisible the degree of work involved in achieving this appearance. The art of painting is wholly absorbed by the need to present sitters in a way that brings them to life, and to establish their personalities. Details such as the veins on the woman's temple lull the viewer into unquestioningly accepting the verisimilitude, and hence the authority, of the portrait. Mor's portraits are nothing if not authoritative and this quality guaranteed his continued success and struck a chord with his Spanish patrons, who also informed the taste for portraits among their subjects in Spain and the Low Countries.[5]

The physical state of the portrait gives some indication of how Mor achieved his seamless effects. On the face and hands there are areas of diagonal striations. They appear because the painting has been slightly abraded and also because Mor applied such thin, milky layers over the white priming. Applying thin flesh-tones and building successive layers gives the painting a translucency that denies evidence of brushstrokes.

The identity of this sitter is unknown. In the nineteenth century she was thought to represent Mary I of England (1516–1558). There is, however, no similarity between this sitter's features and those of Mary in Mor's portrait of 1554 at the Prado, Madrid,[6] and the attire in the Melbourne portrait is inappropriate for a monarch. Through his connections Mor had many opportunities to portray members of the upper classes, and men and women attached to the Hapsburg court. The sitter in the present work might be the wife of a wealthy courtier or merchant. The garments she wears are southern Netherlandish and the portrait can be dated to 1555–60, the time during which Mor was resident in Brussels and Utrecht. There are relatively few works by the artist from this period, so the Melbourne portrait is important for understanding Mor's style and clientele. During his career Mor was bound by the demands of his clients but his freedom came from the style of portraiture that he defined and that remained dominant in Spain and her territories until well after his death. From beneath his contrived and highly finished technique emerges his ability to capture the essence of the sitter and transcend the constrictions of narrative detail.

Mark McDonald

9. JACOPO TINTORETTO
(Jacopo Robusti) Venetian, 1519–1594

Doge Pietro Loredano

Unsigned, undated; painted between 1567 and 1570
Oil on canvas
109.5 x 93.0 cm (43 x 36 1/2 in.)
Felton Bequest 1928 (3677–3)

Sometime between 1567 and 1570, Jacopo Tintoretto stood in front of Doge Pietro Loredano (1482–1570) and began to draw, with a brush loaded with lead white, directly onto a canvas prepared with a dark, reddish-brown ground layer. Tintoretto was nearing fifty, his career as a painter was well established, and he had taken up the office of court painter, allowing him to paint the portraits of the Venetian doges, in 1559. Pietro Loredano was in his mid eighties and, though he had just assumed the office of doge (in 1567), was feeling the weight of responsibility in a period when the power and influence of the Venetian state appeared to be unravelling. Tintoretto had taken over from Titian the role of painter of the ducal portraits. The older Venetian painter was by this time well past seventy years of age.

The outcome of the encounter between Tintoretto and the doge is most likely the painting that is now in the collection of the National Gallery of Victoria. *Doge Pietro Loredano* is a portrait of a vulnerable old man, in a position of tremendous power, painted by a middle-aged artist – an artist who is confident in his means of expression, and now taken up with the influential role of painter to the court, but who is, nonetheless, respectful of and perhaps deferential to the old painter who had been there before and whom he much admired.

The present portrait was worked up from an initial rendition of the sitter in a formal posture. Tintoretto began by depicting the doge with an upright, regal stance, a slight turning away of the head, the neck vertical – all reflecting the conventions for these portraits. But the more the artist studied the subject, the more he altered the painting, changing the neckline to bring the head more into the shoulders, lifting the waistline to increase the sense of age. An X-radiograph made in 1987 gives evidence of these developments and it is the reworking of the essential features of the posture, the redistribution of the body mass, the revealing of the old man within the powerful figure, which direct our attention to Tintoretto's achievement.[1] It is likely this painting was not the work intended to satisfy the artist's portrait commission. Tintoretto was most probably putting together a 'reference', which needed to carry the likeness of the sitter and the essential elements of the portrait, in order that he or studio assistants, or both, could produce a final formal portrait to meet the commission and could subsequently make further versions of the picture. In the end, at least two paintings were derived from this initial version. One, which took its place in the Hall of the Great Council in the Doge's Palace, was destroyed by fire in 1577. The other hangs in the Kimbell Art Museum in Fort Worth, Texas.[2]

We can only speculate about how long the painting process took: probably not long – perhaps only one sitting. For use in the studio, the painting was most likely temporarily stretched onto a simple loom and may have remained there for years. It would not at the time have necessarily been regarded as a finished portrait; indeed it is perhaps only to a modern audience that it reads as complete. It provides, however, a rare insight into the working method of a great painter and is a marvellous example of the power of paint to communicate a complex reflection of reality.

John Payne

10. PAOLO VERONESE (Paolo Caliari) AND STUDIO
Veronese (active in Venice), 1528–1588

Nobleman between Active and Contemplative Life

Unsigned, undated
Oil on canvas
134.0 x 204.5 cm (52 3/4 x 80 1/2 in.)
Felton Bequest 1947 (1707–4)

An intelligent, inventive artist, and not just a mindless 'decorator', Paolo Veronese first acquired the style of his master, Antonio Badile.[1] Moving to Venice in the early 1550s, Veronese integrated the technical audacity and the sensuality of central Italian Mannerism with the weighty figures and chromatic brilliance of Titian. A sharp observer of social customs, gorgeous clothing and decorous behaviour, but given to experimenting with the limits of what was appropriate in religious iconography, Veronese came to the attention of the Inquisition in 1573.[2] Talking his way out of trouble, he continued producing paintings of notable originality, although his assistants were frequently engaged in the late commissions.

This work has survived on the margins of Veronese's oeuvre since being catalogued in the Cook collection at Richmond in 1913 as 'School of Veronese'.[3] Berenson included the picture in his 1936 list as an autograph later work.[4] The painting was included in Pignatti's 1976 works catalogue under attributed works,[5] and was omitted from Pedrocco's complete catalogues of 1991[6] and 1995.[7]

The subject matter has proved elusive. Several figures are in sixteenth-century dress, and the architecture is a mixture of classicizing and contemporary. The semi-nude female to the right, who gestures towards the seated man, is accompanied by a winged, nude child, who also gestures spiritedly. She may be Venus, and the putto with her, Cupid, but he has no bow, quiver of arrows, or blindfold. The three winged, nude children in the left foreground seem to be putti or *amorini*. All seem related somehow to the imperfect cube on which rests the right foot of the woman at the left. The reclining, somnolent child in front, who perhaps plays with his genitals, touches the cube with both feet.

Tietze-Conrat suggested that the subject relates both to the Choice of Hercules and to the Judgement of Paris. Minerva, Juno and Venus were the three nude goddesses exposed to the visual judgement of Paris. Tietze-Conrat identified the clothed woman at the far left as Minerva and the other as Juno, personifying respectively Contemplative Life and Active Life.[8] The square block often symbolizes Steadfastness (*stabilitas*),[9] but sometimes Wisdom, or Virtue,[10] and would therefore belong with Minerva.

The well-dressed young man reads a folio-sized book. Juno, protector of women and chaste marriage, extends towards him a tiara, her attribute as the queen of heaven. Here the iconography leans towards the Choice of Hercules, between Vice and Virtue. The nobleman, in his reflective consciousness perhaps aware of the competing moral forces and temptations of the senses, concentrates on his learning, safe from idle pursuits and the pleasures of love. These are represented vividly by the child who appears to be fondling his genitals. This figure, and the putto with Venus, may be adapted from a painting of *Charity* (Musée du Louvre, Paris) by a Fontainebleau School artist, a work engraved by Marten Peeters of Antwerp no later than 1565.[11] Veronese was interested in prints and they are therefore not an unlikely source of inspiration. The *Charity*'s artist drew on Andrea del Sarto's *Charity* (Musée du Louvre, Paris) painted for Francis I,[12] where the eroticized child may signify the self-love surpassed by Charity's love of one's neighbour (*amor proximi*). Michelangelo's drawing of a *Children's Bacchanal* (Royal Library, Windsor), subsequently engraved, includes a sleeping child in a pose similar to that in Andrea's painting and perhaps representing the children's sexuality.[13] In the Veronese, however, the implication is that learning and wisdom, if they are attended to, should displace the pleasures of the senses. Or perhaps that an equilibrium between the two forces should be present in the perfect life.[14]

Robert W. Gaston

PROVENANCE

Sir Francis Cook (1817–1901), Doughty House, Richmond, Surrey; Cook family, Doughty House, 1913; Sir Herbert Cook (1868–1939), Doughty House, 1932; with Agnew's, London, 1946; from whom acquired by the Felton Bequest, for the National Gallery of Victoria, 1946.

TECHNICAL NOTE

The picture is patently unfinished and there are several visible pentimenti, indicating, among other adjustments, the change in profile of the woman at the far left, and the lowering, from the waistline to the hips, of the garment of the woman to the right, whose right leg should be her left. A technical examination by John Payne at the National Gallery of Victoria discovered remarkable inconsistency in the brushwork of the yellow garments of the falconer and groom at the right, and found that the field of colour of the background was originally blue (a mixture of expensive azurite with lead white) but now, 'owing to accumulated layers of discoloured varnish and extensive deteriorated retouching',[15] is 'pale khaki in colour'.[16] Payne identifies 'a sense of struggle with the detailing of the work', but leaves open the question of whose responsibility that was, the master's or his assistants'.[17] He concludes: 'The complexity in the development of the image precludes notions of it being a copy or a simple pastiche'.[18] Thoughtful research by Brown on the means by which 'replication' was achieved in Veronese's studio, through his collaboration with assistants,[19] could be extended to the present picture.

11. SEBASTIAEN VRANCX
Flemish, 1573–1647

The Crossing of the Red Sea

Signed l.r.: *S. Vrancx. fe*, undated; painted *c*.1597–1600
Oil on canvas
116.0 x 183.0 cm (45 3/4 x 72 in.)
Purchased through The Art Foundation of Victoria with the assistance
of the National Australia Bank Limited, Founder Benefactor, 1989 (E1–1989)

Born in Antwerp, an almost exact contemporary of Rubens, Sebastiaen Vrancx probably trained with Adam van Noort, subsequently becoming a free master in the painters' guild of Antwerp. He was dean of the guild 1612–13. Vrancx was also a rhetorician and wrote poems and stage plays. Early in his career he belonged to the Antwerp militia, and military subjects account for about half his oeuvre. He is best known as a painter of battle scenes, although his work included landscapes, domestic and church interiors, allegorical scenes, and history paintings. In the late 1590s Vrancx travelled to Italy, perhaps to capitalize on the current vogue that Northern landscape artists were enjoying in Rome, and the *Crossing of the Red Sea*, dated by Vander Auwera to *c*.1597–1600, was painted during this three-year visit.[1] The Melbourne picture was probably commissioned by a wealthy Italian patron with a taste for the Netherlandish style best epitomized by the works of Jan 'Velvet' Brueghel and Paul Bril. In the *Crossing of the Red Sea*, Vrancx is clearly indebted to both these masters, in the large number of small, detailed figures engaged in their various activities, and in the fantastic, decorative qualities of the landscape. Yet in the dynamism of horses and riders the Italian influence of Antonio Tempesta (1555–1630), famous for his hunting and battle scenes, can also be detected.[2]

The Old Testament book of Exodus tells how the Jews, under Moses' leadership, journeyed out of captivity in Egypt to the Promised Land. God guided them with a pillar of cloud during the day and a pillar of fire at night. When they reached the Red Sea, Moses, instructed by God, parted the waters, and the Israelites marched safely across the sea bed. But when the pursuing Egyptian army followed, the waters returned, drowning them. The theme had great significance in the Counter-Reformation period, when the basic tenets of Roman Catholic faith were being restated in the face of Protestant reform. The biblical event was associated not only with Christian baptism but with the punishment of heretics, symbolized by the death of Pharaoh and the destruction of his armies. The painting abounds with distracting and entertaining details – for instance at the lower right, where a drowning Egyptian, his head submerged, is about to be given the coup de grâce by an armed Israelite hurling a rock from the shore. Yet this detail also heightens the notion of punishment.

The theme of heresy is emphasized by the depiction of members of Pharaoh's army as Germans, wearing old-fashioned red uniforms slashed with black, and as Turks, wearing turbans and carrying a banner with the star and crescent moon. Respectively, these two groups represent Protestantism and Islam, the two most prevalent heresies threatening the Church of Rome. Moses, distinguished by the rays of light issuing from his forehead, is placed at the centre of the picture, accompanied by Aaron the priest, who reminds us of Rome's sole authority to dispense the sacraments, of which baptism promised new life, symbolized by the Israelites' new-found freedom. Moses prefigured Christ, a connection Vrancx makes clear by situating Moses below a Holy Family–like group. To the right are a young woman kneeling in thanksgiving, and an older woman holding a swaddled infant; both figures reinforce this New Testament prefiguration. These different groupings form the apex and base of a pyramid at the very centre of the painting. Their significance is clearly indicated by the vertical line Vrancx creates from the pillar of cloud at the upper centre, through the tree trunk, to the group below. Vrancx, however, has successfully synthesized the symbolic aspects of his composition with a delightful sense of actuality.

Susan Russell

PROVENANCE

Private collection, Germany; sale, Christie's, London, 11 December 1987, lot 35; with Chaucer Fine Arts, London, 1988, 1989; from whom acquired by the National Gallery of Victoria 1989.

SELECTED EXHIBITIONS

Eau, mythe et symbole dans la peinture occidentale, Shimane Prefectural Museum of Art, Shimane, Museum of Modern Art, Kamakura, 1999, cat. no. 18.

SEVENTEENTH CENTURY

12. EL GRECO
(Domenikos Theotokopoulos) Greek/Spanish, c.1541–1614

Portrait of a Cardinal

Unsigned, undated; painted c.1600–05
Oil on canvas
57.0 x 46.0 cm (22 1/2 x 18 in.)
Felton Bequest 1950 (2253–4)

In his biographical *Lives of the Eminent Spanish Painters and Sculptors* (1724), Palomino observed that El Greco 'was without question a superior portrait painter'.[1] Palomino's assessment holds true and El Greco's portraits are counted among his most remarkable achievements. Painted around 1600–05, the National Gallery of Victoria's portrait corresponds typologically with a number of other portraits from the same period and exemplifies El Greco's unique approach to the genre.

As revealed by an early photograph, sometime after 1908 the portrait was severely cut down.[2] The figure originally stood before a desk, with a quill in his right hand. It is not known why the painting was reduced, but the head and probably the mantle, the most accomplished passages, were painted by El Greco and compare well with other autograph portraits from the same period.[3] The other parts were probably painted by an assistant. After 1600 there was a sharp increase in the number of portraits El Greco painted, a fact that raises questions about the organization of his studio and the degree to which assistants contributed to his paintings.[4] Little is known about his assistants, except for his son, Jorge Manuel, who became the most important.[5]

The identity of the sitter for the Melbourne portrait is not known. The name of St Bonaventure has been suggested but the portrait probably represents a contemporary of El Greco, an ecclesiastic from Toledo[6] (the title *Portrait of a Cardinal* may require further examination, since the sitter's costume calls this description into some question). After El Greco moved from Italy to Toledo in 1577 and established himself as that city's leading painter, there was no shortage of patrons eager to commission portraits from him.[7]

A hallmark of El Greco's portrait style is his capacity to grasp the psychological character of the sitter. In the present portrait the sitter gazes out towards the viewer but avoids direct eye contact and wears an expression of contemplative diffidence. El Greco's figures are often described as having an 'inner glow', a quality that is discernible in the present work and that can be related to the artist's aesthetic and intellectual interests, in particular Neoplatonism.[8] Neoplatonism was underpinned by the concept of the subordination of the physical to the spiritual world, and the higher plane was that to which man ideally aspired. In Neoplatonic thought, light was an expression of Christian doctrine and in many of El Greco's paintings figures appear to emit their own light, an indication of their spiritual illumination. In his portraits El Greco expresses the beauty of spirit through the manipulation of light and colour. The colour and the handling of paint in this portrait are characteristic of El Greco and testify to the importance of his early contact with the work of Titian and Tintoretto in Venice.[9] The crimson mantle and yellowish complexion of the sitter contrast with the neutral background. The mantle and collar have been abraded, so the intensity and dramatic relief of the colours have somewhat diminished. El Greco considered colour the principal conveyor of meaning, a view that he derived from the Italian Mannerist painters and developed further. He also simplified the Venetians' technique of superimposing glazes over layers of pigment, instead applying oil glazes directly onto the underpainting, as can be seen in this work.

El Greco introduced to Spain a highly personal style of portraiture that is represented well by this portrait. His technique of scumbling impasto paint, to give a general impression of the sitter's countenance while conveying his or her physical character and psychology, proved critical to his continued Toledan patronage and marks him as one of the most innovative portrait painters during his period.

Mark McDonald

PROVENANCE

Dalborgo di Primo, Baron del Asilo; from whose estate purchased by the 1st Marquis de Pidal, 1858; 2nd Marquis de Pidal, 1902; Pidal family, 1908; with Tomás Harris, London, 1950; from whom acquired by the Felton Bequest, for the National Gallery of Victoria, 1950.

13. NICOLAS RÉGNIER

(Niccolò Renieri) Flemish (active in Italy), 1591–1667

Hero and Leander

Unsigned, undated; painted c.1625–26
Oil on canvas
155.3 x 209.5 cm (61 1/2 x 82 1/2 in.)
Felton Bequest 1955 (3262–4)

Nicolas Régnier, a Flemish painter trained in Antwerp, travelled in 1615 to Rome, where he was employed by Caravaggio's former patron Vincenzo Giustiniani.[1] Régnier modelled his early works on the half-length figure groups of the Caravaggist Bartolomeo Manfredi, establishing the basis for his way of composing pictures for the rest of his life. By the mid 1620s, together with French painters such as Simon Vouet, he was turning away from Caravaggism towards the style of the Bolognese painters, especially Guido Reni. In 1625 or 1626,[2] Régnier moved to Venice, where he lived until his death in 1667, working also as a dealer.

Regnier's style developed little after his move to Venice, and dating his works therefore becomes difficult. Fantelli, pointing out similarities between the *Hero and Leander* and the mature Venetian works, dated the Melbourne picture to the later 1650s.[3] The evident influence of Reni during this period can be adduced in support of this dating, since at this time Régnier seems to have been in contact with his half-brother Michele Desubleo (c.1601–1676), who was a close follower of Reni and who had been established in Bologna from the 1630s. Cottino observes that the *Hero and Leander* is very close to works by Desubleo of the 1640s, and traces the figure of Hero to Desubleo's *Venus and Adonis* at the Pinacoteca Nazionale, Bologna.[4] Other of Desubleo's Reniesque works, such as the *Death of Sophonisba* (private collection, Turin),[5] also invite comparisons with the *Hero and Leander*.

Yet an earlier dating to around 1625–26, proposed by Voss[6] and by Ivanoff,[7] is to be preferred. The figure of Leander is much closer, in both pose and handling, to the figure of St Sebastian in the *St Sebastian Tended by St Irene* (Musée des Beaux-Arts, Rouen) – datable to the later Roman period (1624–25) by its Vouetesque women[8] – than to the later Venetian version of the same subject (Ferens Art Gallery, Kingston-upon-Hull), a work that Fantelli dated to c.1645–50.[9] Besides, the sharply modelled draperies and coolly subtle colour harmonies of Hero's upper garments are unlike the overworked forms and unsubtle colouring of Desubleo, and could have been achieved only through direct contact with Reni's works of the 1620s, in particular his *Judith with the Head of Holofernes*, c.1625–26 (Sedlmayer Collection, Geneva).[10] The warm orange of the damask of Hero's dress, on the other hand, may be a residue of Caravaggio, who used a very similar pattern and colour in the *Magdalene* in the Palazzo Doria-Pamphili, Rome.[11] Régnier uses this fabric on a number of occasions in the Venetian period.

The story of Hero and Leander is found in a poem by the Greek poet Musaeus (4th–5th century AD). Leander, a youth of Abydos, on the Asian side of the Hellespont, would swim the strait nightly to meet his lover, Hero, a priestess of Aphrodite, at Sestos on the opposite shore. Hero would light a torch to guide Leander to the tower where she dwelled, but on a stormy night the light went out and Leander drowned. Distraught, Hero plunged to her death.

Musaeus does not place the living Hero on the beach beside Leander, and Hoff has suggested that Régnier drew on the version of the story in Ovid's *Heroides*, in which Leander, in a letter to Hero, envisions his death.[12] While Ovid may have suggested the motif of the lamentation over the dead Leander, a two-figure composition was almost inevitable given Régnier's limited compositional vocabulary, and there is little reason to suppose that the painting is to be understood other than as a depiction of the moment following Leander's drowning, as narrated by Musaeus.

David Marshall

PROVENANCE

P. D. Nicholls, Gloucestershire; with Colnaghi, London, 1955; from whom acquired by the Felton Bequest, for the National Gallery of Victoria, 1955.

14. ANTHONY VAN DYCK
Flemish (active in Italy and England), 1599–1641

Philip Herbert, 4th Earl of Pembroke

Unsigned, undated; painted c.1634
Oil on canvas
105.0 x 83.0 cm (41 1/2 x 32 3/4 in.)
Felton Bequest 1938 (457–4)

Addressing the viewer with a subtly melancholic air, this depiction invests the formal conventions of portrait painting with a nervous restlessness. Philip Herbert was Earl of Montgomery (from 1605) during the reign of James I, and 4th Earl of Pembroke (from 1630) under the rule of Charles I. Herbert's aplomb and authority are heightened by the contained solidity and restraint of the pose, by his position slightly above the viewer's level and by his display of the wand of office of Lord Chamberlain. The sense of magnificence is increased by the glimpse of a dramatic landscape, the rich yellow curtain, and the luxurious lace and other expensive materials of his costume. Yet these assertions of rank and power are combined with signs of intellectual reflection and temperamental sensitivity. The beautifully painted hand is alive with an unusual combination of delicacy and electric energy, reinforcing the complexity of character perceptible in the refined elegance of the face.

When Anthony van Dyck arrived in England in 1632, the court of Charles I was one of the leading cultural centres in Europe.[1] Charles I's love of the arts and his awareness of their potential to promote a desirable self-image for the monarch gave rise to a lively atmosphere that encouraged ideals of sophisticated learning and civilized behaviour. The portrait of Philip Herbert should be seen in the context of this courtly community, and van Dyck as the artist who could capture its concerns without resorting to stiff formalities. The earl, who performed in masques conducted at the court, exudes a persuasive bearing. In emphasizing this suave self-presentation, the portrait complements the aesthetics of grace promoted by the court's Caroline poets.[2]

Herbert wears the ribbon of the Order of the Garter, an honour highly prized as a way of enhancing the prestige of the bearer.[3] The earl was an enlightened and lavish patron of the arts, and in particular of van Dyck, commissioning an unusually large and theatrical group portrait of the Pembroke family, c.1633–34, which has been described as 'operatic' in its scope.[4] This work still hangs in the Double Cube Room designed by Inigo Jones at the Pembroke family seat at Wilton House, Wiltshire, a monument to enlightened patronage of architects, painters, interior designers and gardeners.[5]

Born in Antwerp, van Dyck was a favoured student and assistant of Peter Paul Rubens, and worked in the Netherlands, France and Spain before his second stay in England, where he remained for the latter part of his life. In 1632 he was knighted by Charles I and described as Principal Painter in Ordinary to Their Majesties. His depiction of the Earl of Pembroke is indicative of the development of his style in England towards more intimate informality. Van Dyck had absorbed from Rubens an audacious fluency of brushwork and a sumptuous emphasis on colour, tone and surface texture. In works such as this portrait, these qualities evolved into a style of lively linear rhythms, theatrical compositional structure and keen characterization that became one of the most influential in the history of portraiture thereafter.

Vivien Gaston

PROVENANCE

Philip Herbert, 4th Earl of Pembroke (1584–1650), Wilton, Salisbury, Wiltshire; Jonathan Pytts (1730–1807), Kyre Park, Tenbury Wells, Worcestershire; Baldwyn-Childe family, Kyre Park, 1882; William Lacon Childe; by descent to Mrs Baldwyn-Childe, Kyre Park, 1930; Charles Edward Childe-Freeman, Kyre Park, 1930; from whom purchased, with Kyre Park estate, by George H. Heath; with Colnaghi, London, 1931, 1934, 1937; from whom acquired by the Felton Bequest, for the National Gallery of Victoria, 1937.

SELECTED EXHIBITIONS

Van Dyck in England, National Portrait Gallery, London, 1982–83, cat. no. 12; *Van Dyck 1599–1641*, Koninklijk Museum voor Schone Kunsten, Antwerp, Royal Academy of Arts, London, 1999, cat. no. 75.

47

15. ANTHONY VAN DYCK

Rachel de Ruvigny, Countess of Southampton

Unsigned, undated; painted *c.*1640
Oil on canvas (mounted on plywood panel)
222.4 x 131.6 cm (87 1/2 x 51 3/4 in.)
Felton Bequest 1922 (1246–3)

PROVENANCE

Thomas Wriothesley, 4th Earl of
Southampton (1606–1667),
Southampton House, London;
Lady Frances Seymour, Countess of
Southampton (later Lady Darcy)
(d. 1681), Southampton House, 1667;
Conyers Darcy, Lord Darcy and
Baron Conyers (d. 1692), 1681; from
whom purchased by Anthony Grey,
11th Earl of Kent (1645–1702), 1683;
Henry Grey, 1st Duke of Kent
(1671–1740), 1702; Lady Jemima
Campbell (later Baroness Lucas and
Marchioness de Grey) (d. 1797),
1740, 1758; Amabel, Lady Lucas
(later Countess de Grey) (d. 1833),
1815; Thomas Philip de Grey, 2nd
Earl de Grey and Baron Lucas
(d. 1859), 1833, 1834, 1852, 1857;
Anne Florence de Grey (later
Countess Cowper), Panshanger,
Hertfordshire, 1859, 1873; Thomas
de Grey Cowper, 7th Earl Cowper
and 7th Baron Lucas (d. 1905),
Panshanger, 1885, 1887; Lord Lucas
(d. 1916), Panshanger, 1905 (on loan
to National Gallery, London,
1909–22); Lady Lucas (d. 1959),
1916, 1922; from whom acquired by
the Felton Bequest, for the National
Gallery of Victoria, 1922.

SELECTED EXHIBITIONS

Van Dyck 1599–1641, Koninklijk
Museum voor Schone Kunsten,
Antwerp, Royal Academy of Arts,
London, 1999, cat. no. 104.

At the time of her marriage to Thomas Wriothesley, 4th Earl of Southampton, in 1634, Rachel de Ruvigny was described as beautiful, virtuous and religious, 'of a goodly Personage, somewhat taller than ordinarily French Women are, excellent Eyes, black Hair, and of a most sweet and affable Nature'.[1] Born at Charenton (near Paris) in 1603, she was a widow for several years before her marriage to Wriothesley, in France. The Earl and Countess of Southampton were at the English court by November 1634, and the countess took part in Inigo Jones's court masque *Luminalia* in 1638. She bore five children and died in childbed in 1640.[2]

Van Dyck's portrait shows the Countess of Southampton seated above swirling clouds, her arm resting on a sphere of dark, reflective crystal, a skull at the hem of her dress.[3] The sun's rays break through dark clouds behind her. Her fluttering veil borrows grandeur from the antique, while the sheen and movement of her blue draperies show the painter's deep admiration for Titian's light and colour.[4] The face is painted with that admirable freshness which comes from working directly from the model: the painting is the primary version among several, including one at the Fitzwilliam Museum, Cambridge.[5] The figure in the Melbourne portrait may once have held a sceptre in her right hand, as in the work in Cambridge,[6] but the sceptre was not there when the court miniaturist Jean Petitot painted his enamel version dated 1643 (Devonshire Collection, Chatsworth, Derbyshire).[7]

As a young assistant to Rubens in Antwerp, van Dyck was familiar with the rhetorical style of the Baroque, and apparitions in the clouds were common in contemporary theatre. This painting, which suggests an apotheosis,[8] is nevertheless, for van Dyck, unusually overt in its allegorical content. The picture recalls Rubens's *Apotheosis of James I*, *c.*1630 (Mrs Humphrey Brand collection, Glynde Place, Sussex),[9] with its vision of ascension into heavenly splendour. This ancient idea places the spirit of a deceased person above the earthly elements, with that spirit sometimes identified with a star. Since the skull, which recalls the vanity of earthly things, can in portraits signify that the sitter is deceased, the painting may have been completed after the death of the Countess of Southampton in 1640.[10] Hoff has concluded that the portrait was painted, or at least finished, on the occasion of the sitter's death,[11] while Devapriam has pointed rather to the theme of virtue escaping the grave.[12]

According to Bellori in his life of van Dyck, published in 1672, the artist painted the countess 'in the form of the goddess Fortune seated on the globe of the earth',[13] although the painting in fact shows the crystal sphere associated with the world in a broader sense. Fortune rules the cosmos, and governs through the stars. She shares the glassy fragility of a crystalline sphere,[14] and remains subject to the Eternal, which is represented in the Melbourne painting as rays of light.

In 1635 Wriothesley had serious difficulties over land title.[15] He was restored to Fortune's favour in 1636, however, with the help of Charles I,[16] and this was the year associated with the present portrait when engraved by James McArdell in 1758.[17] Does the imagery compliment the countess in an allusion to this episode? Even if this is so, she seems gentler than the indifferent Fortune of the Stoics, and more like beneficent Providence, said to govern like a good mother.[18]

In all, the work has the tone of Henry Drummond's elegy 'Teares on the Death of Moeliades' of 1613, written at the death of Henry, Prince of Wales: 'Rest, blessed spright, rest satiate with the sight / Of him whose beams both dazzle and delight … Rest, happy ghost, and wonder in that glass / Where seen is all that shall be, is, or was, / While shall be, is, or was do pass away, / And nought remain but an eternal day'.

Margaret Legge

16. CLAUDE LORRAIN
(Claude Gellée) French (active in Italy), 1604/05–1682

River Landscape with Tiburtine Temple at Tivoli

Unsigned, undated; painted c.1635
Oil on canvas
38.0 x 53.0 cm (15 x 20 3/4 in.)
Felton Bequest 1967 (1796–5)

Claude Gellée, born in the village of Chamagne, south of Nancy in the duchy of Lorraine, was to become known as Claude Lorrain, a reference to his place of birth. A skilled draughtsman and etcher, Claude is chiefly known as one of the first professional landscape painters, as well as one of the genre's greatest exponents. Landscape painting did not exist in its own right until the seventeenth century, and Claude was instrumental in raising its status to the level of acceptance and popularity it subsequently enjoyed. Known to his contemporaries as the Raphael of landscape painting, Claude achieved success and fame early in his career, and his works were so often forged or unscrupulously imitated that in 1635 he began a graphic record of his major works, the *Liber Veritatis* (British Museum, Department of Prints and Drawings, London).

Claude went to Rome in his teens, but moved to Naples c.1618 and there studied with Goffredo Wals, a landscape painter from Cologne. Returning to Rome, Claude joined the workshop of Agostino Tassi, who specialized in illusionistic fresco decorations, marine views and landscapes. In 1625 Claude returned to Lorraine, where he worked for the court painter Claude Deruet, but was back in Rome by c.1627, staying there for the rest of his life. His art developed from a combination of influences, in which northern manners (as, for example, in the work of Wals, Adam Elsheimer, Jacques Callot, Bartholomeus Breenbergh, Paul Bril and Herman van Swanevelt) were important, but into which he synthesized Italian characteristics, notably from Tassi, Filippo Napoletano, the Carracci and Domenichino.

The *River Landscape with Tiburtine Temple at Tivoli* belongs to the mid 1630s, considered by Roethlisberger as the artist's 'romantic' phase.[1] A small work, it may have been painted as a 'souvenir' for one of Claude's foreign patrons, who were particularly numerous during this decade (Tivoli, south of Rome, was a popular spot for visitors and for artists to sketch). Claude has depicted the Temple of Vesta (1st century BC), but has relocated it from its actual position at the edge of an extremely steep precipice and has changed its proportions to accommodate it to the imaginary setting. Even so, the composition suggests the actual locale, and thus would have evoked strong classical associations for the viewer: the Tiburtine Sibyl, who was closely connected with this site, was traditionally said to have predicted the coming of Christ to Augustus Caesar, and the Roman poets Cicero, Catullus and Propertius had frequented the area. While not following a particular narrative, Claude recalls a pastoral Roman literary tradition where herders, playing pipes – instruments especially reminiscent of antiquity – tend their animals in a carefree, Arcadian landscape evocative of a golden age.

For Claude, the oil medium was most sympathetic to his handling of a particular quality of light: a dominating characteristic of the artist's works. Claude is today primarily known as a painter of 'classical' landscapes – in the sense not only of quality but also of subject matter, structure and mood – but in his own day it was the natural effects he achieved which were most admired. He managed to fuse accurately observed aspects of nature into an idealized construction, uniting them into a cohesive whole with his poetic use of light. In the *River Landscape* he frames the view with the dark foreground slope and the silhouetted trees to the left, balancing these with the temple and its grove of trees to the right, but this artificial arrangement is lent reality by the golden light, which blurs the forms, and by the pale, hazy landscape beyond, convincingly evoking the atmosphere of the Roman countryside.

Susan Russell

PROVENANCE

Adelbert Wellington, 3rd Earl Brownlow (1844–1921), Ashridge, Berkhamsted, Hertfordshire, 1921; the late Earl Brownlow sale, Christie's, London, 4 May 1923, lot 161; from which purchased by Lady Cust; her sale, Christie's, London, 4 December 1964, lot 79; from which purchased by Agnew's, London; with Agnew's, London, 1967; from whom acquired by the Felton Bequest, for the National Gallery of Victoria, 1967.

SELECTED EXHIBITIONS

Claude Lorrain 1600–1682, National Gallery of Art, Washington DC, Galeries Nationales du Grand Palais, Paris, 1982–83, cat. no. 7.

51

17. JACOB JORDAENS
Flemish, 1593–1678

Mercury and Argus

Unsigned, undated; painted *c*.1635–40
Oil on wood panel
49.3 x 64.5 cm (19 1/2 x 25 1/2 in.)
Presented through The Art Foundation of Victoria by
Mr James Fairfax, AO, Honorary Life Benefactor, 1996 (1996.658)

Jacob Jordaens based his *Mercury and Argus* on an episode from Ovid's *Metamorphoses* (1.588–723), in which the god Jupiter seduced the nymph Io and then changed her into a white heifer to hide his infidelity from his wife, Juno. Suspicious of her husband, Juno asked for the animal as a gift and entrusted hundred-eyed Argus, who never slept, to guard it. Jupiter sent his son Mercury to free Io by killing Argus. Disguised as a herdsman, Mercury played a reed pipe to make Argus drowsy, told him a story about the reed pipe's invention, then deepened his sleep with a magic wand and used a hooked sword to decapitate him. Juno subsequently took Argus's hundred eyes and placed them on the feathers of her own bird, the peacock.[1]

Jordaens portrays the moment preceding the decapitation and shows Argus being overcome by sleep as Mercury cautiously withdraws his hooked sword. Mercury, following Ovid's description, wears a shepherd's hat instead of his magical winged cap and winged sandals, and has set aside his pipe at the left and his sleep-producing wand directly below his right foot. Argus is depicted not as a monster with a hundred eyes but as a flabby-skinned old man with grey hair and beard, who still grips his herdsman's staff but slouches to the right as sleep overtakes him.[2] Io is the white heifer behind Argus, but Jordaens has added three more cows and a drowsing dog, which testify to his love of painting animals.[3] The scene is set in a pastoral landscape with lush green vegetation, but the figures are placed close to the picture plane, with little spatial recession. Bright light from the left focuses our attention especially upon Mercury and upon Io. Jordaens uses red and blue draperies to contrast Argus and Mercury and unifies the composition by harmonizing the warm golden-brown tones, luxuriant greens and cool whites. The light blue sky streaked with white clouds suggests the calm before the turbulent moment when Mercury beheads Argus.

The panel is a replica of Jordaens's canvas of *Mercury and Argus* painted in the early 1620s and now at the Musée des Beaux-Arts, Lyon.[4] The two works are identical in composition, modelling and colouring, but the Melbourne picture is more smoothly painted and much smaller, its size and handling suggesting, as Jaffé believes, that it was painted later, about 1635–40,[5] and probably for a private collector. Jordaens returned to this same subject numerous times, and in a version of *c*.1646, now in an American private collection, he greatly expanded the landscape at the left and right and the sky above.[6] This version in turn, as d'Hulst has shown, inspired an engraving by Schelte à Bolswert.[7]

Jordaens's contemporaries were familiar with the moralized Christian meanings given to Ovid's story of Mercury and Argus. Bolswert's engraving carries a Latin caption that includes the following moral lesson: 'Virginal modesty is a guardian with eyes as vigilant as those of Argus, but it is conquered as soon as it listens to the commands of love'.[8] A somewhat similar interpretation is given to Ovid's story in Carel van Mander's *Wtlegghingh op den Metamorphosis Pub. Ovidij Nasonis*, first published in Haarlem in 1604. According to van Mander, when reason, symbolized by Argus, is seduced by sensual desire, represented by Mercury, one is led to a pernicious life.[9] By contrasting the fleshy young Mercury with the flabby-skinned old Argus, Jordaens does seem to suggest the physical consequences of a material life based on sensual pleasure and excess. In the Melbourne panel, therefore, Jordaens not only endows Ovid's Mercury and Argus with realistic flesh-and-blood existence but also implies that human desires, when not controlled by reason, lead to tragic physical and moral consequences.

Frank I. Heckes

PROVENANCE

Baron Descamps; private collection, Brussels; with Colnaghi, London, 1991; James Fairfax, Sydney, 1991; by whom presented to the National Gallery of Victoria, through The Art Foundation of Victoria, 1996.

18. THOMAS DE KEYSER

Dutch, 1596/97–1667

Frederick van Velthuysen and His Wife Josina

Signed and dated c.l.: *TDK.* [monogram] *1636*
Oil on wood panel
114.9 x 80.5 cm (45 1/4 x 31 3/4 in.)
Presented through The Art Foundation of Victoria by Lynton and Nigel Morgan,
in memory of their parents, Eric and Marian Morgan, Founder Benefactors, 1987 (E1–1987)

In the 1630s, Thomas de Keyser was the most fashionable portrait painter in Amsterdam, and his work was popular with the middle and upper classes of that city. His paintings are characterized by a highly detailed style and by realistically painted figures posed in a rather formal manner. This style of painting was in vogue in Amsterdam in the early seventeenth century, and de Keyser, as one of its leading exponents, had a strong influence on other artists, including the young Rembrandt.

The Melbourne picture shows de Keyser at his most brilliant, particularly in his masterly way of representing a variety of fabrics and textures. The clothes worn by the woman in this portrait are made of black silk damask, and the contrasts in textures unique to that fabric are clearly distinguished. The lace, too, is meticulously detailed, even to the point of de Keyser's grading the strength of the black that shows through the white cloth of the collars: he has painted the different areas of black at different densities to reflect the effect of the folds in the white fabric. Indeed he was noted for his ability to paint contrasting blacks and greys, his technical virtuosity giving a tangible and realistic volume to his figures.

The sitters in this portrait are Frederick and Josina van Velthuysen, and the work is a variant of the 'marriage portrait', a genre that originated in Netherlandish painting.[1] Marriage portraits were usually commissioned to celebrate the wedding of the sitters; however, in this case the painting is dated 1636, whereas the couple were married in 1632.[2] A further inscription, *ANNO 1634*, appears on the base of the statue at the right, but is painted into a background of a similar colour and is therefore difficult to read. The significance of this date has yet to be discovered. In most cases, marriage portraits were expressions of the perceived social and economic status of the sitters. Costume was of primary importance, and here the quality of the clothing is indicative of wealth and high social standing. However, in keeping with Netherlandish Protestant traditions, the outfits are rich but not ostentatious. Frederick van Velthuysen was the son of the burgomaster of Utrecht, and the couple would have been among that city's elite citizens.

Seventeenth-century marriage portraits often describe the respective roles of the man and woman within the marriage and are patriarchal in character. The portraits conform to a stereotype of what a marriage should be – as dictated by Dutch society and reinforced in Dutch art. Here, the couple are set on the terrace of a classical building, against the background of an Italianate town and landscape, this imaginary setting indicating the sitters' intellectual – and possibly mercantile – interest in Italy. Frederick is placed nearest to the building and Josina closer to the garden, this positioning indicating his predilection for the pursuit of scholarly and contemplative endeavours, and her alignment with the sensory pleasures associated with nature.

The sculpture on the right has particular significance, as it would have been thought at the time to be a statue of Homer.[3] The inclusion of this sculpture, and its location in close proximity to the figure of Josina van Velthuysen, could indicate that marriage, and with it the active encouragement of his wife, is perceived as being likely to enhance rather than constrain Frederick's potential for engaging in intellectual pursuits. His scholarly interests are confirmed by a painting by de Keyser dated 1660 (Pakzad collection, Hannover). In this posthumous portrait, Frederick is portrayed curiously unaffected by time, in the same pose and setting as in the Melbourne picture, but shown handing a book to his twelve-year-old son.[4]

Laurie Benson

PROVENANCE

Frederick van Velthuysen (d. 1658), Amsterdam, 1636; Lord Hampden; Rochelle Thomas, 1920; her sale, Christie's, London, 20 February 1920, lot 97; from which purchased by Agnew's, London; from whom purchased by Asscher, Koetser & Welker, London, 1920; with Asscher & Welker, London, 1934; Sir George Leon; Alan P. Good, Glympton Park, Woodstock, Oxfordshire; the late Alan. P. Good sale, Sotheby's, London, 15 July 1953, lot 33; from which purchased by Davies; Eric Morgan, Melbourne; Lynton Morgan and Nigel Morgan, Melbourne, 1987; by whom presented to the National Gallery of Victoria, through The Art Foundation of Victoria, 1987.

19. AELBERT CUYP
Dutch, 1620–1691

Landscape with Cattle

Signed l.r.: *A. cuijp*, undated; painted between 1639 and 1649
Oil on wood panel
65.0 x 90.8 cm (25 1/2 x 35 3/4 in.)
Felton Bequest 1932 (4664–3)

Aelbert Cuyp is now considered one of the leading landscape artists of the 'golden age' of Dutch painting. His style changed in subtle ways during his lifetime, and this work is from a period when, concentrating on natural atmospheric effects, he executed idyllic landscapes bathed in the diffuse golden light of dawn or dusk. Throughout his career he almost always placed the horizon line above only a third of the canvas, making the sky and natural conditions a dominant force in his work. He demonstrated a keen observation of nature, and the animals in his landscapes are always healthy and robust. In their idyllic settings, they attest to the buoyant economy and sense of prosperity that was prevalent in Holland in the early seventeenth century. In particular the dairy industry was a subject of great pride, and the depiction of cattle was a special genre in Dutch painting.

Although Cuyp did not travel outside the Netherlands, he was far from being an isolated painter unaffected by other artists. Dordrecht, where he lived and worked, was a prosperous port town, and its wealth attracted a number of leading Dutch artists. Cuyp was also strongly influenced by the great landscape painters Claude Lorrain and Salvator Rosa, coming into contact with their work through Dutch artists, such as Jan Both, who travelled to Italy and worked with these masters. Also, judging from Cuyp's sketches and paintings, he travelled widely through Holland and had contact with artists from Amsterdam, Rotterdam, The Hague, Utrecht and other centres. In the Melbourne painting, the town depicted in the background is Leiden, birthplace of Rembrandt, Jan Lievens and Gerrit Dou. However, a major building, the 'Marekerk', is not apparent. Our knowledge of when this church was constructed (between 1639 and 1649)[1] helps us date the painting: it must have been executed before 1649, and almost certainly after 1639 (since no works by Cuyp are known before this date).

Cuyp's landscapes are always a setting for human activity, most often people fishing, sailing, or herding cattle, sheep or goats – all very popular subjects in seventeenth-century Dutch painting and printmaking. As the locations of Cuyp's landscapes are so clearly identifiable and the landmarks so obvious, perhaps his paintings had particular relevance as 'portraits of property', and thus functioned as status symbols for the artist's clientele. Cuyp often included a building, or in this case a tree, of monumental proportions, lending a sense of grandeur and providing a stabilizing element to the composition.

Cuyp can perhaps be considered a specialist painter of animals, as he demonstrated an almost clinical observation of their musculature and habits, both when animated and when in repose. The cow beneath the tree at the right of this composition has its back arched and its tail lifted, as though it is urinating. An undated photograph of the painting, which appears to have been taken prior to the work's restoration before entering the National Gallery of Victoria's collection, clearly shows the cow performing this most natural act.[2] It has been proposed by Chong that this detail, a testament to the artist's keen powers of observation, may have offended the then prevailing sensibility, and was painted out.[3]

In the later part of his life, Cuyp was independently wealthy and did not rely solely on painting for his income. Indeed, he virtually ceased artistic pursuits as he furthered his career performing clerical and civic duties. His paintings were almost ignored until the late eighteenth century, when British artists such as Richard Wilson and J. M. W. Turner were influenced by his work.

Laurie Benson

PROVENANCE

4th Lord Huntingfield, Heveningham Hall, Yoxford, Suffolk; the late Lord Huntingfield sale, Christie's, London, 25 June 1915, lot 76; from which purchased by Peel; private collection, 1932; from which acquired by the Felton Bequest, for the National Gallery of Victoria, 1932.

20. ATTRIBUTED TO GIANLORENZO BERNINI
Neapolitan (active in Rome), 1598–1680

Portrait of a Young Man (formerly *Self-Portrait*)

Unsigned, undated
Oil on canvas
57.0 x 42.0 cm (22 1/2 x 16 1/2 in.)
Everard Studley Miller Bequest 1976 (E3–1976)

The earliest record of this portrait dates from 1780, when it was thought to be by Diego Velázquez (1599–1660).[1] Velázquez's name continued to be associated with it until it was acquired by the London dealer David Carritt, who identified it as a self-portrait by Gianlorenzo Bernini, and it was acquired as such by the National Gallery of Victoria in 1976. At the time, the Bernini attribution received support from those who knew the picture in London, although not all were convinced that it was a self-portrait. More recent opinions recorded in the National Gallery of Victoria files are sceptical of the attribution to Bernini, and hence of the identification of the sitter.[2] Most consider the painting to be more Spanish than Italian. Tomory and Gaston have cast doubt on the attribution in print,[3] and Tomory has tentatively given the picture to Juan Bautista Martínez del Mazo (c.1613–1667).

There are a range of Bernini self-portraits with which the Melbourne portrait can be compared.[4] A painting at the Galleria Borghese, Rome,[5] can be dated to before 1622 – when Ottavio Leoni's engraved portrait of Bernini as a Knight of the Order of Christ was published[6] – on the basis of the apparent age of the sitter and the nature of the moustache. In the Galleria Borghese portrait, Bernini wears only a thin moustache and no chin tuft. In the Leoni portrait he wears a thick moustache, and a tuft of hair on the chin. In the Melbourne painting there is no chin tuft and the moustache is modest, so that if the work represents Bernini it ought to date from before 1622, and slightly earlier than the Galleria Borghese portrait.

The sitter in the Borghese portrait stares at the viewer with a fierce intensity that reflects the physiognomical explorations of his own features that Bernini made in his early years and that culminated in his statue of *David*, 1623–24, also at the Galleria Borghese. In Bernini's later portraits the gaze becomes less theatrical, modulating into a more controlled intensity, especially in a second portrait at the Galleria Borghese, datable to the 1630s.[7] More mellow is a self-portrait of *c*.1640 at the Galleria degli Uffizi, Florence.[8] This work, the most formal of the group, nevertheless still radiates a force of character and an intense engagement with the viewer that are the hallmarks of Bernini's self-portraits. All these self-portraits are rendered with a controlled plasticity that is unsurprising in a sculptor. The National Gallery of Victoria portrait has neither the intensity nor the plasticity of these. The sitter does not engage the viewer in the direct, confrontational way of Bernini's early self-portraits. His gaze is softer, sliding away to the left as if nervous of catching the viewer's eye too directly. The role played by the hand touching the collar finds no counterpart in secure Bernini self-portraits, which in most cases are head studies. Physiognomically, too, the Melbourne painting has less in common with Bernini's self-portraits than may at first appear from the turn of the head and the angular chin.

In all but the Leoni portrait Bernini wears a plain white linen collar attached to a dark costume. In Bernini's later portraits this collar is fuller than in the earlier works but retains their austerity. By the 1640s such collars were often enlarged into a square panel with front and back trimmed with lace points, producing a much fancier effect. It is evidently a collar of this kind which the sitter in the Melbourne portrait wears, over a dark jacket with leather shoulder-pieces. The costume, therefore, implies a dating somewhat later than the *c*.1620 that follows from an identification of the sitter as Bernini. The loose handling of the collar, and the atmospheric background, also suggest a later date, and there are enough hints of Velázquez to make an attribution to a Spanish artist, or at least to a painter affected by Spanish art, plausible.

David Marshall

PROVENANCE

Karl Theodor, Elector Palatine of the Rhine and Elector of Bavaria (1724–1799), Elector's Palace, Mannheim, 1780, Schloss Nymphenburg, Munich, 1799; Maximilian IV Joseph, Duke of Zweibrücken, Elector Palatine of the Rhine and Elector of Bavaria (1756–1825), 1799, 1802, 1822; Ludwig I, King of Bavaria (1786–1868); Maximilian II, King of Bavaria (1811–1864), Schloss Schleissheim, Munich, 1851; Royal Gallery, Schleissheim, sale, 1851, lot 448; from which purchased by Prof. Sepp; Prof. Franz von Rinecker (1811–1883), Würzburg, 1868; his sale, Paris, 30 March 1868, lot 112; A. Casso, 1895; sale, Hôtel Drouot, Paris, 28 June 1934, lot 24; with David Carritt, London, 1976; from whom acquired by the National Gallery of Victoria, under the terms of the Everard Studley Miller Bequest, 1976.

21. DUTCH (formerly attributed to Jan Victors)

Portrait of a Lady

Unsigned, undated; painted *c*.1640
Oil on canvas
126.0 x 104.0 cm (49 1/2 x 41 in.)
Purchased 1979 (E1–1979)

As Rembrandt scholars continue to assess existing attributions to the Dutch master, the close examination of the work of his many pupils and followers has become a critical part of the process.[1] Over the last two decades, various exhibitions have been devoted to connoisseurship and Dutch art, and the number of publications on Rembrandt's followers is increasing.[2] As the knowledge base and the understanding of these artists grows, traditional attributions to them also come under scrutiny. Such is the case with the present painting, which has been attributed to Jan Victors (1619–*c*.1676) since 1904 (when it appeared in the sale of works belonging to the late Princesse Mathilde), an attribution challenged by some scholars and supported by others. The Dutch scholar I. Q. van Regteren Altena, in a handwritten note on a copy of the 1904 sale catalogue,[3] suggested that the painting might be by Govaert Flinck (1615–1660). Other artists, including Ferdinand Bol, Jacob Backer and Gerbrand van den Eeckhout, have also been proposed as the author of this painting.[4]

Central to the dilemma of attribution is the fact that the painting has characteristics of a number of seventeenth-century Dutch masters, without obviously conforming to the style of any one artist. The work is clearly influenced by Rembrandt, although it does not have the inventive qualities and high level of emotional intensity seen in his portraits. However, the unidentified artist is very accomplished and confident in technique, a quality indicated in fine details and subtle touches. The lace of the sitter's left sleeve is masterly in execution, with the sharp end of the brush having been lightly, and with a very free hand, incised into the wet paint to articulate the translucent pattern of the lace. This is a technique favoured by many Dutch artists, notably Rembrandt, and its use in the Melbourne portrait may indicate that the artist responsible had spent some time in the master's studio, as a pupil or assistant.

The attribution to Victors seems untenable, because the dating of the *Portrait of a Lady*, based on the costume of the sitter, places the work at *c*.1640, a time when Victors was not painting in the manner evidenced in the Melbourne portrait. Close comparison with two of Victors's finest portraits, dated 1650 – the *Portrait of a Gentleman* and the *Portrait of a Lady* (Milwaukee Art Museum), both of which were hung with the Melbourne painting in the 1997–98 exhibition *Rembrandt: A Genius and His Impact* – has clearly demonstrated this point.[5] Victors's earlier portrait style was markedly conventional and conservative and his figures lack the lively presence of the woman in the Melbourne painting. By 1650, however, his style had developed to the point where the figures in the Milwaukee paintings are more animated than in any work he had produced to that date. Thus it is unlikely that *c*.1640 he could have painted a portrait with the degree of informal intimacy present in our *Portrait of a Lady*.

Sumowski tentatively supports van Regteren Altena's assertion that the Melbourne painting is by Govaert Flinck.[6] Flinck possessed the technical skill and experience to have produced a painting of this quality, and there is a liveliness in his manner that is comparable to that revealed by the present work. However, Flinck's technique in the 1640s was perhaps more painterly and less polished than that of our unidentified artist, and doubt is therefore cast on this attribution.

A solution to the dilemma might be found if the pendant to the Melbourne portrait could be located. At the time of the Paris sale of 1904, the *Portrait of a Lady* was paired with a *Portrait of a Gentleman*, the two pictures probably being marriage portraits (in 1918 the *Portrait of a Gentleman* was sold in a New York sale).[7] It is hoped that the exposure of the Melbourne portrait in the United States during the present exhibition might lead to the re-emergence of the pendant portrait.

Laurie Benson

PROVENANCE

Princesse Mathilde (1820–1904), 1904; the late Princesse Mathilde sale, Galerie Georges Petit, Paris, 17–21 May 1904, lot 22; from which purchased by Agnew's, London; Mrs Robert Wallach, 'Hopefield', Warrenton, Virginia; Cross Johnson (on loan to Smithsonian Institution, Washington DC); Pinakos Inc. (Dr Rudolph Heinemann), New York, 1943; from whom half share purchased by Knoedler's, New York, 1943; from whom half share repurchased by Pinakos Inc., New York, 1968; with Agnew's, London, 1976; from whom purchased by Norman Salter, Melbourne, 1976; Mrs Salter, Melbourne, 1979; from whom acquired by the National Gallery of Victoria, 1979.

SELECTED EXHIBITIONS

Rembrandt: A Genius and His Impact, National Gallery of Victoria, Melbourne, National Gallery of Australia, Canberra, 1997–98, cat. no. 52.

22. JAN DAVIDSZ DE HEEM
Dutch, 1606–1683/84

Still Life with Fruit

Signed u.r.: *J. D. de Heem f*, undated; painted *c*.1640–50
Oil on canvas
67.3 x 79.8 cm (26 1/2 x 31 1/2 in.)
Felton Bequest 1935 (231–4)

Jan Davidsz de Heem's technical brilliance, and the seductive realism that results from it, masks, initially at least, the superbly contrived nature of this painting. The stone table supports an abundance of fruits, all of them produce of the autumn harvest, except for the summer-fruiting cherries. There are also two pewter plates, a large blue and white Chinese ceramic platter and a similar bowl, three fancy glasses (a *roemer*, a flute and a wine glass) and a sumptuous German silver-gilt cup. The light falls from the upper left, through a window whose pearly reflections may be seen in the tall, wine-filled flute, the green *roemer* and the embossed cup. These vessels also reflect each other and the local colours of the adjacent fruits. Colour is carefully orchestrated to achieve both variety and balance. At the lower right the prominent white accent of the cloth, together with the broken bread, acts as a counterweight to the strong vertical that runs through the silver cup and the edge of the velvet cloth; the elements at the right are, in turn, balanced by the scattered white of the citrus blooms and the milky flesh of the oysters at the lower left. All of the objects are represented at about their natural size. Despite its relatively small dimensions, the painting conveys a sense of grandeur and of restrained luxury.

De Heem's earliest still lifes are simpler and much more sober compositions that reflect the influence of his older Utrecht contemporary, the still life painter Balthasar van der Ast (1593/94–1657). By 1626 de Heem had moved from Utrecht to Leiden (where Rembrandt was still working), and his paintings from this period show a preference for subdued tonalities and for *vanitas* subject matter. With his move to Antwerp in the mid 1630s de Heem came into direct contact with the exuberant manner of Flemish still-life painting, and its impact on him was decisive. Here at last he was able to find his own distinctive approach, by combining Dutch and Flemish elements. Sandrart, writing in 1675, claimed that de Heem moved to Antwerp because:

> [I]t seemed to him sensible, since one could have there rare fruits of all kinds, large plums, peaches, morellos, oranges, lemons, bunches of grapes, and others in finer condition and state of ripeness to draw them from life. He copied them ... with exceeding excellence so that ... he surpassed all others in the Netherlands and therefore obtained great praise, honour and profit.[1]

From the 1640s de Heem was the most important and influential still-life painter in the Netherlands. The *Still Life with Fruit* probably dates from this very decade. The painting belongs to an iconographic type whose invention is credited to de Heem: the *pronk*, or sumptuous, still life. Some of de Heem's *pronk* still lifes are cabinet pictures like the present one, while others are over two hundred centimetres (seven feet) in width. The disparity of sizes and, especially, the existence of canvases of such huge dimensions would seem to suggest that the artist may have received commissions for still lifes, for it is unlikely that such large pictures would have been made for the open market. However, no documents have been found to support this hypothesis. What is certain is that, although the still life was accorded a very lowly rank in the hierarchy of subject matter in the seventeenth century, the genre's popularity with collectors was not in the least affected.

Irena Zdanowicz

PROVENANCE

Comte de l'Espine, Paris; Princesse de Croy, Paris; with O. Hirschmann, Amsterdam, 1934; from whom acquired by the Felton Bequest, for the National Gallery of Victoria, 1934.

SELECTED EXHIBITIONS
Still-Life Still Lives, Art Gallery of South Australia, Adelaide, 1997.

23. SALOMON VAN RUYSDAEL
Dutch, *c.*1600–1670

River Landscape with Boats

Unsigned, undated; painted *c.*1640–50
Oil on canvas
105.2 x 111.0 cm (41 1/2 x 43 3/4 in.)
Felton Bequest 1933 (4729–3)

The National Gallery of Victoria has a strong representation of seventeenth-century landscapes by artists of the school of Haarlem. The most discernible characteristic distinguishing the art of this group from that of artists from other Dutch regions is a naturalistic approach to the landscape: the Haarlem school painters accurately depicted scenes unmistakably drawn from their local surroundings, and included details unique to their region. They gave their works spiritual and narrative content, while using recognizable details to convey their meaning, in a way highly relevant to their local audience. However, their works are not bereft of invention in composition or in the creative use of motifs.

Salomon van Ruysdael is considered a pioneer of the movement towards naturalism and he was a strong influence on other Haarlem artists such as his nephew Jacob van Ruisdael and Meindert Hobbema. When viewed in its entirety, Ruysdael's work seems formulaic, as he settled on representing a narrow subject range and often repeated the same motifs. Although his use of colour changed throughout his career, he employed a basic compositional structure of a cloudy sky, monumental trees, and a landscape or river anchoring the composition. He painted river scenes more than any other type of landscape, depicting calm waters as the setting for the busy activity of river life, critical to the economic and social welfare of Holland and, in particular, of Haarlem, which is an inland city, reliant on rivers as a critical means of transport.

River Landscape with Boats has a number of characteristics that Ruysdael repeated in many compositions, such as flocks of birds in the sky, horsemen, people and animals on barges, fishermen casting nets, a floating barrel, and majestic trees dominating the painting. While superficially the repetition of such elements may seem uninventive, it is the subtle inclusion of rather curious and intriguing details which makes each of the artist's paintings interesting. In this instance, the viewer's attention is drawn to the vessel in the centre of the composition, which has the coat of arms of the city of Amsterdam on its stern.[1] It is also flying the *Prinsenvlag* of orange, white and blue, derived from the time of William I of Orange, whose orange livery, in a mark of allegiance to the House of Orange, was adopted for the national flag. Oddly, here, the flag is being flown upside down, and as the *Prinsenvlag* was also known as the '*Oranje Boven*' (orange on top) it is unlikely that the sailors had made a mistake. It is most probable that this is a signal of some kind and it can be interpreted as indicating that the vessel is in distress. However, the boat does not appear to be damaged or sinking. Clearly identifiable as a two-masted transport vessel, a *speeljacht*,[2] it is sitting in the water at a level to be expected if it were intact.

Other intriguing points are that the sails are rather casually draped over the spar and down the masts and, strangely, no one is seen on deck. On the viewer's right two men are swimming towards the moored boat, and a man in a small boat is rowing away from the swimmers. The *speeljacht* has its leeboard – a mooring device dropped into the water when a boat is stationary, to steady it against the wind – still tied to its side. These details are difficult to explain, but imply that there is a unique narrative element to this painting. Unfortunately it is unlikely that a particular event can be identified to help explain the narrative, as the precise date of the work is unknown.

Laurie Benson

PROVENANCE

Lord Castletown, Upper Ossory, 1924; his sale, Christie's, London, 18 July 1924, lot 151; from which purchased by Colnaghi, London; with Colnaghi, London, 1933; from whom acquired by the Felton Bequest, for the National Gallery of Victoria, 1933.

24. BERNARDO CAVALLINO
Neapolitan, 1616 – c.1656

The Virgin Annunciate

Unsigned, undated; painted c.1645–50
Oil on canvas (mounted on wood panel)
85.5 x 70.0 cm (33 3/4 x 27 1/2 in.)
Felton Bequest 1968 (1829–5)

The *Virgin Annunciate* dates to the period of Bernardo Cavallino's maturity, in the second half of the 1640s.[1] The picture was originally paired with a painting of the Archangel Gabriel, which, although lost, is probably reflected in a composition by one of Cavallino's imitators.[2] From this work it is apparent that the light falling on the Virgin emanated originally from above Gabriel's right shoulder. The light is, therefore, that of the Holy Spirit descending to reveal the Virgin at the moment of Incarnation. For her part, the Virgin registers her humble yet resolute acquiescence by leaning forward, in a gesture traditionally employed to denote her acceptance of the Incarnation after an initial moment of uncertainty.[3] The miraculous spotlight casts her face into an oval shape, leaving her neck in shadow. This distinctive effect provides one of the clearest indications of Cavallino's close association with Massimo Stanzione and Artemisia Gentileschi, who developed similar refined female facial types and lighting effects from the 1620s onward.[4]

Many of Cavallino's paintings have not fared well with the passing of time, and the current work is no exception. The Virgin's drapery has sunk into the dark background, particularly in the area of her right arm, which is now difficult to discern. Preliminary technical analysis recently undertaken at the National Gallery of Victoria has revealed particles of blue pigment among the acid green highlights of her mantle.[5] This finding, together with the darkness of the mantle, suggests that the picture has suffered from a common form of paint deterioration, which has been noted in a number of other pictures by Cavallino. Cavallino frequently built up his figures (particularly those in the background) from thin glazes to which he added an unusually high proportion of medium relative to pigment. These delicate and partially transparent glazes have proved unstable over time and have in many cases merged into the dark backgrounds against which they originally stood out.[6] An indication of the original appearance of the mantle in the Melbourne picture may be provided by a closely related painting by Cavallino of the *Nursing Madonna* (Oblastní Galerie, Olomouc, Czechoslovakia).[7] The Virgin in this painting wears a cerise dress under a transparent veil worn around her neck, just as in the *Virgin Annunciate*. But her mantle is blue, thus further suggesting that the green in the National Gallery of Victoria's painting may originally have been combined with blue, in keeping with traditional Marian iconography.

The *Virgin Annunciate* has suffered further from having been cut down at some stage from its original octagonal format, in order to fit a rectangular frame. An indication of the original proportions and dimensions of the canvas might be provided by an unmodified pair of octagonal half-lengths by Cavallino, depicting St Peter and St Paul.[8] Cavallino frequently paired single half-length figures of this kind. The important early bourgeois collector Pompilio Gagliano owned two pairs of the artist's half-length saints, while the aristocratic Francesco de Palma, duca di Sant'Elia, owned a pair of his small tondo paintings of heads of women.[9] These pairings appear to have been conceived with the interior design requirements of Cavallino's early collectors in mind. Paired paintings offered a useful means of integrating an otherwise heterogeneous group of paintings, by bracketing certain pictures among the tightly packed wall-to-ceiling hangs that were then in vogue.[10] The original viewing experience of the *Virgin Annunciate* may thus have differed considerably from the contemplation of a relatively isolated painting in an art museum, as is the norm today. The Virgin and Gabriel may, instead, have once communicated to each other the sacred intimacy of the Incarnation from across the clamour of a crowded wall, being located on either side of or underneath larger gallery paintings by one of the leading large-scale figure painters of the day, such as Stanzione or Gentileschi themselves.

Christopher Marshall

PROVENANCE

Private collection, France; from which purchased by Hazlitt Gallery, London; with Hazlitt Gallery, London, 1968; from whom acquired by the Felton Bequest, for the National Gallery of Victoria, 1968.

SELECTED EXHIBITIONS

Bernardo Cavallino of Naples 1616–1656, Cleveland Museum of Art, Cleveland, Kimbell Art Museum, Fort Worth, Museo Pignatelli Cortes, Naples, 1984–85, cat. no. 49.

25. SALVATOR ROSA
Neapolitan (active in Florence and Rome), 1615–1673

Romantic Landscape with Mercury and Argus

Signed l.l.: s. r. [monogram], undated; painted c.1655–60
Oil on canvas
123.5 x 203.4 cm (48 1/2 x 80 in.)
Felton Bequest 1951 (2883–4)

Salvator Rosa – poet, actor, artist – was born at Arenella in Naples, where he trained as a painter. He painted battle scenes, historical subjects, allegories, allegorical portraits and macabre themes, as well as being an accomplished printmaker. He went to Rome in 1635 and, after trips outside the city to execute commissions, returned there in 1639, becoming the focus of a group of poets and writers. He also founded a company of actors, with whom he performed, and during one performance insulted the most powerful artist in Rome, Gianlorenzo Bernini. The incident may have prompted Rosa to accept an invitation from Cardinal Giovanni Carlo de' Medici to visit Florence, for by c.1640 the artist was living there, his house a centre for learned activities, and it was here that he wrote many of his satirical poems. Rosa returned to Rome in 1649 and remained there until his death.

The story depicted in *Romantic Landscape with Mercury and Argus* comes from Ovid's *Metamorphoses* (1.588–723).[1] Jupiter, king of the gods, fell in love with Io, an Argive princess. To spare her from the jealousy of his wife, Juno, Jupiter turned Io into a white heifer. Juno, not deceived, asked for the cow as a gift, which, to avert suspicion, Jupiter granted her. Juno had Io guarded by the shepherd Argus but Jupiter sent his son, the crafty young Mercury, to reclaim her and he lulled Argus to sleep with music, preparatory to stealing Io away. This is the moment Rosa shows: Mercury, distinguished by his winged hat (petasus), plays his pipe, as Argus, apparently rapt, listens at his feet. In the background Io, the white heifer, seems similarly charmed as she faces Mercury and the viewer, as though inviting us to await with her the outcome of her fate. The story has a bloody ending – Mercury decapitates Argus and throws his body down a cliff – a denouement Rosa suggests by the threatening rocky outcrop directly opposite the figures on the right, and by the sense of foreboding expressed in the moody sky, wind-tossed branches and inhospitable terrain. The landscape thereby assumes a narrative function, a phenomenon that Rosa developed from the landscapes of Nicolas Poussin, but with distinct emotional and scenographic characteristics (the *Romantic* of the title) far removed from Poussin's restrained classicism.

In the late 1650s Rosa painted at least two other pictures on the theme of Mercury and Argus, but the term 'variants' for these works (one of which is at the Nelson-Atkins Museum of Art, Kansas City) seems misleading.[2] In the *Romantic Landscape*, Rosa has created an original composition that differs significantly from the other versions, not only in its scale and organization but also in its conception: the painting has a grandeur consistent with the best of the artist's work from the late 1650s. Describing these pictures, Rosa's biographer, Baldinucci, wrote: 'He had excelled himself'.[3] The works are characterized by the rockiness of the landscape; cloudy, threatening skies; stretches of murky water; and vegetation that appears at the mercy – as do the figures – of the elements. It is to this period that the Melbourne picture should be consigned.[4] Although Rosa was not a landscape specialist, his landscapes were his most important legacy, making him a much admired figure in eighteenth-century England, where the concept of the Sublime in nature held sway. With his professional independence, expressive works and turbulent personality, he was for the nineteenth century the embodiment of the Romantic artist.

Susan Russell

PROVENANCE

Aston Bruce, 1824; Viscount Combermere, Combermere Abbey, Combermere, Shropshire; from whom purchased by an English dealer; from whom purchased by Arthur Tooth & Sons, London; from whom purchased by Colnaghi, London; from whom acquired by the Felton Bequest, for the National Gallery of Victoria, 1950.

69

26. JACOB VAN RUISDAEL
Dutch, 1628/29–1682

The Watermill

Signed l.l.: V. R. [monogram], undated; painted *c*.1660
Oil on canvas
65.0 x 71.3 cm (25 1/2 x 28 in.)
Felton Bequest 1922 (1249–3)

In many respects Jacob van Ruisdael is regarded as the finest Dutch landscape artist of the seventeenth century and as one of the most influential internationally. He was technically brilliant even as a teenager – several outstanding signed and dated works were painted when he was seventeen – and he had a prolific career, with some seven hundred paintings ascribed to him.[1] He was also an accomplished printmaker and draughtsman. Unlike many artists of his time he did not specialize in a particular landscape type, painting a wide variety of subjects, including seascapes, townscapes and winter scenes, with equal passion and virtuosity.

Ruisdael was a gifted artist who employed a meticulous technique, delineating practically every leaf and twig with astounding accuracy and he brilliantly conveyed the texture of objects. This virtuosity did not result in his producing boring works that were just demonstrations of skill; rather he utilized his technique to clearly convey his meaning. He did not paint idyllic landscapes, but charged his subjects with great drama and strong emotional content and he is regarded as the most romantic of the Dutch landscape artists, producing works with strong spiritual and moralizing content. His best works combine high drama with an earthy quality and a degree of tangibility, which make his scenes appear familiar and believable.

The versatility Ruisdael demonstrated is reflected in his sources of inspiration. He was also inspired by other artists, particularly his uncle, Salomon van Ruysdael, and Cornelis Vroom, Allart van Everdingen and Rembrandt. Ruisdael was widely travelled in Holland and elsewhere in northern Europe, and the sights he saw fuelled his imagination. Such is the case with the *Watermill*, the subject of which has been identified as a type used in the Veluwe near Apeldoorn.[2] A drawing by Ruisdael of the mill, *c*.1660 (Teylers Museum, Haarlem) – which was also sketched by Meindert Hobbema, when the two artists travelled together – shows that the subject was undoubtedly drawn from life and then juxtaposed against a dramatically stormy sky. Thus an intense painting was created from a naturalistic drawing.

Here, Ruisdael has focused our attention on the mill with the cascading water driving its wheel. By cropping the building quite tightly and leaving much of it outside the canvas, he has made it appear quite large in scale by comparison with the woods around it and the man and his dog venturing into the forest. Ruisdael often used buildings, be they houses, windmills, or watermills, to symbolize the impact of human beings on a natural setting. In some cases his portrayal of this conflict is extreme, such as when he depicts ruins being overwhelmed by nature. And while the *Watermill* does not have the overtly dramatic content of many of his other paintings, the battle between nature and the attempts to manipulate and control it is still in evidence here, albeit quite subtly suggested.

The *Watermill* exemplifies many of the higher achievements of Ruisdael's art, such as his attention to fine detail and his ability to convey to his audience that they are witnessing the scene first-hand. He is truly an engaging painter. Intriguingly, Ruisdael also had a career as a doctor and surgeon, and the analogy between the requirement for a steady hand in his painting technique and in this other highly skilled profession is not lost on art historians. He had a successful career as an artist and, presumably, as a surgeon.[3]

Laurie Benson

27. JAN STEEN
Dutch, 1626–1679

Interior

Signed l.l.: *J Steen* [*J* and *S* in ligature], undated; painted *c*.1661–65
Oil on wood panel
55.6 x 43.0 cm (22 x 17 in.)
Felton Bequest 1922 (1248–3)

PROVENANCE
William Wells, Redleaf, 1833; the late William Wells sale, Christie's, London, 12 May 1848, lot 86; from which purchased by Henry Vane, 2nd Duke of Cleveland, Raby Castle, Durham; Lord Barnard, Raby Castle, 1922; from whom acquired by the Felton Bequest, for the National Gallery of Victoria, 1922.

SELECTED EXHIBITIONS
The Golden Age of Dutch Art: Seventeenth Century Paintings from the Rijksmuseum and Australian Collections, Art Gallery of Western Australia, Perth, Art Gallery of South Australia, Adelaide, Queensland Art Gallery, Brisbane, 1997–98, cat. no. 37.

Jan Steen's bawdy *Interior*, like his portrayals of dissolute households, is a catalogue of domestic vices, the virtuous family turned upside down, with its moral transgressions recorded with humour. The meticulous execution reflects the influence of such Leiden 'fine painters' (*fijnschilders*) as Gerrit Dou and Frans van Mieris, but the greater emphasis on the narrative linking of the gestures and expressions of the main figures suggests that this painting was created *c*.1661–65, while Steen was living in Haarlem.

Light from the left illuminates ten people, most of whom carouse and merrily enjoy themselves. They are grouped together in the smoky, littered interior of an inn; at the left is a bed with open curtains and a chandelier and, at the right, plates and jugs are displayed on a shelf, and a mortar and pestle are shown on a cupboard. An amorous cavalier, wearing a red cap adorned with a long white feather, touches the breast of a mother, who looks approvingly at him as she suckles her baby at her other breast and reaches for the bedclothes from a foreground cradle. This woman's elderly husband, slumped in a chair near a fireplace at the right, appears not only drunk but also resigned to the cavalier's lustful action. There is a three-quarter-empty gin bottle next to the husband, who is unable to light his pipe with a burning coal, just as he is unable to kindle his young wife's passion. An old photograph of the painting shows that on the wall above the husband there was originally a drawing of an owl.[1] Very slight traces of this drawing are still visible, and X-radiographic examination has confirmed the form of an owl in this area. In Dutch art the owl is a traditional symbol of drunkenness, stupidity and folly, because of such popular folk sayings as 'He is as drunk as an owl' and 'What good are a candle and spectacles if the owl simply refuses to see?', the latter saying implying that foolish people will always be morally blind.[2] These words are inscribed below a print of an owl, a candle and a pair of spectacles that hangs above a drunken woman and man in Steen's painting *The Drunken Couple*, *c*.1664–68 (Rijksmuseum, Amsterdam).

Other details in the painting, such as the mussel shell in the left foreground, the cat staring at the mother, the mortar and pestle, and the woman's red-stockinged foot elevated on a footwarmer, emphasize the lustful intentions of the cavalier and the mother. Mussels, like oysters, were considered an aphrodisiac and their appearance was likened to that of the female genitals; the cat probably serves as a symbol of sensuality or lasciviousness; the mortar and pestle often suggest the sexual act; and the red-stockinged foot reveals the mother's sexual wantonness.[3] The standing man in the background who laughs and proposes a toast has Jan Steen's features, as seen in his *Self-Portrait as a Lutenist* of *c*.1663–65 (Museo Thyssen-Bornemisza, Madrid).[4] Like an actor, Steen represented himself as various personae in his paintings. However, he was basically a moralist and in this work, as in many others, he showed the moral chaos affecting the family and society in general as a result of self-indulgence, lust and drunkenness.

Frank I. Heckes

28. JAN STEEN

The Wedding Party

Signed l.r.: *J Steen* [J and S in ligature], undated; painted *c*.1667–68
Oil on wood panel
45.5 x 37.3 cm (18 x 14 3/4 in.)
Presented through The Art Foundation of Victoria by Mr James Fairfax,
Honorary Life Benefactor, 1992 (E1–1992)

Jan Steen's *Wedding Party*, although containing passages, such as the dress of the young woman in the foreground, that recall the Leiden 'fine painting' (*fijnschilderij*) technique, has the dynamic movement of figures and the basically free, illusionistic brushstrokes that are characteristic of Steen's style in *c*.1667–68.

Steen portrays a wedding celebration, which takes place at an inn.[1] Through an archway, in a back room, the bride sits at a table with her contented father at the left and her roundfaced mother barely visible at the right.[2] A floral marriage wreath hangs above the young bride's head while a second wreath hangs above the head of the much older bridegroom, who stands in front of the table to propose a toast. The bride, wearing a small bridal crown and her hair loose as a symbol of chastity, looks rather sad and does not raise up the glass in front of her.[3] This unequal marriage between a young woman and an old, wealthy man is paralleled in the foreground by another, equally ill-matched, couple, who are also placed under a marriage wreath. An elderly man, who, as indicated by his white apron is the innkeeper, tips his flower-decorated hat and bends over, extending his right hand, to invite an attractive young lady to dance while an old woman, probably the girl's mother, smiles and looks approvingly at the possible match.[4] The elderly man wears an antiquated sixteenth-century doublet and slashed sleeves, his costume recalling those worn by the greybeard Pantalone in the Italian commedia dell'arte; the younger man dancing in the background, who also raises up his hat, has a long phallic nose and a costume similar to that of another Italian character, Giangurgolo, famous for his insatiable appetite.[5]

The young seated woman, elegantly attired in a blue-grey dress and orange cloak, raises up her right hand while bending her left hand limply backwards, as if hesitant to accept the old suitor's offer. She looks directly at him but does not gaze amorously into the man's eyes, as does the woman in front of the archway; nor, however, is the seated woman downcast like the woman behind her, whose grinning male companion does not take advantage of the passion of youth, and turns away. The sculpted cupids holding dolphins by the tail, which appear under the table beside the foreground woman, suggest that she will accept. They have been shown to relate to an emblem in *Le Théâtre des bons engins* (1539) by Guillaume de La Perrière, wherein a man is depicted seizing a large dolphin by its tail. The explanation for the emblem states: 'It is easier to hold fast a dolphin than control the fickle heart of a woman. However skilfully cunning a man may be, a woman's mind is smarter … When a husband believes he has her subject to his will … then she suddenly tears herself away from the halter'.[6] Steen may refer to this emblem to suggest that the young woman will seek marriage with the wealthy old innkeeper in order to gain greater freedom, but that he will be deceived because of her fickle heart.

The innkeeper resembles the wealthy old suitor in Steen's *Choice between Old Age and Youth* of *c*.1662–65 (Muzeum Narodowe, Warsaw). In that work, which conflates two poems by Gerbrand Adriaensz Bredero (1585–1618) about two pairs of unequal lovers, a maiden and her young beau sit together and smile, but show no interest as the old man offers the maiden money, and a rich crone in the background approaches with a purse, to try to tempt the young man (this painting includes a print depicting people acting appropriately for their stage on the stairway of life).[7] Steen's *Wedding Party* similarly portrays ill-matched couples, and the point in both works is that marriages should be based not on financial interest but on love between partners who are equal in age and socioeconomic standing.

Frank I. Heckes

PROVENANCE

Anton Meynts, Amsterdam, 1823; the late Anton Meynts sale, de Vries, Amsterdam, 15 July 1823, lot 118; from which purchased by Nieuwenhuys; van Cranenburgh, Amsterdam; Lord Charles Townshend, London; William Wells, Redleaf; C. J. Nieuwenhuys, 1886; the late C. J. Nieuwenhuys sale, Christie's, London, 17 July 1886, lot 98; from which purchased by Galerie Sedelmeyer, Paris; Maurice Kann, Paris, 1911; with Agnew's, London, 1946; R. P. Silcock; with Agnew's, London, 1974; James Fairfax, Sydney; by whom presented to the National Gallery of Victoria, through The Art Foundation of Victoria, 1992.

29. MEINDERT HOBBEMA
Dutch, 1638–1709

The Old Oak

Signed and dated l.l.: *M. Hobbema. / F 1662*
Oil on canvas
101.0 x 144.0 cm (39 3/4 x 56 3/4 in.)
Felton Bequest 1950 (2252–4)

PROVENANCE
Jonkheer Alberda, Castle
Dijksterhuis, Pieterburen, 1829;
Alberda family, Castle Dijksterhuis,
1834; from whom purchased by van
Arnhem and Goekinga, Groningen,
1834; Colonel de Biré, Brussels
(collection assembled by Héris),
1841; Héris sale, Paillet/Bonnefons,
Paris, 25 March 1841, lot 1 (bought
in); private collection, France; sale,
Hôtel Drouot, Paris, 25 May 1945,
lot A; with Agnew's, London, 1949;
from whom acquired by the Felton
Bequest, for the National Gallery of
Victoria, 1949.

Around 1655, at the age of fifteen or sixteen, Meindert Hobbema became one of the few apprentices to enter the studio of the landscape artist Jacob van Ruisdael (1628/29–1682).[1] Ruisdael had a profound effect on Hobbema's work, with the two artists often portraying the same scenes (Hobbema drew and painted the same mill as appears in Ruisdael's painting *The Watermill* in this exhibition (cat. no. 26)).

Hobbema specialized in producing heavily wooded landscapes, which were romantic in character like those of his master, although he did not imbue his works with the same degree of drama or eerie atmosphere as did Ruisdael. This difference in treatment is clearly demonstrated in *The Old Oak*, which has its source in Ruisdael's etching *Travellers, c.*1655.[2] In the print, the composition is tightly focused on the trees and the swamp, which take up nearly all of the picture space, with only a small portion of sky visible in the top right corner. If the viewer can imagine both artists standing before this scene, Hobbema has seemingly taken many steps back from Ruisdael, and has expanded the scope of his vision; thus the viewer is both more distant and slightly more elevated from the point of view shown in the print. Moreover, Hobbema has contained the composition very much within the boundaries of the canvas, whereas the print, in giving the impression that the swamp extends outside the image into the viewer's space, perhaps engages and involves the viewer more directly than does the painting.

In the print, the figures are so dominated by the swamp, and so dwarfed by the natural surroundings, that the work has a more sinister and mysterious atmosphere than does Hobbema's painting. Interestingly, as Ruisdael worked towards the final state of the print, he added more vegetation, leaves and branches, thus darkening the final version and intensifying the bleak atmosphere.[3] In comparison, the painting is light and airy, as not only is the sky more dominant, but the vegetation is less dense and, although the foreground is in shadow, the background is brightly illuminated by sunlight.

These differences are so stark that they indicate that Hobbema was not trying to replicate the artistic intention of Ruisdael, or produce a coloured version of the print, as Stechow and others have suggested;[4] rather, Hobbema has interpreted his master's work, giving it an alternative narrative content. In Ruisdael's print, the swamp is the subject, and is a dominant entity, overwhelming the figures who travel through it. Hobbema, by contrast, has placed far greater emphasis on the oak tree, and by doing so he has created a melancholic study, more about the struggle of the water-bound majestic tree than the predicament of people. Both artists depict almost identical leafless limbs emanating from the oak tree. In Ruisdael's hands, however, the limbs are jagged and sharply pointed, almost weapon-like, posing a danger to the figures. Hobbema has isolated these limbs, thereby drawing our attention to them, and suggesting the inevitable death of the oak. The small tree in the centre of the composition has even less chance of survival and the sharply leaning tree on the right seems also to be succumbing to the inevitable force of the water. The still water appears as a calm lake, which even has ducks swimming on it, rather than as the murky, threatening swamp of Ruisdael.

The differences in the two works exemplify the contrasting approaches that Ruisdael and Hobbema had to their art. Ruisdael usually sought the most dramatic twist to a scene, while Hobbema took a subtler and more gentle approach, downplaying the human drama.

Laurie Benson

30. REMBRANDT
(Rembrandt Harmensz van Rijn) Dutch, 1606–1669

Portrait of a White-Haired Man

Signed and dated u.c.: *Rembrandt f. / 1667*
Oil on canvas
108.9 x 92.7 cm (42 3/4 x 36 1/2 in.)
Felton Bequest 1951 (2372–4)

This frontal three-quarter-length portrait of a man[1] employs a classic pyramidal portrait format, but one animated by a slight baroque twist that provides a note of selfconscious alertness. The sitter, whose identity is unknown, is dressed in contemporary attire, his long hair styled in the fashion of the later seventeenth century, and very like that of the painter Gérard de Lairesse in Rembrandt's 1665 portrait (Metropolitan Museum of Art, New York).[2] The subject of the Melbourne portrait wears the standard black garments of the well-to-do burgher and rests his left hand on his hat, which is now very difficult to distinguish. His right hand is cropped, a detail that has given rise to speculation that the canvas has been cut. Technical evidence, however, indicates that this has not been the case and that the composition is exactly as Rembrandt intended it to be.

The man is seated in an armchair, set against a neutral background at the upper right of which is a swathe of red drapery, which is painted with bold, broad brushwork. Level with the loosely painted drapery is the face, which, by contrast, is modelled in great detail, its accumulated layers of visible brushstrokes building up into a surface that is palpable both as flesh and as paint. The sitter's curling hair is in some areas depicted suggestively, and, in other areas, with carefully applied detail: one area of waves at the right has been defined with the blunt end of a brush pushed through wet paint, whereas elsewhere individual strands have been carefully isolated. The collar, like the drapery, the brown undergarment and the white cuffs, is daring in its broad handling. The sitter's lips are slightly parted. His gaze, which seems to slip in and out of focus,[3] is like the brushwork, which alternates between illusionistic representation and an assertive, painterly presence.

Although trained as a history painter in his native Leiden, Rembrandt first achieved wide fame as a portraitist not long after arriving in Amsterdam in the early 1630s. From that time on, portraits – both of individuals and of groups – became his financial mainstay. If one includes his character heads (*tronies*), portraiture comprises almost two-thirds of his entire oeuvre.

This painting is an outstanding example of Rembrandt's late style and is one of the last two signed and dated portraits he made in 1667, just two years before his death. The other is the *Portrait of an Elderly Man* at Cowdray Park, Sussex; that work, however, is painted with more uniformly broad brushstrokes.[4] The Melbourne picture is unusual among the very late portraits for its comparatively detailed treatment of the head.[5] During the 1660s, when fashion in painting was turning to a smoother style of brushwork and a higher degree of finish, Rembrandt continued to uphold a different aesthetic, preferring broadly handled paint. According to Houbraken, Rembrandt maintained that a painting was finished not when convention would have it, but when the painter determined that it was.[6] His achievements were nevertheless still appreciated by connoisseurs. He continued to receive significant commissions from wealthy individuals and in 1662 was commissioned to paint his last official group portrait, of the Syndics of the Cloth Merchants' Guild, the so-called *Staalmeesters* (Rijksmuseum, Amsterdam). In the year that the Melbourne portrait was painted, Rembrandt was visited by Cosimo III de' Medici, Prince of Tuscany, who recorded in a travel journal his visit to 'the famous painter Rembrandt'; it is also likely that in 1669, the year of Rembrandt's death, Cosimo again visited the artist, and bought one of his last self-portraits,[7] a work now at the Galleria degli Uffizi, Florence.[8]

Irena Zdanowicz

PROVENANCE

Vincent Donjeux, 1793; his sale, Lebrun Paillet, Paris, 29 April 1793, lot 148; Heneage Finch, 5th Earl of Aylesford (1786–1859), Packington Hall, Meriden, Coventry, Warwickshire; Sir Alfred Beit (1853–1906), 1899, 1905, 1906; Sir Otto Beit (1865–1930); Sir Alfred Lane Beit (1903–1994); with C. Marshall Spink, London, 1951; from whom acquired by the Felton Bequest, for the National Gallery of Victoria, 1951.

SELECTED EXHIBITIONS

Rembrandt: The Master and His Workshop – Paintings, Gemäldegalerie, Staatliche Museen zu Berlin – Preußischer Kulturbesitz, Berlin, Rijksmuseum, Amsterdam, National Gallery, London, 1991–92, cat. no. 50; *Rembrandt: A Genius and His Impact*, National Gallery of Victoria, Melbourne, National Gallery of Australia, Canberra, 1997–98, cat. no. 27.

31. ARENT DE GELDER
Dutch, 1645–1727

King Ahasuerus Condemning Haman

Signed u.r.: *A de Gelder f*, undated; painted *c*.1680
Oil on canvas
80.5 x 96.5 cm (31 3/4 x 38 in.)
Felton Bequest 1934 (216–4)

The subject of this painting is an incident from the Book of Esther. Esther, wife of Ahasuerus, King of Babylon, has learned from her uncle Mordecai of Haman's plot to slaughter the entire Jewish population in the kingdom. Esther has bravely petitioned the king to spare the Jews, at the same time revealing her own, hitherto secret, Jewish identity. Arent de Gelder's painting shows the second of two banquets that Esther has arranged, and the moment depicted is that in which she unmasks Haman as the true enemy. 'Then was Haman afraid before the king and the queen' (Esther 7:6). Haman is seen here slumped in the darkness behind the table, covering his face in fear and horror. Esther, dressed in pearls and gold raiment, is partly hidden in the left background. Dominating the picture is Ahasuerus. Anger at the duplicity and evil intentions of the scheming Haman has impelled the king to push aside his armchair and to lean sharply forward, causing his royal chain to slip. His clenched fists, and the glinting dagger that he holds in his left hand, indicate both his anger and his resolve to punish Haman. The action depicted appears to be the very moment before Ahasuerus leaves the table in wrath, to go into the palace gardens (Esther 7:7). He will return to order Haman's death, on the gallows that Haman himself had constructed for Mordecai. Only then 'was the king's wrath pacified' (Esther 7:10).

This canvas is one of no fewer than ten extant paintings by de Gelder of subjects from the Book of Esther. All of these works, executed in the 1680s, depict three-quarter-length figures against a neutral background. The paring down of details, and a close-up focus on the action, allowed the artist to maximize the dramatic and psychological impact of the story. In this he reveals his debt to Rembrandt, whose workshop he attended for two years, probably from 1660, after which time he returned to his native Dordrecht.

De Gelder's painting technique is also indebted to Rembrandt's late manner: it is free and painterly, with some areas selected for a higher degree of finish. This differentiation is not merely a stylistic mannerism or an exercise in painterly bravura, but serves to focus attention on details important to the narrative or to convey the illusion of three-dimensionality (such as is seen in the heavily impastoed chain, the gold dagger and the elaborate turban). Abundant use is made of a kind of sgraffito, whereby details of the design are scratched out from a layer of wet paint. The effect is one of extraordinary spontaneity. De Gelder achieves this with an astonishing variety of strokes, both broad – as in the drapery on Ahasuerus's right knee, which appears almost as though it might have been smeared by a finger dragged over the surface of the wet paint – and fine, as in the bouncing feathers that adorn the king's turban.

We do not know exactly why the story of Esther featured more prominently in the work of de Gelder than it did in the work of any other seventeenth-century Dutch painter. The popularity of the theme accelerated following the 1564 publication of Philips Galle's eight engravings after Maarten van Heemskerck's illustrations of the Esther story, a series that must have been known to de Gelder, as he found in it a model for the exotic turban worn by Ahasuerus.[1] Rembrandt treated the subject on canvas as well as in etching.[2] Throughout the seventeenth century, Esther's story of the salvation of the Jews from mortal danger had wide cultural currency among the Dutch, who identified in the biblical narrative their own struggle to free themselves from the yoke of Catholic Spain. However, by the 1680s, these political issues had been resolved, and, as a history painter, de Gelder was probably more interested in the dramatic potential of the story.[3]

Irena Zdanowicz

PROVENANCE

Private collection, Paris; from which purchased by Douwes, Amsterdam; with Douwes, Amsterdam, 1934; from whom acquired by the Felton Bequest, for the National Gallery of Victoria, 1934.

SELECTED EXHIBITIONS

Rembrandt: A Genius and His Impact, National Gallery of Victoria, Melbourne, National Gallery of Australia, Canberra, 1997–98, cat. no. 69.

EIGHTEENTH CENTURY

32. NICOLAS DE LARGILLIERRE
French, 1656–1746

Crown Prince Frederick Augustus of Saxony

Unsigned, undated; painted between 1714 and 1715
Oil on canvas
137.1 x 103.8 cm (54 x 40 3/4 in.)
Everard Studley Miller Bequest 1968 (1819–5)

This impressive portrait depicts Frederick Augustus II (1697–1763), Elector of Saxony and King of Poland (as Augustus III), with a remarkable sense of presence and alertness of address. He stands in a magnificently shining suit of armour, and crisply painted red cloak lined with yellow, amid a rocky outcrop, against a background windswept landscape and stormy sky. His right hand firmly grasps the plumed helmet of the Polish cavalry (Hussarian), while his left holds his right glove and rests by his sword. The effect is awe-inspiring and daunting. Yet the viewer is also struck by the expression of magnanimous confidence, which suffuses the picture with a sense of benevolence as well as power.

The portrait was painted when Frederick, as a young man, spent a year in Paris in 1714–15. It appears that the painting was intended as a pendant to the portrait of the prince's father, Augustus the Strong, painted at about the same time and now at the Nelson-Atkins Museum of Art, Kansas City.[1] Equally robust and confident, Frederick Augustus I sports similar armour, and points back into the picture space, towards a distant landscape, in a gesture of command. Both father and son are shown wearing the sash of the Danish Order of the Elephant, conferred on Augustus II in 1711. The existence of copies of the portraits (both Musée Cantonal des Beaux-Arts, Lausanne), attributed to Jean-Baptiste Oudry, supports the hypothesis that the two paintings on which the copies are based were executed at the same time.[2] Only in hairstyle is there a difference in presentation – between the father's more relaxed coiffure and the extreme contrivance evident in the powdered wig of Augustus II, with its fashionable peaks.[3]

Frederick Augustus I was keenly interested in French art and employed the French architect Raymond le Plat as his artistic adviser. Frederick Augustus II was also an enthusiastic collector and patron of the arts. Of particular interest is his acquisition of Giambattista Tiepolo's *Banquet of Cleopatra*, c.1743–44, which hung in the elector's hunting castle, Hubertusburg, and is now in the collection of the National Gallery of Victoria (reproduced on p. 12 of this catalogue).

Nicolas de Largillierre was born in Paris, studied in Antwerp, and from 1674 worked in London, where he met Peter Lely (1618–1680), who was successor to van Dyck as court painter to the English Crown. After returning to Paris, probably in mid-1679, Largillierre was elected to the Académie; he was eventually elected director, in 1738. Together with his close friend Hyacinthe Rigaud,[4] he became one of the two leading French portraitists of his time, adept at the flattering enhancements so sought after by his patrons. His technique is notable for its facility and fluency, effects influenced by the baroque energy of van Dyck's brushwork. Largillierre's depictions are to be valued for their direct engagement with the viewer; their lavish attention to textures, colouristic detail and sparkling light effects; and the sprightly, incipiently rococo, quality of the artist's brushstrokes. His works mark the transition from the heavier rhetoric of the Baroque to the softer atmospheres and more delicate intimacies of eighteenth-century portraiture.

Vivien Gaston

PROVENANCE

Princess von Hohenlohe, Paris; Baron d'Huart, Paris, 1938; his sale, Hôtel Drouot, Paris, 7 December 1938, lot 38; private collection, Paris, 1966; with Heim, Paris; with Heim, London, 1968; from whom acquired by the National Gallery of Victoria, under the terms of the Everard Studley Miller Bequest, 1968.

SELECTED EXHIBITIONS

The Great Eighteenth Century Exhibition in the National Gallery of Victoria, National Gallery of Victoria, Melbourne, 1983.

33. CANALETTO
(Giovanni Antonio Canal) Italian, 1697–1768

Bacino di S. Marco: From the Piazzetta

Unsigned, undated; painted *c*.1735–45
Oil on canvas
131.4 x 163.2 cm (51 3/4 x 64 1/4 in.)
Felton Bequest 1986 (E1–1986)

After learning his craft painting scenery with his father, Bernardo Canal, for the thriving Venetian opera and theatre, the young Canaletto found a niche painting landscapes for a growing clientele. His career subsequently developed to the point where he became exclusively an urban landscape artist, taking his native Venice as the main subject of his art.

Canaletto's views of Venice were disseminated widely in Europe as both paintings and prints, which he produced primarily for the burgeoning tourist market in Italy, and particularly for wealthy Englishmen on the Grand Tour.[1] To this day, more of his works are found outside Italy than in his native land. The present painting is one of four views of Venice that were commissioned from Canaletto by William Holbech, for the dining room of his family home, Farnborough Hall, in Warwickshire. Holbech had spent fifteen years in Venice and knew Canaletto well, and the artist may have had a hand in designing the elaborate stucco settings within which the works were installed in Holbech's home.[2]

Canaletto painted evocative rather than topographically accurate renderings of Venice, as he took subtle and very effective liberties with the placement, proportions and perspectives of buildings, to create balanced and appealing compositions. The view in the Melbourne painting is that looking southwest into the Bacino di S. Marco, the stretch of water between the Piazzetta S. Marco, the island of S. Giorgio Maggiore, the Giudecca and the opening of the Grand Canal.[3] To the right is the Sansovino Library and the column of St Theodore, which dominate and anchor the composition. Canaletto has manipulated the placement of the Sansovino Library, so that it appears in line with the picture plane rather than at an angle to it. Across the Grand Canal we can see a dome of S. Maria della Salute, which would in fact have been obscured completely by the Sansovino Library if viewed from the point where Canaletto would have stood to survey this scene. He has also shifted the column of St Theodore to the left to allow this glimpse of the dome. Adjacent to S. Maria della Salute is the Dogana di Mare with its golden orb, a structure that seems closer to the Piazzetta than it appears in reality. Had Canaletto obeyed the constraints of geographic accuracy, the column of St Mark, topped by a statue of a winged lion, would have further obscured the view across the Bacino; therefore he excluded the column from the painting.[4] Our view thus unhindered, we see in the distance the Giudecca, highlighted by the domed Il Redentore, a Franciscan church designed by Andrea Palladio (1508–1580). Canaletto has also brought the distant islands closer to the viewer, allowing the buildings to be seen clearly, at a more impressive scale.

Canaletto developed a painting technique and style that suited his aim of quickly producing his popular paintings. From the 1730s onward, his works are quite linear and tightly structured, so that they present a detailed appearance. Yet the artist did not overwork the paint or labour in minute detail, and close examination of this painting reveals his use of quite broad brushstrokes: he cleverly used a rapid application of paint to give this work energy and vitality, despite its rather formulaic and controlled structure. The light is clear and even, and highlights of red, green and blue in the costumes of the busy figures contrast with the masses of sky, sea and the paving of the Piazzetta. These technical qualities reveal the supreme confidence of the artist.[5] Canaletto consistently produced these idealized scenes, showing Venice at its most splendid, and it is little wonder that he was the artist chosen by Holbech to paint mementos of the Englishman's favourite city.

Laurie Benson

PROVENANCE

Commissioned by William Holbech (d. 1771), Farnborough Hall, Warwickshire; Captain Ronald Holbech, Farnborough Hall, 1930; from whom purchased by Savile Gallery, London; with Savile Gallery, London, 1940; with Arthur Tooth & Sons, London, 1944; with Agnew's, London, 1976, 1982, 1985; from whom acquired by the Felton Bequest, for the National Gallery of Victoria, 1985.

SELECTED EXHIBITIONS

The Great Eighteenth Century Exhibition in the National Gallery of Victoria, National Gallery of Victoria, Melbourne, 1983.

34. BERNARDO BELLOTTO
Italian (active in Dresden and Warsaw), 1720–1780

Ruins of the Forum, Rome

Unsigned, undated; painted *c.*1743
Oil on canvas
87.0 x 148.0 cm (34 1/4 x 58 1/4 in.)
Felton Bequest 1919 (964–3)

The eighteenth-century Venetian view painter Bernardo Bellotto painted this view of the west end of the Forum in Rome around 1743, when he was still in his early twenties. Bellotto was the nephew and pupil of Venice's most famous view painter, Giovanni Antonio Canal, il Canaletto. By the time he left Canaletto's busy studio in the early 1740s to commence his career as an independent artist, Bellotto had quite thoroughly absorbed his uncle's painting manner and techniques. Bellotto was, however, an independent-minded person who, at an early age, decided to leave the security of Venice and explore Italy and, eventually, central and northern Europe. These travels stimulated the young artist to develop his own distinctive images of towns and landscapes, images that were themselves to become highly valued. *Ruins of the Forum, Rome* dates from his very first sojourn, as a solo artist, in that city. The painting is one of a group of seven large views showing the most famous landmarks of Rome.[1]

By the eighteenth century, the old Forum was popularly known as the 'Campo Vaccino', literally 'cow paddock'. Some of the most famous architectural ruins of ancient Rome, such as the three prominent columns of the Temple of Castor and Pollux seen in the foreground of this view, were still visible, though others were wholly or partly submerged in the soil of the Campo. Full archaeological excavation of the area did not take place until the nineteenth century, so the Forum of Bellotto's time remained a sleepy and poetic reminder of the decay of ancient Rome's former glories. In this view Bellotto contrasts the ruins of the ancient temples with the still formidable presence of Michelangelo's bell tower for the Senatorial Palace on the Capitol, and also with the comings and goings of daily life in Rome, including the eager 'Grand Tourists' playfully exploring the monuments.

Bellotto was a painter who delighted in rendering both the geometry and the surfaces of the architecture he painted. The slightly telescopic effect of the receding architectural elements in the present work was achieved with the accentuated diagonal lines of the interconnecting smaller buildings, set against the solid vertical forms of the major architectural components. Strong light from the right of the painting shows the variety of colours and surface textures of the worn terracotta brick, plaster, stone and travertine surfaces on the various buildings. Fine, incised outlines of most of the buildings are evident over the surface of the painting. This use of outline reveals the influence of Canaletto's methodical working process, in which the lines of the composition were transcribed from a detailed preparatory drawing.

This view of the Forum is based on a sketch attributed to Canaletto and made about twenty years earlier (British Museum, Department of Prints and Drawings, London).[2] On his arrival in Rome, Bellotto revived the view by making numerous amendments. A similar Canaletto painting of the same view, deriving more directly from the original drawing and executed around 1742, is in the Royal Collection at Windsor Castle.[3]

In 1748 Bellotto left Italy for good and was to find acclaim for his large views of Vienna, Munich, Dresden and Warsaw. These paintings are characterized by a wide, horizontal format and by inventive positioning of the primary architectural components. The present view of Rome is one of Bellotto's first attempts at this kind of large architectural view and prefigures the fine finish and complexity of composition found in his mature works.

Carl Villis

PROVENANCE

7th Earl of Bessborough, Bessborough, Kilkenny; the late Earl of Bessborough sale, Christie's, London, 14 March 1891, lot 149; from which purchased by Agnew's, London; Hope Heirlooms (Lord Francis Pelham-Clinton-Hope), Dorking, 1917; his sale, Christie's, London, 20 July 1917, lot 76; from which purchased by Pawsey and Paine; A. H. Buttery, London; from whom acquired by the Felton Bequest, for the National Gallery of Victoria, 1918.

SELECTED EXHIBITIONS

The Great Eighteenth Century Exhibition in the National Gallery of Victoria, National Gallery of Victoria, Melbourne, 1983.

35. 36. EDWARD HAYTLEY
English, active 1740–1761

The Brockman Family at Beachborough
Temple Pond with Temple in Right Foreground
Temple Pond with Temple in the Distance on Left

Unsigned, undated; painted *c*.1744–46
Oil on canvas
Each canvas 52.7 x 65.0 cm (20 3/4 x 25 1/2 in.)
Everard Studley Miller Bequest 1963 (1246A–5, 1246B–5)

During the 1730s and 1740s in England, the expanding and 'improving' of country estates was a favourite preoccupation among leisured landowners. Squire James Brockman (1696–1767) of Beachborough Manor in Kent was no exception. Indeed it would appear that he had his garden temple – surely modelled on Lord Cobham's Rotunda in the celebrated gardens at Stowe – sketched, in preparation for these delightful portraits of his estate, before the temple was even built. According to the Brockman family accounts, payments were made in 1744 for 'building of great pond'[1] and for 'ceiling of temple at pond'.[2] Yet already in December 1743, Brockman's neighbour, Mrs Robinson, had written to her daughter, the celebrated bluestocking Mrs Elizabeth Montagu (1720–1800), describing Edward Haytley's first sketches for his painted views:

> M[r] Haytely is come back from my Neighbours where he has been drawing a landskip from y[e] life it is a veiw of his pond & his Temple that is to be built … with some figuers to adorn it the principle of which are y[e] Squire & Miss Molly. She is sett on a stool and drawing & he is … smiling very graciously on her … all this is to be put into a Picture & painted by M[r] Hayteley.[3]

Mrs Robinson goes on to say that Haytley also sketched Miss Highmore, presumably Susanna, a family friend and the daughter of the artist Joseph Highmore, falling into the water and being pulled out by her leg! Mrs Robinson identifies all the figures in the painting now known as *Temple Pond with Temple in the Distance on Left*: Miss Highmore walking with the local parson, the Reverend Edmund Parker; Brockman's cousins, Mary ('Miss Molly', who kept house at Beachborough) and Elizabeth ('Miss Betty', in the blue riding habit); little Miss Henckle and her parents.

In the second painting, of the pool seen from the opposite end, with the temple now on the right, the two young women appear to be Miss Molly and Miss Betty, while the seated gentleman is probably the squire again, or perhaps the young women's father, Henry Brockman of Cheriton. The scale of the works, so characteristic of the English conversation piece, makes it difficult to tell. However, Mrs Robinson considered that Haytley's 'genius' was in capturing, even in miniature, real likenesses rather than merely 'something of a caricatura'.[4] The original red-brick Tudor house is clearly identifiable in the middle distance, as is the view beyond the estate to the English Channel and the cliffs of France on the horizon.

Little is known about Edward Haytley – although in 1754 Mrs Robinson hoped he might 'succeed, as he is a young man of great merits'.[5] He appears in the Brockman cash books between 1740 and 1748;[6] was certainly at Beachborough in December 1743; and executed a portrait of Mrs Montagu and her family at their country house (private collection) the following year. In 1760 and 1761 he exhibited three-quarter-length portraits with the Society of Artists in London. It is possible that, like Arthur Devis, Haytley was a native of Preston in Lancashire, in the north of England. Both artists were largely forgotten by the end of the eighteenth century. While the informality of their small family portraits was a welcome change from the exuberant baroque of the early 1700s, and spread from the aristocracy to the middle classes, this approach was eclipsed later in the century by Joshua Reynolds's 'grand style'.[7]

Jane Clark

PROVENANCE

James Brockman (1696–1767), Beachborough Manor, Kent; Drake-Brockman family; by descent to Mrs W. Arkle, Western Australia, 1961; with Leggatt's, London, 1961, 1963; from whom acquired by the National Gallery of Victoria, under the terms of the Everard Studley Miller Bequest, 1963.

SELECTED EXHIBITIONS

The Great Eighteenth Century Exhibition in the National Gallery of Victoria, National Gallery of Victoria, Melbourne, 1983; *Manners and Morals: Hogarth and British Painting 1700–1760*, Tate Gallery, London, 1987–88, cat. nos 127, 128.

37. JOSEPH HIGHMORE
English, 1692–1780

Self-Portrait

Unsigned, undated; painted c.1745–47
Oil on canvas
126.4 x 101.0 cm (49 3/4 x 39 3/4 in.)
Felton Bequest 1947 (1760–4)

PROVENANCE

Collection of the artist; Anthony
Highmore (1718–1799) (the artist's
son); John Field Highmore
(1749–1794); Maria Highmore
(later Mrs William Payler)
(1783–1814), Patricksbourne,
Kent; Charlotte Clara Payler (later
Mrs F. Morgan Payler), Biddlesden
Park, Buckinghamshire; Frederick
Morgan Payler; Frederick Trafford
Morgan Payler (1872–1954), Ballarat,
Victoria, 1947; from whom acquired
by the Felton Bequest, for the
National Gallery of Victoria, 1947.

SELECTED EXHIBITIONS

*The Great Eighteenth Century
Exhibition in the National Gallery of
Victoria*, National Gallery of Victoria,
Melbourne, 1983; Art Gallery of
South Australia, Adelaide, 1996
(loaned for display with *The Artist's
Wife Susanna, Daughter Susanna
and Son Anthony, c.1727*, then
recently acquired by the Art Gallery
of South Australia).

Trained first as clerk to an attorney, Joseph Highmore switched professions in about 1714, entering Sir Godfrey Kneller's Academy to study painting. By 1715 Highmore was established as a portraitist, painting citizens of London 'in the Very habit they appear in'.[1] He evidently met William Hogarth at the St Martin's Lane Academy in 1720, and Highmore's portraits certainly share some of Hogarth's innovative warmth in interpretation of character. Three or four years later, Highmore moved from the City of London to Lincoln's Inn Fields, where his friend the writer Samuel Richardson described him as 'an eminent painter, in Holborn-row'.[2] Richardson's novel *Pamela; or, Virtue Rewarded* (1740–41) later inspired Highmore's remarkable series of twelve narrative paintings of 1744 (now divided between the National Gallery of Victoria,[3] the Tate Gallery in London and the Fitzwilliam Museum, Cambridge), which reveal his knowledge of modern French art. Highmore had spent two months in Paris in 1734 and also visited Antwerp and Düsseldorf to see portraits by Rubens – whom he discussed in scholarly articles for the *Gentleman's Magazine*. Indeed he was an artist of considerable intellect, possessing, in the poetical words of his son-in-law: 'An eye, a hand, whose magic powers could save / From age and death the beauteous and the brave; / A head, which daily added to its store / Of useful knowledge, and yet sought for more'.[4]

Highmore was recognized by contemporaries as a master of two portrait styles, which he varied according to his sitter: the elegantly modish, and what George Vertue, the eighteenth-century chronicler of British art, called a 'natural easy style'. This handsome self-portrait epitomizes the latter. Highmore presents himself in the dual role of professional artist and educated gentleman. His 'morning' dress is consciously informal: a loose coat, and a soft cap on his shaven head – which would have been covered by a powdered wig on more formal occasions. Such attire was considered just as appropriate for eighteenth-century artists and men of letters as for gentlemen and aristocrats who wished to suggest the intellectual nature of their leisure pursuits.

This portrait is one of an important group by Highmore brought to Australia by a direct descendant of the artist. A lovely group portrait, c.1727, of the artist's wife, Susanna, with the Highmore children, Anthony (b. 1718) and young Susanna (b. 1725), is now at the Art Gallery of South Australia, Adelaide. Another portrait of daughter Susanna, as a very young woman, c.1740–45, with her pet parrot and a cat named Brue, is at the National Gallery of Victoria,[5] along with a portrait of a good-looking young man presumed to be an older Anthony, c.1745–47.[6] Highmore brought up his children with great thought and care. Both were trained as artists, and Highmore once wrote an article describing his success in educating a teenage daughter[7]: Susanna spoke fluent French and proficient Italian, published her poetry and was named one of Samuel Richardson's adopted 'literary daughters'.[8] Interestingly, she is probably one of the delightful cast of characters in Edward Haytley's *Brockman Family at Beachborough* (cat. no. 36), and her father is believed to have painted a portrait of Beachborough's squire, James Brockman.

Highmore's career spanned more than three decades before he retired in 1762 to live in Canterbury with his daughter and her husband, the Reverend John Duncombe. It was Duncombe who wrote of him, in a warmly respectful obituary in 1780: 'No man had more clearness and precision of ideas, or a more ardent desire to know the truth; and when known, conscientiously to pursue it … He retained [his talents] to the last'.[9]

Jane Clark

38. 39. FRANÇOIS BOUCHER
French, 1703–1770

The Mysterious Basket

Signed and dated l.l.: *F. Boucher – / 1748.*
Oil on canvas (oval)
92.7 x 78.9 cm (36 1/2 x 31 in.)
Purchased through The Art Foundation of Victoria with the assistance of Coles Myer Ltd, Fellow,
Mr Henry Krongold, CBE, and Mrs Dinah Krongold, Founder Benefactors, and the Westpac Banking
Corporation, Founder Benefactor, 1982 (E2–1982)

The Enjoyable Lesson

Signed and dated c.l.: *f Boucher / 1748*
Oil on canvas (oval)
92.5 x 78.6 cm (36 1/2 x 31 in.)
Felton Bequest 1982 (E1–1982)

PROVENANCE

The Enjoyable Lesson exhibited by
the artist, Salon, Paris, 1748, no. 19;
both works exhibited by the artist,
Salon, Paris, 1750, no. 24 (as two of
four paintings);[a] Countess of Rosebery
(1851–1890), Mentmore Towers,
Buckinghamshire, 1884;[b] on the US
art market; with Knoedler's, New
York, 1956; from whom purchased by
Rosenberg & Stiebel, New York, 1956;
from whom purchased by Durand-
Matthiesen, Geneva, 1956; Ortiz-Patiño
Collection; Georges Ortiz-Patiño; with
David Carritt, London, 1982;[c] from
whom acquired by the National
Gallery of Victoria: *The Mysterious
Basket* through The Art Foundation
of Victoria; *The Enjoyable Lesson*
through the Felton Bequest.

SELECTED EXHIBITIONS

*The Great Eighteenth Century
Exhibition in the National Gallery of
Victoria*, National Gallery of
Victoria, Melbourne, 1983.

At the Salon of 1750, François Boucher exhibited four oval paintings representing 'The sleep of a shepherdess to whom a rustic brings flowers on behalf of her shepherd'; 'A shepherd who shows his shepherdess how to play the flute'; 'A shepherd tuning his bagpipes near his shepherdess'; and 'Two lovers surprised in the backwoods'. The first two pictures can be identified with *The Enjoyable Lesson* and *The Mysterious Basket*, both signed and dated 1748; the third, also signed and dated 1748, is in the collection of Major John Mills, Hampshire;[1] and the fourth is now lost. A set of engravings by René Gaillard, corresponding to the four compositions but in a rectangular format, was made in 1758, when the paintings on which the engravings were based belonged to a certain Monsieur Perinet in Paris. The oval set of paintings has therefore been thought to have belonged to him.

As Laing[2] has argued, however, Perinet's images were probably based on a different (rectangular) set, perhaps painted especially for the engraver, since it was not customary for Boucher's engravers to adjust the format of compositions they reproduced. Laing has also cast doubt on the account of the early provenance of the Melbourne pictures as provided by Ananoff and Wildenstein, an account that implied a complicated story of separation and reunification.[3] Laing suggests instead that we know only that the oval set may have been broken up by 26 December 1827, when what appears to have been the oval version of *The Lovers Surprised* was sold at auction in Paris;[4] he further proposes that the two Melbourne pictures, which apparently remained together, were probably later acquired by Mayer Amschel de Rothschild (1818–1874), passing to his daughter, Hannah, Countess of Rosebery (1851–1890), at Mentmore, Buckinghamshire, where they are recorded in 1884 in the boudoir.

The Enjoyable Lesson and *The Mysterious Basket* are fine examples of Boucher's particular contribution to the genre of the painted pastoral. In contrast to Watteau's *fêtes galantes*, where the protagonists are aristocrats and the rustics are relegated to subsidiary roles, in Boucher's pastorals the protagonists are rustics. Their costumes are prettified versions of contemporary peasant dress, rather than the archaizing fancy dress of Watteau, the generalized classical draperies of mythological painting, or the elaborate hooped dresses and plumes of opera. Boucher's source of inspiration is not the elevated literary pastoral, but contemporary popular theatre.[5]

Boucher was a friend of the theatrical producer Charles-Simon Favart, whose company produced plays in the 1740s at one of the fairs near Paris, the Foire Saint-Laurent. These spectacles departed from the coarse, and somewhat cruel, humour of the commedia dell'arte, which had hitherto dominated such performances. The humour of Favart's rustic protagonists lay in their ingenuity rather than their stupidity. He introduced sentimental themes, especially the blooming of young love between shepherd and shepherdess, and dressed his actors in more realistic costumes. One such production, a pantomime called *Les Vendanges de Tempé*, met with such success in 1745 that it was reworked in 1752 as a

ballet-pantomime called *La Vallée de Montmorency*. The play tells the story of the love of a shepherdess, Lisette, and a shepherd referred to only as 'the Little Shepherd'. They suffer from a jealous rival and hostile parents, but their love eventually prevails. The play consisted of a series of tableaux with musical airs, many of which were plagiarized from popular songs (spoken dialogue was forbidden, since this was the monopoly of the official theatres). Hence the *Vendanges* was like a series of pictorial compositions, and some scenes may have been inspired by pictorial traditions. The influence soon flowed the other way, and within a year Boucher was producing paintings inspired by the play.

The Mysterious Basket and *The Enjoyable Lesson* are not straightforward illustrations of *Les Vendanges de Tempé*, as the differences between Boucher's imagery and the plot summary provided by the Parfaict brothers in 1756[6] are often considerable. The episode corresponding to *The Mysterious Basket* occurs in scene IV. After being scolded by her mother, Lisette sulks and falls asleep. The Little Shepherd comes across her and tries unsuccessfully to wake her. He retires, taking her basket in order to fill it with grapes, and later places it beside her. She continues to sleep, and he tries to wake her by tickling her lips with a straw. She awakens slowly, rubbing her lips, while the shepherd hides behind a thicket of flowers. The shepherdess awakens fully and is surprised to find her basket full beside her. She listens with pleasure to the singing of birds, and calls to her cousin Babet to help her catch them.

Boucher's painting tells a somewhat different story, the key to which is the Salon description. The man depicted is not the Little Shepherd, but a rustic acting on his behalf. The basket contains flowers rather than grapes, and also a note, as was traditionally delivered by third parties. These elements, and residual echoes of the pictorial tradition from which the composition ultimately derives – that of the satyr discovering a sleeping nymph – explain the young man's intense gaze and mature masculinity. The bagpipes behind the shepherdess seem to hint at a moment shortly after that shown in the engraving of *The Shepherd Tuning His Bagpipes*, the one composition in Boucher's set of four paintings that cannot be readily connected to a particular scene in the *Vendanges*. In *The Mysterious Basket*, the shepherd has departed, and the shepherdess has fallen asleep beside his bagpipes (the same garlanded log appears in the foreground of both works, perhaps a residual stage prop).

The Enjoyable Lesson is more closely tied to the story of the *Vendanges* as it has come down to us. In scene V, Babet and Lisette, in attempting to catch birds in a net, capture the Little Shepherd instead. After freeing and caressing him, they are invited to dance to the sound of his flute. After a few steps Lisette wants to play the flute, and the Little Shepherd teaches her, allowing her to blow while he does the fingering. Babet, though, not happy to dance alone to their music, wrests the flute from Lisette, and makes the Little Shepherd dance with her. Lisette then joins the dance, and the three perform a jealous *pas de trois*. The shepherd prefers Lisette, and Babet retires, uttering menaces. Although Boucher gives no hint of this amorous triangle, the androgynously youthful shepherd and girlish shepherdess have the sweet sentimentality of young love awakening that was Favart's innovation in the theatre; indeed, the motif of the boy fingering the flute while the girl blows seems to have been Favart's invention.[7]

We cannot be sure that the Parfaicts' plot summary accurately records the original performances of Favart's play, and there may have been versions of the *Vendanges* that corresponded better to Boucher's paintings.[8] In other respects, though, the paintings are based less in the theatre than in the pictorial traditions of Netherlandish art, in which accessory objects allude to the central theme. In *The Enjoyable Lesson* the phallic significance of the flute is discreetly underlined by the way the shepherdess strokes the shepherd's crook, resting between his knees. The goat, emblem of lust, attracts our attention, while the sheep direct our attention to the stone lion (an animal associated with such virtues as pride, faith, or fortitude), which crouches on the 'fontana de la verità' (fountain of truth).[9] Similarly, in *The Mysterious Basket*, we see a dog, a common symbol of faithfulness, while the ram's head on the vase may again allude to lust. The head of a boy on the relief also needs explanation. In some of Boucher's pastorals connected with Favart's productions there appears, in addition to the shepherd and shepherdess, a boy, who, as Laing suggests, may be a character from the original performances.[10] The boy apparently spies on the lovers, and is no doubt the means by which the angry parents are informed. It is possible that the relief in *The Mysterious Basket* may allude to such a character. The surroundings in both pictures thus hint at issues traditional in the iconography of amorous encounters.

David Marshall

40. JACOPO AMIGONI
Italian, c.1685–1752

Portrait Group: The Singer Farinelli and Friends

Signed on handle of one of the artist's brushes: *G. Amiconi*, undated; painted between 1750 and 1752
Oil on canvas
172.8 x 245.1 cm (68 x 96 1/2 in.)
Felton Bequest 1950 (2226–4)

PROVENANCE

Carlo Broschi Farinelli (1705–1782), Bologna, 1761; Antonio Canova (1757–1822); Mrs Clinton Dawkins, 1885; Lady Templemore, 1926; Ronald Tree, Ditchley, Oxfordshire, 1949; with Agnew's, London, 1949; from whom acquired by the Felton Bequest, for the National Gallery of Victoria, 1949.

SELECTED EXHIBITIONS

The Great Eighteenth Century Exhibition in the National Gallery of Victoria, National Gallery of Victoria, Melbourne, 1983; *Splendori del Settecento veneziano*, Museo del Settecento Veneziano di Ca' Rezzonico, Gallerie dell'Accademia, Palazzo Mocenigo, Venice, 1995, cat. no. 24.

This striking portrait presents the renowned Italian castrato Carlo Farinelli (1705–1782) in Madrid in the early 1750s, at the culmination of a brilliant career. Farinelli sits at the centre of an intimate circle of friends, including the artist, who stands behind him in the act of 'completing' the portrait, while wearing a modish satin painter's smock and turban.[1] Jacopo Amigoni's self-portrait in the act of painting is a witty transposition of Velázquez's appearance in *Las Meninas*, 1656 (Museo del Prado, Madrid), to a more relaxed and intimate outdoor setting.[2] The artist's representation of himself in this way also distinguishes him from the seated trio of musical celebrities. Teresa Castellini, the prima donna of the Madrid opera, sits alongside Farinelli. Further to the left sits the Abate Metastasio, Farinelli's lifelong friend and the librettist for many of his most famous performances. Metastasio, in his dark clerical attire, is distanced slightly from the others. He is also portrayed in a half-length format, and with a less animated and open posture. These features suggest that his likeness derives from one of two now lost portraits, which Metastasio had sent to Farinelli in 1748 and 1751. But Amigoni's depiction of the Abate also functions in a more metaphorical sense, to convey Metastasio's less direct presence within the group.

From 1730, Metastasio had served as poet to the court at Vienna. His main contact with Farinelli was through a voluminous correspondence, which is preserved today in the form of his letters only. He also sent Farinelli copies of his work, including the poem (here set to music) that Farinelli places in Castellini's hand. This poem constitutes one of Metastasio's most famous compositions and had been sent to Farinelli as recently as January 1750. Amigoni's transcription records an otherwise unknown musical setting for it, penned by none other than Farinelli himself.[3] Metastasio's poem describes the sadness of a lover's departure. The inclusion of the poem might refer to Castellini's intention at that time to leave Spain.[4] She and Farinelli were certainly close. She had been Farinelli's favourite pupil as well as, so the rumours suggested, the focus of an impossible love on his part.[5] Yet the poem might be better understood as an expression of the mood of the group as a whole. As itinerant professionals serving the European courts, all four would have identified with Metastasio's emphasis on the strains created by the tyranny of departure. Farinelli's portrait, nonetheless, acts as a powerful rejoinder to the question posed at the poem's conclusion: 'Yet who can tell if thou will ever think of me?'. By commemorating the group's companionship, even as they consider the inevitability of separation, Amigoni celebrates the ability of true friendship to withstand all.

Such sentiments must have proved increasingly consoling to Farinelli with the passing of time. Amigoni was dead within a year or two of the portrait's completion, while Castellini eventually made good on her intention to leave Madrid, doing so in 1757, ostensibly for reasons of health. Two years later, as a result of a reversal of fortunes brought about by the coronation of a new king, Farinelli was forced to retire from public life to a villa on the outskirts of Bologna. There the present painting took on a new meaning as a key exhibit in an extraordinary private museum of memory, which Farinelli cultivated in his final years through the imagery of his paintings and the personal associations attached to his belongings. In 1761 the English commentator Charles Burney singled out this painting from among Farinelli's numerous portraits of 'great personages, chiefly sovereign princes, who have been his patrons'.[6] Burney correctly identified the portrait's significance in bringing together Farinelli, Metastasio and Amigoni. But he mistook the beautiful prima donna for a Venetian singer of the 1720s. Such are the injustices of memory. But if time can bring about oblivion it can also provide for the eventual recovery of true identity – in this instance, the identities of all the intimate friends here united for posterity.

Christopher Marshall

41. ARTHUR DEVIS
English, 1712–1787

The Clavey Family in Their Garden at Hampstead

Signed and dated l.l.: *Art*ʳ: *Devis. fe. / 1754.*
Oil on canvas
124.5 x 99.0 cm (49 x 39 in.)
Everard Studley Miller Bequest 1976 (E1–1976)

Arthur Devis made his career as a painter *par excellence* of the conversation piece, a portrait genre that became very popular in England in the first half of the eighteenth century. The term *conversation piece* is earliest seen in print in 1706 and derives from Latin via the Italian *conversazione* (a recreational gathering of friends or family). Usually modest in scale, these group portraits in domestic settings were defined by George Vertue, the eighteenth-century engraver and chronicler of art history, as 'peices of Conversations – family peeces – small figures from the life in their habits and dress of the Times'.[1]

A native of Preston in Lancashire, Devis was the son of a cabinetmaker, whose influential connections in town brought the young artist early patronage. Devis left Preston in the 1720s and worked for a time with the Flemish-born Peter Tillemans, a specialist in topographical landscapes and sporting subjects. By 1735, however, Devis had decided that he could make a better living from portraiture – despite his lack of training in that branch of art – and by 1742 he had moved permanently to London. He was undoubtedly influenced by William Hogarth, among the earliest and most accomplished painters of the distinctively English conversation piece. Hogarth, in turn, would have been familiar with seventeenth-century Dutch family groups and scenes of everyday life, and, importantly, with the work of French rococo artists such as Jean-Antoine Watteau and Philippe Mercier (both were in England during the 1720s).[2]

Devis's carefully constructed interiors and landscape backgrounds are, in fact, almost never real places (several are repeated in portraits of completely different families). Instead, they are idealized settings created to demonstrate his sitters' position in the world.[3] Thus Devis has placed the Clavey family in what purports to be their garden at Hampstead, overlooking the cool green wilds of the Heath. Charles Clavey Esquire (1714–1782), of Frome in Somerset and Hampstead, Middlesex, was a substantial citizen, Master of the Worshipful Company of Masons and a Common Councilman of Farringdon Ward Without, in the City of London. Here he is presented as a country gentleman on *his* land. The third adult figure is probably Mrs Clavey's brother, in a pose used very frequently by Devis to convey a tone of elegant relaxation: the man is shown leaning nonchalantly and crossing his legs like a famous ancient Roman statue, the 'Uffizi Mercury'.[4]

Devis was particularly sensitive in his rendering of fabrics, especially silk and lace, which he painted in meticulous detail. Nevertheless, his figures are doll-like, charmingly stilted – however carefully delineated their features and costumes – the result, at least in part, of his use of an articulated lay figure, about seventy-six centimetres (thirty inches) high, complete with a miniature wardrobe of clothes, which still survive.

Although the children are dressed like little replicas of their elders, their freedom to share in the pleasures of their parents' lives was something quite new in eighteenth-century Europe. It seems to be summer, when the son and heir, also Charles, then aged eleven, was home from school, and the younger Thomas and Patty Maria could gather flowers for their mother's bouquet. In this time of great social change, children were increasingly seen as individuals, and childhood as an important stage in life. Here the children animate the scene. For all the genteel poise and conscious refinement of this group of figures, there is also a sense of warm affection between them, and, somewhat unusually in Devis's art, a suggestion that when they have finished posing there will be real and lively 'conversation'.

Jane Clark

PROVENANCE

Charles Clavey (1714–1782), Hampstead, Middlesex, 1754; Mrs John Griffith (née Sarah Clavey); Griffith family, 1930; H. E. Griffith, 1933; his sale, Christie's, London, 31 March 1933, lot 100; from which purchased by Lee; Mrs Edward Griffith, 1966; her sale, Sotheby's, London, 23 March 1966, lot 65; from which purchased by Leggatt's, London; R. Graham, 1975; sale, Christie's, London, 21 March 1975, lot 157; from which purchased by Leger Galleries, London; from whom acquired by the National Gallery of Victoria, under the terms of the Everard Studley Miller Bequest, 1975.

SELECTED EXHIBITIONS

The Great Eighteenth Century Exhibition in the National Gallery of Victoria, National Gallery of Victoria, Melbourne, 1983.

42. JOHAN ZOFFANY

(Johannes Josephus Zauffaly) German (active in England), 1733–1810

Self-Portrait as David with the Head of Goliath

Signed and dated on belt: *1756 I. Zauffalij inv. et pinx.*
Oil on canvas
92.2 x 74.7 cm (36 1/4 x 29 1/2 in.)
Purchased with the assistance of the Isabella Mary Curnick Bequest and
The Art Foundation of Victoria, 1994 (IC1–1994)

Johan Zoffany was born near Frankfurt on 13 March 1733. His family later moved to Regensburg, where Zoffany's father was court cabinetmaker and architect, and the young Zoffany was apprenticed to Martin Speer. In 1750, at the age of seventeen, Zoffany went to Rome, where he studied under the fashionable portrait painter Agostino Masucci and received instruction from the German expatriate Anton Raphael Mengs (1728–1779). Zoffany returned briefly to Regensburg in 1757 before settling in London in 1760, establishing himself as a fashionable painter of portraits and conversation pieces. He became a Royal Academician on the recommendation of George III in 1769. Thus began a pattern of aristocratic patronage and acceptance in high society, which, although the artist's career included significant periods in Italy and India, saw him as an important member of the British school. He died in London in 1810.

This, the earliest known self-portrait by Zoffany, was sold at auction in 1989 with an attribution to Mengs. Subsequent cleaning revealed the signature and date on David's belt. Zoffany was twenty-three years old and towards the end of his first stay in Rome when he decided to represent himself as the biblical hero David, having just slain the Philistine Goliath (1 Sam. 17:50). Zoffany depicts himself as the young and beautiful David wearing a sheepskin hat at a rakish angle and with heavy swathes of a sheepskin cape draped behind him. His right elbow rests nonchalantly on Goliath's head, while his right hand supports his own chin. In his left hand he holds the stone with which he – a young and relatively diminutive shepherd boy – has struck Goliath on the brow, felling, and thus slaying, the powerful giant. Zoffany plays down the gruesome aspects of the scene, concealing the neck wound and making only subtle allusions to blood. Rather, the interpretation of the subject is sensual, even homoerotic, in the emphasis on the muscled, yet smooth and effeminate, nudity of the figure of David, the undulating silhouette of the back against the cape, the tactile quality suggested by the sheepskin against skin, the slightly parted lips, and the intense engagement of the gaze. The facial features, while clearly those of Zoffany, have been idealized, particularly in the narrowing of the nose. The Bible describes David as 'of a beautiful countenance' (1 Sam. 17:42). The emphasis on David's physical beauty has precedents in earlier interpretations of this subject, by Donatello, Guido Reni and others. The sexual subtext is continued in the phallic configuration of the sling, used to hurl the stone at Goliath but here suggesting another level of humiliation for the vanquished Philistine.[1]

Pressly has suggested that, in representing himself as David victorious over Goliath, the young painter conceived himself as 'the anointed one', victorious in his challenge to the old masters.[2] The shepherd's staff leaning inside the crook of David's left arm, replacing the traditional sword, and the stone that he holds, could be interpreted as the artist's mahlstick and chalk respectively. However, if the slain Goliath is intended to represent the tradition of the old masters, his unexpectedly 'conscious' expression suggests that this rival has not been finally vanquished. The triumph of the impetuous, confident young painter may not be complete.

Ruth Pullin

PROVENANCE

Sale, Gersaint, Strasbourg,
17 November 1989, lot 265; from
which purchased by Richard L. Feigen,
New York; with Richard L. Feigen,
New York, 1994; from whom
acquired by the National Gallery of
Victoria with the assistance of the
Isabella Mary Curnick Bequest and
The Art Foundation of Victoria, 1994.

44. RICHARD WILSON
Welsh (active in Italy), 1713/14–1782

Llyn Peris and Dolbadarn Castle

Unsigned, undated; painted c.1760–63
Oil on canvas
96.0 x 131.0 cm (37 3/4 x 51 1/2 in.)
Felton Bequest 1949 (2055–4)

PROVENANCE

Sale, Christie's, London, 15 July
1899, lot 67; from which purchased
by Arthur Tooth, London; J. Pierpont
Morgan (1837–1913), New York; Mrs
Herbert L. Satterlee (née Louise
Pierpont Morgan), New York;
Herbert L. Satterlee (1863–1947),
New York, 1947; the late Herbert L.
Satterlee sale, Park-Bernet, New
York, 22 April 1948, lot 21; from
which purchased by Weitzner, New
York; with Arthur Tooth & Sons,
London, 1948; from whom acquired
by the Felton Bequest, for the
National Gallery of Victoria, 1948.

SELECTED EXHIBITIONS

Richard Wilson: The Landscape of
Reaction, Tate Gallery, London,
1982–83, cat. no. 105; The Great
Eighteenth Century Exhibition in the
National Gallery of Victoria, National
Gallery of Victoria, Melbourne, 1983.

This landscape was painted c.1760–63, at least four years after Richard Wilson returned to Wales from Italy, where he had been persuaded by Joseph Vernet, the French marine artist, to exchange portrait painting for landscape. This Wilson did, modelling his compositions and imagery on the works of the pioneer landscapists of the seventeenth century. In fact the subject in the present painting was consistently identified as Italian, until the picture was acquired by the National Gallery of Victoria. This identification was due to the fact that the imagery – the lake, the castle, the trees, the boys fishing and the distant mountain – had originated with Nicolas Poussin, Claude Lorrain and Gaspard Dughet, who drew it from the Roman Campagna, the same countryside that had inspired the Roman poets like Horace, Juvenal and Propertius. The painting thus reflects Wilson's six to seven years in Italy: in Venice, where he seems to have noticed the painting techniques of both Antonio and Francesco Guardi, among others; in Rome and Naples, where he developed a direct link between classical associations and the Romantic actuality of his Welsh landscapes. The process was no different from that practised by the neoclassical figure painters.

Wilson was to suffer a lack of recognition in his lifetime, due to the prevailing opinion among collectors, carefully schooled by the tastemakers, that regional landscape was too familiar to lend itself to anything other than purely topographical representation. But it is interesting to note that in his lecture on 'Invention', in 1801, Henry Fuseli says that Titian, Poussin, Salvator Rosa, Claude, Rubens, Rembrandt and Wilson, among others, 'spurn ... this kind of map-work'.[1] With these artists, Fuseli says, 'We tread on classic or romantic ground'.[2] In fact, topographic artists since the seventeenth century had never been overly accurate, and the painting here – while it clearly demonstrates a fusion of the two impulses – is by no means an accurate view, for the artist has employed a kind of poetic licence in disposing his motifs, justified, no doubt, by a Greek epigram that had been popularized by Horace and was much quoted in the eighteenth century: 'Poetry is spoken painting; painting is silent poetry'.

Dolbadarn Castle, in Gwynedd, north Wales, was abandoned after the conquest of Wales by Edward I (1272–1307) but not before serving as a prison for Owain Goch, the brother of Llewellyn the Last, for twenty-three years. In 1774 Thomas Jones, a pupil of Wilson's, painted The Bard (National Gallery of Wales, Cardiff) from a poem by Thomas Gray in memory of Edward I's edict ordering all the poets of Wales to be killed. In these different pictorial responses, then, are the local triggers for romantic nationalism, which was to be taken up in Scotland by Walter Scott a generation later. There were many, like Joshua Reynolds, however, who objected to the combination of classical myth or reference with regional landscape, fearing that art itself would betray its creative heritage – and not recognizing that it was Wilson's perceptive familiarity with his native countryside which allowed him to merge ancient and modern, and thus enable regional landscape to exercise the same power over following generations as had the Tiber, Lake Nemi and the Sabine hills over Roman predecessors.

Peter Tomory

45. ALLAN RAMSAY
Scottish, 1713–1784

Richard Grenville, 2nd Earl Temple

Signed and dated c.r.: *A. Ramsay / 1762*
Oil on canvas
234.3 x 152.4 cm (92 1/4 x 60 in.)
Everard Studley Miller Bequest 1965 (1554–5)

Allan Ramsay's full-length portrait of Richard Grenville (1711–1779) is undoubtedly one of his finest works, and indeed one of the finest British portraits of the mid to late eighteenth century.[1] The subject is represented in the robes of a Knight of the Garter (to which he had been appointed in 1760), and the commission offered Ramsay a magnificent opportunity to depict in sumptuous van Dyck style one of the wealthiest, most politically powerful and, above all, fashionable, men in England.

We now know that Grenville commissioned the picture as a presentation to his brother-in-law William Pitt, later Lord Chatham, who, like Grenville's own brother George, at one time held the office of prime minister. The picture follows chronologically Ramsay's hugely successful coronation portraits of George III and Queen Charlotte, and in stylistic terms represents a new phase of painterly bravura in the artist's work. It has been suggested that Ramsay, already de facto Principal Painter to the King (the appointment could be formalized only in 1767, upon the death of Ramsay's predecessor), increasingly felt a need to respond to the new public attention accorded to Joshua Reynolds and other prominent contemporary portrait painters, and this representation of Lord Temple belongs firmly to the tradition of the 'swagger portrait'.

There has been some discussion about the rather impressionistic townscape in the left background. It has been proposed – and this is highly plausible – that it represents a rather free view of the city of Oxford, dominated by the dome of the recently completed Radcliffe Camera. Oxford is geographically close to Stowe, and the inclusion of a representation of the city may simply reflect local interest.

The attention art historians have always given to Reynolds and Gainsborough has served until fairly recently to obscure our understanding not only of Ramsay's high contemporary reputation but also of the quality of his portraits. He made two extended visits to Italy during his working career, the first in 1736–38 when he studied under Imperiali in Rome and Francesco Solimena in Naples, at which time he developed a friendship with that other great painter of contemporary portraits, Pompeo Batoni, whose polished style and attention to detail Ramsay's work could be said to reflect. When Ramsay returned to Italy in 1754 he was also closely involved with a group of artists and architects, including Robert Adam, Charles-Louis Clérisseau and Giovanni Battista Piranesi, who were laying the foundations of the neoclassical revolution that was soon to dominate European taste and style.

At the time of the commissioning of the Melbourne portrait, Richard Temple was indisputably established not only as a powerful political figure but also as one of his period's great arbiters of taste. In 1749 he had inherited from his uncle, Lord Cobham, the house and estate at Stowe; the garden at Stowe was already one of the most celebrated in Europe, with William Kent, Alexander Pope and later 'Capability' Brown all contributing, through their work there, to the creation of a new landscape aesthetic based on the primacy of nature. Grenville himself undertook major changes to the grounds, including monuments that reflected his own interests (he had been First Lord of the Admiralty in 1756–57 during the Seven Years War with France): he placed a one-hundred-foot obelisk to commemorate General Wolfe's victories in Canada, and later in 1777 he erected a monument to the Pacific navigator Captain James Cook. Throughout the 1770s, Robert Adam was engaged by Grenville to rebuild the vast south front of Stowe, making it one of the most magnificent of all European neoclassical houses, rivalling in size and grandeur many royal residences on the Continent.

Gerard Vaughan

PROVENANCE

Richard Grenville, 2nd Earl Temple (1711–1779), Stowe, Buckinghamshire, 1762; by whom presented to William Pitt, 1st Earl of Chatham (1708–1778); John Pitt, 2nd Earl of Chatham (1756–1835); by whom presented to 1st Baron Glastonbury (d. 1825), Butleigh Court, Glastonbury, Somerset; by descent to Robert Neville Grenville (d. 1936); Captain Richard Neville, Butleigh Court, 1946; his sale, Christie's, London, 5 April 1946, lot 54; from which purchased by Harbord; Mrs Alan Palmer, Farley Hall, 1964; her sale, Sotheby's, London, 15 July 1964, lot 105; from which purchased jointly by Agnew's and Leggatt's, London; acquired from Leggatt's by the National Gallery of Victoria, under the terms of the Everard Studley Miller Bequest, 1965.

SELECTED EXHIBITIONS

The Great Eighteenth Century Exhibition in the National Gallery of Victoria, National Gallery of Victoria, Melbourne, 1983; *Allan Ramsay 1713–1784*, Scottish National Portrait Gallery, Edinburgh; National Portrait Gallery, London, 1992–93, cat. no. 77.

46. FRANÇOIS-HUBERT DROUAIS
French, 1727–1775

Madame Sophie de France

Signed and dated c.r.: *Drouais le fils / 1763*
Oil on canvas
73.7 x 59.8 cm (29 x 23 1/2 in.)
Everard Studley Miller Bequest 1964 (1359–5)

Mme Sophie[1] epitomizes composure, in her serene expression, controlled address to the viewer, upright pose and carefully arranged hands. She holds a small open book in one hand and what is probably a fan in the other; the implication is that we have interrupted her pursuit of the desirable feminine occupation of reading. She leans elegantly against a balustrade, her head surrounded by an abstractly atmospheric background. The effect of harmony and control is further conveyed in the subtle tones and the restricted palette, which ranges from apricot and flesh pinks to powdery blues and soft greys. The work, with its delicacy of treatment and mild gentility of temperament, is characteristic of rococo taste and sentiment.

Sophie-Philippe-Élisabeth-Justine (1734–1782) was the eighth child of Louis XV, King of France, and Queen Marie Leszczynska. As a very young woman, Mme Sophie was described by the Marquise de Pompadour: 'Madame Sophie is almost as tall as myself, very good, plump, a fine throat, well built, fine skin and eyes and in profile as like the King as one drop of water to another'.[2] François-Hubert Drouais's portrait is in keeping with this description, the artist depicting in apparently glowing health the twenty-nine-year-old sitter, who shows no diffidence or shy aspects, but only confident self-possession, in the clarity and unstrained expression of her eyes and mouth.

The other source of this appearance of wellbeing is the sitter's dress, which is remarkably decorative, seemingly belying her sister's opinion that Mme Sophie's chief virtue was simplicity.[3] Yet in donning this complex and intricate apparel, in which she is effectively festooned with flowers, she is merely reflecting aristocratic standards of attire. A close comparison can be made with François Boucher's well-known portrait of Madame de Pompadour, 1756 (Alte Pinakothek, Munich), in which the sitter also looks up from an open book and wears a dress similarly encrusted with three-dimensional flowers.[4] The myriad of flowers trimming Mme Sophie's dress of brocaded silk stand out from it, especially on the stomacher (the front panel of the bodice), the ruche encircling her throat, and the edges of her sleeves. In her powdered hair is a matching topknot of flowers. The desired end is to transform the sitter into a flower herself, so that she becomes part of this effusion of 'natural' beauty.

Drouais was born in Paris, the son of the painter Hubert Drouais, and studied with his father and with François Boucher, among others. At the court of Louis XV, Drouais's work was sought after within the royal circle: his patrons included Mme de Pompadour and Mme du Barry. In their playful ornamentation, his depictions of the French aristocracy epitomize full-blown rococo fantasies, which in this portrait are barely contained by the sitter's innate restraint and poise.

Vivien Gaston

47. JOSHUA REYNOLDS
English, 1723–1792

Miss Susanna Gale

Unsigned, undated; painted between 1763 and 1764
Oil on canvas
210.0 x 118.8 cm (82 3/4 x 46 3/4 in.)
Felton Bequest 1934 (158–4)

PROVENANCE

Francis Gale (d. 1774), Liguanea,
Jamaica; Lady Gardner (née
Susanna Gale) (1749–1823), 1809;
Hon. Susannah Cornwall (d. 1853),
Ashcroft House, Wootton-under-
Edge, Gloucestershire, 1809;
Rev. Alan Gardner Cornwall,
Ashcroft House, 1853, 1867, 1872;
the late Reverend Alan Gardner
Cornwall sale, Christie's, London,
16 November 1872, lot 46 (bought
in); Bertram Currie; Laurence
Currie; with Spink, London, 1933;
from whom acquired by the Felton
Bequest, for the National Gallery of
Victoria, 1933.

SELECTED EXHIBITIONS

*The Great Eighteenth Century
Exhibition in the National Gallery of
Victoria*, National Gallery of Victoria,
Melbourne, 1983.

When Miss Susanna Gale (1749–1823) sat for Joshua Reynolds, she was just fourteen years of age, and had travelled to London, from her home in Jamaica, to complete her education. As the daughter of Francis Gale Esquire, a British sugar planter, Miss Gale was a wealthy heiress and she is presented here as a young lady and 'the fairest flower in the garden'.[1] After returning to Jamaica, Susanna married Sabine Turner, who died only nine months later. Her second marriage took place in May 1769, to Captain Alan Gardner, RN, who went on to become commander-in-chief in Jamaica and was made the first Baron Gardner of Uttoxeter in 1806. Lady Gardner died in London at the age of seventy-four, leaving a family of seven sons and one daughter.

By the summer of 1760, Reynolds had established himself in Leicester Fields (now Leicester Square) as the pre-eminent portrait painter in London. His notebooks demonstrate his popularity, recording that in one year, for example, he had more than 150 different sitters. Reynolds's working practice is revealed in a letter written by him to a potential sitter in 1777. The artist advised:

> It requires in general three sittings, about an hour and a half each time but if the sitter chooses it the face could be begun and finished in one day. It is divided into separate times for the convenience of the person who sits. When the face is finished the rest is done without troubling the sitter.[2]

To paint 'the rest' – that is, the hands and the clothes – Reynolds would use his servants and pupils to model for him. The efficiencies of such a practice included the frequent reuse of popular settings and poses, particularly for the artist's female sitters.[3] In fact, at around the time the Melbourne portrait was painted, Reynolds used a pose very similar to that of Susanna Gale: for his portrait of Mrs Thomas Riddell, *c*.1763 (Laing Art Gallery, Newcastle-upon-Tyne).[4] However, the ultimate inspiration for the pose derives from a portrait of Marchesa Elena Grimaldi, 1623 (National Gallery of Art, Washington DC), by van Dyck.[5] Reynolds knew and admired the work of van Dyck and in this particular instance has adhered to the original model fairly closely, even to the placement of the sitter in a portico.

An important difference between van Dyck's painting and that by Reynolds is the greater emphasis that Reynolds places on the surrounding garden. While van Dyck depicts a manicured and well-ordered garden, Reynolds modernizes the landscape, in line with the growing appreciation of nature in the mid to late eighteenth century. The tree to the left is an essential element of the design, in that it serves to balance the composition, but also important is its prominence – as a pictorial device, it functions to give equal weight to the natural world and the man-made. (Of course, any consideration of compositional balance must take into account the fact that the work was at some stage trimmed, after having suffered seawater damage in the eighteenth century.)[6] Reynolds skilfully combines the neoclassical setting of the portico, and its associations of cultivation and refinement, with the treed landscape, evocative of the pleasures and virtues to be gained through contact with nature. The fact that the sitter is shown poised between the two worlds alludes to her education and background, as well as her natural graces and charms. Another area in which Reynolds shows his virtuosity is in his handling of the colours. The pale skin tones of the youthful Miss Gale are complemented by the pinks and whites of her dress, both of which are offset by the deep greens and russet tones of the foliage and its shadows.

Jennifer Jones-O'Neill

48. JOSHUA REYNOLDS

Lady Frances Finch

Unsigned, undated; painted 1781–82
Oil on canvas
142.1 x 113.3 cm (56 x 44 1/2 in.)
Felton Bequest 1956 (3356A–4)

PROVENANCE

Heneage Finch, 4th Earl of Aylesford
(1751–1812), Packington Hall,
Meriden, Coventry, Warwickshire,
1782; Earl of Aylesford, Packington
Hall, 1881, 1889, 1900; from whom
purchased by Agnew's, London,
1900; with Agnew's, London, 1901;
from whom purchased by
Herbert L. Terrell, New York, 1901;
Mrs Herbert L. Terrell van Ingen,
New York, 1955; from whom
purchased jointly by Agnew's and
Knoedler's, London, 1955; with
Agnew's and Knoedler's, London,
1956; from whom acquired by the
Felton Bequest, for the National
Gallery of Victoria, 1956.

SELECTED EXHIBITIONS

*The Great Eighteenth Century
Exhibition in the National Gallery of
Victoria*, National Gallery of Victoria,
Melbourne, 1983.

In 1781, after a six-week trip to Holland and Flanders, where he evidently went to study the work of Rubens, Reynolds returned to his portrait practice in London with a new appreciation of naturalism. The effect of his study of Rubens can be seen in this portrait of Lady Frances Finch, in which the artist places his sitter, relaxed and comfortable, in a wooded setting with none of the classical allusions that were his trademark. Lady Frances (1761–1838), daughter of the 3rd Earl of Aylesford (1715–1777), was twenty-one at the time the portrait was completed. The final sitting is recorded in March 1782 and by September that same year Lady Frances had married George Legge, Lord Lewisham, and had thus become Lady Lewisham, Countess of Dartmouth.[1] Lady Frances's aristocratic background is not immediately apparent in the informality of the pose and in the proximity of the sitter to the picture plane.

Placing a female sitter in a natural rather than a domestic setting was increasingly popular with eighteenth-century artists as they responded to the fashion, prevalent in literature also, to associate certain qualities of nature with a virtuous character. As Shawe-Taylor suggests, a depiction of a woman as 'an offspring of nature' was a visual sign of her virtue.[2] Poets and novelists explored the significance of nature and identified its appreciation as a mark of refinement and sensibility. James Thomson (1700–1748), for example, noted nature's role in promoting virtue and social harmony, and remarked in the preface to one of his poems: 'I know of no subject more elevating … more ready to awake the poetical enthusiasm, the philosophical reflection, and the moral sentiment, than the works of Nature'.[3] He went on to claim that nature 'enlarges and transports the soul'.[4] The 'quality' of the natural environment was also of considerable importance to artists and writers and, although the setting for this painting was produced in Reynolds's studio, the landscape possibly alludes to the Aylesford estate in Warwickshire, where the grounds had been designed by 'Capability' Brown to have the irregular features and appearance required of a 'picturesque' landscape.[5]

The capacity to feel exquisite sentiments and heightened emotions was a distinctive feature of the eighteenth-century lady of sensibility, and one way to elicit such emotions was through the contemplation of nature. Lady Frances is depicted leaning casually against a tree and engaged in obvious reverie, the subject of which is very likely her surroundings. Reinforcing this idea of the sitter as a woman of sensibility is the blush that is apparent on Lady Frances's cheeks. At one level the blush could simply be the result of an invigorating walk in the woods. At another level, however, a blushing countenance was synonymous with virtue. One critic noted that 'the blush comes forth as an emanation of an intrinsic purity and loveliness, and diffuses through the human form a tinge of the angelic nature'.[6] To his credit, Reynolds has not painted an ethereal being, but a dignified and poised woman, at ease in her surroundings. The characteristic qualities of Reynolds's work in the early 1780s are all evident here, from the confident and open handling of the paint to the fluency and harmonious balancing of light and shade. Another form of balance is achieved by Reynolds's acknowledgement of contemporary trends in the portrayal of women, while successfully integrating them with his own direct and naturalistic portrait style.

Jennifer Jones-O'Neill

49. POMPEO BATONI
Italian, 1708–1787

Sir Sampson Gideon and an Unidentified Companion

Signed and dated beneath tread of lower step: *POMPEO BATONI / PINXIT ROMAE* [A and E in ligature] / *AN. 1767.*
Oil on canvas
275.6 x 189.0 cm (108 1/2 x 74 1/2 in.)
Everard Studley Miller Bequest 1963 (1325–5)

PROVENANCE

Sir Sampson Gideon (later Lord
Eardley) (1745–1824), Belvedere,
Erith, Kent; Gregory William
Twisleton, 14th Baron Saye and
Sele (1769–1844), Belvedere, 1824;
William Thomas Twisleton, 15th
Baron Saye and Sele (d. 1847);
Sir Culling Eardley (1805–1863),
Belvedere, 1847, 1857, Bedwell Park,
Hertfordshire, 1860; Mrs Culling
Hanbury (née Eardley); the Hon.
Mrs William Henry Fremantle (née
Eardley); Sir Francis Eardley
Fremantle, 1944; the late Sir Francis
Fremantle sale, Christie's, London,
14 December 1945, lot 15; from
which purchased by Barnes; Mr
and Mrs Basil Ionides, Buxted Park,
Kent; the late the Hon. Mrs Nellie
Ionides sale, Sotheby's, London,
3 July 1963, lot 34; from which
purchased by Leggatt's, London;
from whom acquired by the National
Gallery of Victoria, under the terms
of the Everard Studley Miller
Bequest, 1963.

SELECTED EXHIBITIONS

*The Great Eighteenth Century
Exhibition in the National Gallery of
Victoria*, National Gallery of Victoria,
Melbourne, 1983.

Pompeo Batoni's portrait of *Sir Sampson Gideon and an Unidentified Companion*[1] is a quintessential document of the taste of the Grand Tour, and is one of the artist's finest portraits of an English visitor to Rome.[2] Batoni, born in Lucca, went to Rome in 1727. A pupil of Sebastiano Conca, he was influenced by, among others, Imperiali, and through this link he came into close contact with foreign visitors to Rome, most particularly the British. Batoni was always close to the British artistic community in Rome and knew, for example, the portrait painter Allan Ramsay. The entry in this catalogue on Ramsay's portrait *Richard Grenville, 2nd Earl Temple*, 1762 (cat. no. 45), refers to the influence of Batoni and it is instructive to compare the present picture with Ramsay's; both are notable for their stylistic polish and for their concentration on elaborate costume. Batoni can be said to have brought the genre of the Grand Tour portrait to a new level of sophistication and he was indisputably the most fashionable and sought-after portrait painter in Rome between the 1750s and the 1770s, when the Grand Tour as a cultural phenomenon reached its apogee. In the decade 1750–60 it is recorded that he produced nearly sixty portraits of British sitters.[3]

The precise subject of our picture remains unresolved. The seated figure is Sir Sampson Gideon (1745–1824), the son of an exceptionally wealthy financier of Portuguese origin.[4] Sir Sampson visited Rome in 1766, and the evidence suggests that the picture, dated 1767, was completed after his return to England.[5] He is depicted showing a portrait miniature to his companion. It can be presumed that the miniature represents Sir Sampson's wife, Maria (the daughter of Sir John Eardley-Wilmot of Belvedere in Kent), whom he married in December 1766. Gideon later assumed his wife's family name, and was created Lord Eardley in 1789. His elegant companion remains unidentified. An old inscription in white paint on the letter in Sir Sampson's left hand read *LORD EARDLY* [sic] *AND HIS TUTOR SIGNOR BASTI* but this identification is clearly incorrect and, as a later addition, was removed in 1963. The misconception may come from some confusion concerning the banker Filippo *Barazzi*, who regularly made himself responsible for the affairs of visiting Englishmen and may well have attended to the picture's consignment to England. While it is not impossible that there was some personal or professional link between Sir Sampson's father and Barazzi, it is unlikely that the sumptuously dressed figure on the left, whose confident pose suggests high rank, could be Barazzi, let alone a tutor, and this assumption can perhaps be supported by the fact that more than one contemporary observer commented upon Sir Sampson's obsession with rank and status.

The picture reflects in every way the eighteenth-century experience of Rome. The Temple of Vesta at Tivoli, included in the background, was one of the most admired of all Roman monuments, and the copy of the bust of the *Minerva Giustiniani*, by then in the Vatican collection, reappears in several other Grand Tour portraits by Batoni and was probably a studio prop. The whippet hound is a charming inclusion and it is recorded that some travelling Englishmen took their favourite dogs with them to Italy. The splendid costumes worn by both sitters are particularly notable. We know from many period accounts that one of the first tasks undertaken by English visitors to Rome was the acquisition of fashionable new clothes, and the stylishness of the Italian dress would not have been lost on contemporary British viewers of the picture.

Gerard Vaughan

50. GEORGE ROMNEY
English, 1734–1802

The Leigh Family

Unsigned, undated; painted *c*.1768
Oil on canvas
185.8 x 202.0 cm (73 1/4 x 79 1/2 in.)
Felton Bequest 1959 (338–5)

Although George Romney chose to remain aloof from the newly established Royal Academy, his skills as a portraitist were nevertheless in demand with London society. Indeed Romney's reputation was rivalled only by the reputations of Joshua Reynolds and Thomas Gainsborough. Exhibited as 'A Large Family Piece' in 1768 at the Free Society of Artists, Romney's portrait of the Leigh family is an accomplished example of the artist's work.[1] The group in this portrait comprises Mr Jarret Leigh (1724–1769), who was a proctor in Doctors' Commons and an amateur artist, with his wife and six children. The family's fine attire, the furnishings and the neoclassical-style setting attest to Leigh's status as a prosperous middle-class gentleman. It was precisely these details that the actor David Garrick (1717–1779) objected to on viewing this painting. Garrick remarked on the 'very bright well-rubbed mahogany table', 'the motherly good lady' and the 'worthy gentleman in the scarlet waistcoat' as constituting 'a very excellent subject' but not one that was suitable for Romney's art.[2] Garrick's comments reflect the popular perception of such conversation pieces as paintings that could be admired as a display of the artist's technical skills and accuracy of observation, but that were not worthy of serious consideration, as they had no intellectual or imaginative content. The most highly regarded artists were those who painted history paintings. Romney would later come to the same conclusion and would express his frustration at being 'shackled' to 'this cursed portrait painting' while his real ambition was to paint subjects from great literature and from history.[3]

Portraits such as *The Leigh Family*, however, earned the artist his living, and Walpole's comments on the exhibition of 1768 demonstrate why Romney's skills as a portrait painter were highly sought after. According to Walpole, 'the whole Picture [was] greatly admired'.[4] He made particular mention of the fine detailing found in such areas as the lace and silk of the garments, and noted that 'the Gloss & Folds of the Sattin' were 'Extremely beautiful'.[5] Technical skill alone does not of course make a good portrait, and Romney's achievement in the present painting is in bringing the figures together in such a way that a comment is made on the character of the family itself.

From the late seventeenth century in Europe, increasing emphasis had been placed on the nature of familial ties and affections. The relationship between parents and children, and the nature of childhood itself, were examined by philosophers such as John Locke and Jean-Jacques Rousseau with a view to promoting a happy and cultivated family unit, and by extension a polite and civilized society.[6] Romney takes advantage of this social and intellectual climate, showing Mrs Leigh gazing lovingly, and, it should be said, dutifully, at her husband, while his demeanour suggests an air of self-satisfaction. The sense that this is a contented and harmonious family is created by the seeming informality of the children. Yet one need only follow the contours of the group to realize that Romney has constructed the composition in perfect balance. He also alludes to classical relief sculpture in the pose of the eldest girl, and thereby imbues the subject with the type of serious neoclassical reference advocated by Joshua Reynolds.[7]

The National Gallery of Victoria also owns a sketchbook in which eleven preparatory sketches for this work have been identified.[8]

Jennifer Jones-O'Neill

PROVENANCE

Exhibited by the artist, Free Society of Artists, London, 1768, no. 180; Jarret Leigh, London; R. F. Meyrick; Mrs Charles Eade, 1958; her sale, Sotheby's, London, 10 December 1958, lot 124; from which purchased by Leggatt's, London; with Leggatt's, London, 1959; from whom acquired by the Felton Bequest, for the National Gallery of Victoria, 1959.

SELECTED EXHIBITIONS

The Great Eighteenth Century Exhibition in the National Gallery of Victoria, National Gallery of Victoria, Melbourne, 1983.

51. THOMAS GAINSBOROUGH
English, 1727–1788

An Officer of the 4th Regiment of Foot

Unsigned, undated; painted between 1776 and 1780
Oil on canvas
230.2 x 156.1 cm (90 3/4 x 61 1/2 in.)
Felton Bequest 1922 (1223–3)

The identity of the officer depicted here is not known, although various suggestions have been made.[1] What is certain is that his uniform identifies him as belonging to the Grenadier and Light Companies of the 4th Foot and he would therefore have taken part in the campaigns in America between 1776 and 1780. After serving in the American War of Independence the regiment left for St Lucia in the West Indies before returning home to England. The gentleman's status as an officer is clearly indicated by the single epaulette worn on the right shoulder; the silver gorget, a symbolic remnant of the armour once worn to protect the throat, and here shown hanging around the neck; and the red silk sash worn around the waist.[2]

Thomas Gainsborough painted a number of portraits of military men, many of them shown full length, standing in a landscape. A strong link can be suggested between the Melbourne picture and the artist's portrait of Colonel John Bullock,[3] who, although leaning on a pedestal, is shown in the same cross-legged pose.[4] Gainsborough, in fact, seems to have liked this pose, and its frequency of use has led one commentator to claim that this sign of 'male casual elegance' is 'all too prevalent'.[5] In this work, however, the pose is effective, as it complements the general air of pensiveness. The atmosphere created is part of the strength of this portrait, a fact that is evident in a comparison with the portrait of Colonel Bullock. For while both officers are accompanied by their loyal dogs, which sit patiently awaiting a word from their masters, Colonel Bullock gazes confidently, and more directly, out at the viewer. The officer depicted in the present work looks beyond the viewer as if in deep thought, his demeanour suggestive of the serious contemplation of his situation – a situation that is more fully explained by the landscape, as it takes on a greater role than that of mere decorative background.

The significant role accorded the landscape is especially relevant in a discussion of Gainsborough's work, as he was one of the rare British portrait artists of his period who painted his own backgrounds. The man-of-war in the distance and the craggy cliffs, together with the weapon, would seem to indicate that the young man has recently been engaged in active warfare. Compositionally, Gainsborough has been able to balance the dark forms of the rocks, and the dominant figure of the officer, with the much lighter seascape and ship at the left of the painting – by means of the dog. This solid triangular shape gives the work stability by continuing the diagonal created by the officer's right arm and thus effectively dividing the composition into two balanced areas.

Gainsborough painted this portrait in the period following his return to London after having resided and worked in Bath for fifteen years. It is a measure of his confidence at this time that in the Melbourne painting he successfully combines the beautifully detailed features of the officer, and a fine portrayal of the uniform, with a looser handling of aspects of the surroundings.

Jennifer Jones-O'Neill

PROVENANCE

Tarner, Brighton, 1867, 1921; his sale, Christie's, London, 18 March 1921, lot 35; from which purchased by W. L. Peacock and A. H. Buttery, London; from whom acquired by the Felton Bequest, for the National Gallery of Victoria, 1921.

SELECTED EXHIBITIONS

The Great Eighteenth Century Exhibition in the National Gallery of Victoria, National Gallery of Victoria, Melbourne, 1983.

52. THOMAS GAINSBOROUGH

A Seapiece, a Calm (A View at the Mouth of the Thames)

Unsigned, undated; painted c.1783
Oil on canvas
156.2 x 190.5 cm (61 1/2 x 75 in.)
Felton Bequest 1948 (1840–4)

The National Gallery of Victoria's *A Seapiece, a Calm* was exhibited at the Royal Academy in 1783.[1] Significant influences on Gainsborough's approach to landscape art can be found in the work of Continental artists such as Jacob van Ruisdael (1628/29–1682) and Joseph Vernet (1714–1789).[2] However, in his late paintings, as, for example, the Melbourne picture, Gainsborough goes beyond his predecessors, imbuing his works with a sense of immediacy and freshness that has led one scholar to claim that the pictures are 'almost wholly original'.[3]

Gainsborough achieves his realistic effects by focusing on the qualities of light, atmosphere and water. The clouds tinged with pink and the blue-green tonalities of the sea do indeed indicate a calm atmosphere, and the boats arranged in the middle distance appear to be moving at a leisurely pace. Similarly, the unhurried human figures, who serve their purpose in the design, pointing – and thus guiding the viewer's eye – across the foreground and into the distance where the gentle breeze fills the sails of the boats.

We know rather a lot about the creation of this work, as X-radiography has shown that Gainsborough reworked the canvas, changing the detail of the figures, adding the boat in the right foreground, and superimposing on landscape the two ships in the middle distance.[4] To effectively render the effects of light, Gainsborough studied painted scenes on glass transparencies and viewed them by means of a 'peep-show box', which he made himself (Victoria and Albert Museum, London). This experiment was inspired by Philippe Jacques de Loutherbourg's *eidophusikon*, a popular spectacle whereby the London public were presented with a variety of weather effects created with candlelight and moving glass transparencies.[5] Gainsborough's own experiments with this medium demonstrate his attention to light and atmosphere, in preference to mere replication of detail.

After Gainsborough's death in 1788, Joshua Reynolds, in his fourteenth Discourse before the members of the Royal Academy, claimed that Gainsborough would go down in history as one of the creators of a distinctive English school of painting. According to Reynolds, Gainsborough's genius lay in his ability to capture 'the powerful effects of nature … in his portraits and landscapes'.[6] Reynolds went on to explain: 'If Gainsborough did not look at nature with a poet's eye, it must be acknowledged that he saw her with the eye of a painter; and gave a faithful, if not poetical, representation of what he had before him'.[7]

While Reynolds's comments compliment Gainsborough on his apparent faithfulness to nature, they serve also to criticize the artist for not endowing his landscapes with the poetical and mythological allusions of Nicolas Poussin or Claude Lorrain. Yet it is in Gainsborough's more literal treatment of his subjects that we can situate his seascapes as precedents for J. M. W. Turner and Richard Parkes Bonington. The qualities in *A Seapiece* that have led Hayes to describe it as 'a masterpiece of delicate beauty'[8] must surely have appealed to later artists interested in representing the interaction of water, light and atmosphere.

Jennifer Jones-O'Neill

PROVENANCE

Exhibited by the artist, Royal Academy, London, 1783, no. 240; Sir Thomas Beauchamp-Proctor (1756–1827), Langley Park, Norwich, 1820; Sir Reginald Proctor-Beauchamp (1853–1912), Langley Park, 1878, 1885, 1912; the late Sir Reginald Proctor-Beauchamp sale, Sotheby's, London, 11 June 1947, lot 23; from which purchased by Agnew's, London; with Arthur Tooth & Sons, London, 1947; from whom acquired by the Felton Bequest, for the National Gallery of Victoria, 1947.

SELECTED EXHIBITIONS

The Great Eighteenth Century Exhibition in the National Gallery of Victoria, National Gallery of Victoria, Melbourne, 1983.

53. JOSEPH WRIGHT OF DERBY
English, 1734–1797

The Synnot Children

Signed and dated l.r.: *I: Wright Pinx^t 1781.*
Oil on canvas
152.4 x 125.8 cm (60 x 49 1/2 in.)
Presented through The Art Foundation of Victoria by Mrs Michael Hawker
(née Patricia Synnot), Founder Benefactor, 1980 (E1–1980)

This group portrait owes its great charm both to the active involvement of the children at play and to the ingenious motif of the birdcage around which they gather. The sitters are the three children of Sir Walter Synnot (1742–1821) of County Armagh: Maria at the left, Marcus who is shown kneeling, and Walter at the centre. The two boys sport seventeenth-century fancy dress in the manner of sitters in a van Dyck portrait, but Maria's dress is more austere and neoclassical in style. As if within a stage set, the children pose in an Arcadian wooded grove; the contrivance of this leafy glade is matched by the enamel-like perfection of their complexions and the intricate counterpoint of their gestures.

Underlying the comeliness of these angelic players are deeper levels of meaning. Most explicitly, the poses and gestures refer to the Annunciation: Maria and Marcus recall Mary and the Archangel Gabriel, while Walter refers to God the Father, with the dove symbolizing the Holy Spirit. Together the figures are combined in a pyramidal composition, characteristic of Wright's depictions of children and deliberately recalling the High Renaissance altarpieces Wright studied during his stay in Italy (1773–75). This rather heavy-handed iconography is accompanied by more convincing and intriguing themes introduced by the cage and the release of the dove. The image of a caged bird was a symbol of childhood popular in the eighteenth century. If innocence is protected through confinement, this portrait evokes the loss of innocence; hence Maria's pose may be seen to express fear for the safety of the bird, and the gestures of Marcus and Walter may be read as indicating comfort and a higher protection. This context is also in keeping with the compositional reference to the Annunciation as a promise of redemption.[1]

Whatever the layers of meaning that may be read into the children's rhetorical gestures, the painting is most eloquent in conveying the Enlightenment fascination with children, and the prevailing confidence in rational inquiry and reflection. The work corresponds subtly with one of Wright's best known paintings, *An Experiment on a Bird in the Air Pump*, 1768 (National Gallery, London). In this work a group of observers, including children, express a variety of reactions to a scientific invention dealing specifically with the life or death of a captive bird, as it depends on the supply of air in the air pump.[2] Likewise, *The Synnot Children* engages the viewer in speculation on the nature of freedom and captivity, a true Enlightenment subject.

Best known for his breathtakingly convincing scenes lit by dramatic candlelight or lamplight, Wright effectively captures in his works the fascination with experiment and industry characteristic of the Age of Reason. The Synnot children, with their cooperative involvement with each other, are seen as the bearers of freedom and enlightenment but are also vulnerable to the dangers and excesses of the new mode of thinking. The marvellously convincing birdcage takes its place among Wright's depictions of clever contraptions, from an orrery to an air pump, to inventions such as the set of cotton-spinning rollers that grace a side table in his portrait of Sir Richard Arkwright, 1789–90 (private collection).[3] All these devices pay homage to the power of invention, so topical at the time of the Industrial Revolution.

It is characteristic of Wright's purpose that the birdcage, here a mere child's wickerwork plaything, is also a refined architectural construction of solidity and grace. Described by Nicolson as a model of 'lucidity and poetry',[4] it is the true object of Wright's artistic attention and, with its door wide open, the repository of the deepest meaning embedded in the work as a whole.

Vivien Gaston

PROVENANCE

Exhibited by the artist, Royal Academy, London, 1781, no. 181; Sir Walter Synnot (1742–1821), Ballymoyer, County Armagh; Synnot and Hart-Synnot family; Hart-Synnot sale, Christie's, London, 5 July 1918, lot 61; from which purchased by Ellis & Smith; Lady Harrison Hughes, London, 1958; from whom purchased by Leggatt's, London, 1958; from whom purchased by William Maxwell Aitken, Lord Beaverbrook (1879–1964), 1958 (on loan to Beaverbrook Art Gallery, Fredericton, New Brunswick, 1959–61); from whom purchased by Mrs Michael Hawker, Menindie, South Australia, 1961; by whom presented to the National Gallery of Victoria, through The Art Foundation of Victoria, 1980.

SELECTED EXHIBITIONS

The Great Eighteenth Century Exhibition in the National Gallery of Victoria, National Gallery of Victoria, Melbourne, 1983.

54. HENRY FUSELI

(Johann Heinrich Füssli) Swiss (active in England), 1741–1825

Milton, when a Youth

Unsigned, undated; painted c.1796–99
Oil on canvas
128.0 x 103.0 cm (50 1/2 x 40 1/2 in.)
Purchased 1981 (E1–1981)

This painting was one of the forty works Fuseli exhibited in London (1799–1800) as the 'Milton Gallery'.[1] The majority of these paintings were of subjects from the poet John Milton's *Paradise Lost* (1667), but there were three representing Milton: as a child, as a youth, and as an adult and blind, dictating to one of his daughters. The first and third are straightforward narrative paintings, but the second is based on a legend (which it does not follow accurately). The legend relates that, when a student, Milton (1608–1674) fell asleep under a tree; in due course a young foreign woman paused near him to write in pencil two lines of Italian verse on a slip of paper, which she left him. He was never to see her but said this episode inspired him to compose *Paradise Lost*.

The artist has posed the sleeping poet in a cave or grotto, while 'the young foreign woman', with no sign of the note, contemplates the young man, as though for ever. The young woman is wearing a *directoire* dress that would have been worn in the lifetime of the artist but not in that of the poet. In Fuseli's time, legends such as the one referred to here were common, attempting to explain the origins of the intuitive imagination of the creative artist, so it seems probable that Fuseli brushed aside the particular legend in order to look at the theme of artistic inspiration in more general terms – hence the anachronisms. Even the young woman loses her original identity to become not only a Muse (probably Kalliope, the Muse of epic poetry) but also, because of the grotto, a sibyl, namely the Cumaean who lived at Cumae (on the coast west of Naples) and wrote her prophecies of destiny on palm leaves. Naples, a city the artist had visited in 1775, was famous for its natural grottos. In the late eighteenth century the building of grottos in the grounds of English country houses became popular and it is worth mentioning that the poet William Wordsworth and his sister Dorothy decorated with seashells the grotto at Coleorton Hall, Leicestershire, the home of the well-known patron Sir George Beaumont.

It has to be remembered that the educated person of the late eighteenth century was very familiar with classical mythology and would have needed no prompting in identifying these ancient associations. Many too would have been familiar with the living muses of the great Italian poets – Dante's Beatrice, Petrarch's Laura, Ariosto's Beatrice and Tasso's Laura – who actively nurtured the poetic spirit of their lovers.

Finally, there is the poet sleeping in the cool comfort of the sibyl's grotto. In Robert Burton's *Anatomy of Melancholy* (1621–52), a work well known to Fuseli, the author wrote of poetic fantasy and imagination: 'In time of sleep this faculty is free, and many times conceives strange, stupend, absurd shapes'.[2] In one of his aphorisms Fuseli agreed: 'One of the most unexplored regions of art are [*sic*] dreams'.[3] At about the same time, Goya titled one of his *Caprichos* (no. 43) as *The Sleep of Reason Produces Monsters*, explaining, in the text accompanying the image, that 'imagination abandoned by reason will produce impossible monsters. United with reason ... imagination is the mother of the arts'. The picture here, with its sleeping poet, illustrates how the creative artist empowered by fantasy and imagination is guided, and his destiny ensured, by the watchful sibyl.[4]

Peter Tomory

PROVENANCE

Exhibited by the artist, *Milton Gallery*, Christie's, London, 1799 and 1800, no. 39; William Roscoe (1753–1831), Liverpool, 1800; private collection, England; Mrs Aubrey Le Blond, 1928; her sale, Sotheby's, London, 5 December 1928, lot 155; from which purchased by A. L. Nicholson; with Bollag, Zurich; from whom purchased by Andrée Stassart, Liège; with Colnaghi, London, 1979; Andrée Stassart, Liège, 1981; from whom acquired by the National Gallery of Victoria, 1981.

SELECTED EXHIBITIONS

The Great Eighteenth Century Exhibition in the National Gallery of Victoria, National Gallery of Victoria, Melbourne, 1983; *Johann Heinrich Füssli: Das Verlorene Paradies*, Stuttgart, Germany, 1997–98, cat. no. 84.

NINETEENTH CENTURY

55. JOSEPH MALLORD WILLIAM TURNER
English, 1775–1851

Walton Bridges

Unsigned, undated; painted c.1806
Oil on canvas
91.2 x 122.5 cm (36 x 48 1/4 in.)
Felton Bequest 1920 (981-3)

PROVENANCE

George Capel-Coningsby, 5th Earl of
Essex (1757–1839), Cassiobury Park,
Watford, Hertfordshire, 1807; Arthur
Algernon Capel, 6th Earl of Essex
(1803–1892), Cassiobury Park, 1878,
1892; the late Earl of Essex sale,
Christie's, London, 22 July 1893, lot
47 (bought in); James Orrock, 1899,
1904; his sale, Christie's, London,
4 June 1904, lot 139; from which
purchased by Agnew's, London; from
whom repurchased by James Orrock,
1905; James Orrock, 1909; Sir Joseph
Beecham (1848–1916), Ewanville,
Huyton, Liverpool, 1910, 1911, 1916;
the late Sir Joseph Beecham sale,
Christie's, London, 3 May 1917, lot
75; from which purchased by Duncan;
acquired by the Felton Bequest, for
the National Gallery of Victoria, 1919.

SELECTED EXHIBITIONS

Turner, National Gallery of Australia,
Canberra, National Gallery of
Victoria, Melbourne, 1996, cat. no. 9.

Throughout his life, J. M. W. Turner painted the river Thames in all its various aspects: from the estuary, sunlit beneath a smoky sky, to the river's winding passage through picturesque outlying towns and farmland. The semi-rural setting of the double bridge at Walton in Surrey was depicted by the artist on a number of occasions during the period when he lived downstream at Isleworth, between 1804 and 1806 (another painting of the bridge c.1806 is in the Loyd Collection). Sketches for the Melbourne composition have been identified in one of the artist's sketchbooks dating to 1805 (Tate Gallery, London).[1] The painting was purchased by the 5th Earl of Essex in 1807 after it had possibly been exhibited in Turner's own gallery during the previous year.

The bridge at Walton lay about halfway between Kew and Windsor Castle. Designed and built by the local architect James Payne in 1783, the bridge featured red-brick arches edged with white stone. This new bridge replaced an earlier wooden structure dating from 1747, which appears in several works by Canaletto.[2] In the shadows at the extreme left of Turner's image is a possible remnant of the old lattice-work bridge. This shaky construction is in stark contrast to the classical gravitas of the new bridge, whose graceful, sunlit geometry is made doubly impressive by its reflection in the still waters below.

Not only the bridge but also the bustling activity in the foreground of the composition serve to capture the viewer's attention. Sheep, dogs and farm labourers crowd the river banks, while ferries and barges narrowly avoid collision as they negotiate the shallow ford. The main focus of attention is a straggly flock of sheep, which are being washed and shorn. Across the water another flock is being encouraged to wade into the stream. An old shepherd waits patiently with his dog at his side, while to his left the scene is being watched from horseback by the owner of the flock, or his overseer. This is a modern working river. Turner's farmhands are no picturesque shepherds – they are part of a vigorous agricultural industry, as they wash and shear their livestock and then use the river to transport the wool to be processed.

During this early period, Turner also used the Thames Valley as the setting for landscapes in which he sought to rival Claude Lorrain (as examples of Claudean versions of contemporary sites, Hill points to *Dido and Aeneas*, 1805–06, and *View of Richmond Hill and Bridge*, 1808 (both Tate Gallery, London)).[3] Some commentators have suggested that the bridge at Walton was the model for plate 13 in Turner's published series of landscape mezzotints, the *Liber Studiorum* (1808–19).[4] Plate 13, published 10 June 1808 and inscribed *EP for Epic(?) Pastoral*, was entitled *The Bridge in the Middle Distance* and was one of the prints most clearly inspired by Claude. The National Gallery of Victoria's painting also has a number of Claudean elements, such as the warm light in which the scene is bathed, the Italianate trees on the far right and the classical pose of the woman on the far left. The golden background provides an idealized setting, in the centre of which Turner has placed a far more realist depiction: of agricultural labourers in an active working relationship with the river. Brown argues that, in these images of the Thames, Turner is motivated by patriotism.[5] At a time of uncertainty and depression during the Napoleonic wars, Turner highlights the vigour of the labourers and the productivity of the land while – in the tradition of artists such as Richard Wilson (1713/14–1782) – he continues to frame his workers in a setting that equates modern rural England with the golden age of classicism.

Alison Inglis and Jennifer Long

56. JOSEPH MALLORD WILLIAM TURNER

A Mountain Scene, Val d'Aosta

Unsigned, undated; painted *c*.1845
Oil on canvas
91.5 x 122.0 cm (36 x 48 in.)
Purchased with the assistance of a special grant from the Government of Victoria and donations from
Associated Securities Limited, the Commonwealth Government (through the Australia Council), the
National Gallery Society of Victoria, the National Art Collections Fund (Great Britain), The Potter
Foundation and other organizations, the Myer family and the people of Victoria, 1973 (E2–1973)

The Val d'Aosta lies high in the Italian Alps, in the Piedmont region just across the border from Mont
Blanc in France. The Alps were a constant source of inspiration for Turner, particularly during the period
1840–44 when he returned every summer to paint. *A Mountain Scene, Val d'Aosta* is a strangely disorienting
image with its mysterious veils of glowing cloud.[1] The rich golden brown of the left foreground acts
as a kind of launching point from which the viewer attempts to penetrate the drifting mist, vainly
seeking to make out the mountain pass, which is hidden from view.

To our twenty-first-century eyes, works such as *Val d'Aosta* appear complete and beautiful, but Turner
scholars agree that the artist would not have exhibited this painting in its present form, without providing
a clearer indication of a theme or subject. Butlin in his analysis of this work drew attention to Turner's
practice of sending canvases in an incomplete state to the Royal Academy or the British Institution and
then finishing the pictures in a last-minute frenzy.[2] Turner used the so-called Varnishing Day to add vital
details that made clear an intended subject, transforming a mass of colour into a recognizable scene or
incident. This process was described in a famous account by an eyewitness:

> The picture when sent in was a mere dab of several colours, and 'without form and void', like
> chaos before the creation. The managers knew that a picture would be sent there, and would not
> have hesitated, knowing to whom it belonged, to have received and hung up a bare canvas, than
> which this was but little better. Such a magician, performing his incantations in public, was an
> object of interest and attraction.[3]

In 1836, *Blackwood Magazine* published a critique of Turner, accusing him of producing works that
were 'a strange jumble'.[4] The young John Ruskin was so incensed by the attacks on the artist that in
1843 he published a defence of Turner's truthfulness to nature. This text marked the beginning of what
would become the five-volume treatise *Modern Painters* (1843–60). Ruskin used his own wonderfully
detailed and poetic language to analyse the types of cloud formations that Turner had studied over a
lifetime. In one particularly apt phrase, Ruskin described the effects of swirling mountain cloud as a
'surge of sky'.[5]

It is impossible to say whether this painting is simply a study of atmospheric effects, complete in itself,
or a background field of colour and texture awaiting its finishing touches. Vaughan has described how
works that were considered unfinished at the time of Turner's death languished uncatalogued in the
basement of the National Gallery, London, only to be discovered at the turn of the new century, when
the artist's treatment of colour and form was re-examined in the light of Impressionism. Vaughan further observes that by the mid twentieth century Turner's late works were once again being re-evaluated –
at a time when abstract expressionism was at its height – in light of their expressionist qualities.[6]

Vaughan demonstrates the extent to which generational ideas and tastes have coloured our understanding
of paintings such as *Val d'Aosta*. However, as Ruskin himself pointed out, regarding Turner: 'The greatest
picture is that which conveys to the mind of the spectator the greatest number of the greatest ideas'.[7]

Alison Inglis and Jennifer Long

PROVENANCE

Camille Groult (1837–1908), Paris,
1894, 1908; by descent to Pierre
Bordeaux-Groult, 1971; from whom
purchased by Agnew's, London,
1971; from whom acquired by the
National Gallery of Victoria, 1973.

SELECTED EXHIBITIONS

Turner, National Gallery of Australia,
Canberra, National Gallery of
Victoria, Melbourne, 1996, cat. no. 33.

57. WILLIAM OWEN
English, 1769–1825

Rachel, Lady Beaumont

Unsigned, undated; painted 1808
Oil on canvas
214.3 x 136.1 cm (84 1/4 x 53 1/2 in.)
Felton Bequest 1955 (3267–4)

Lady Beaumont was ninety-one years old when this portrait was painted. William Owen's very sober style is appropriate for capturing her dignity and powerful physical presence. She sits at an angle to the viewer, her face reflective but not self-absorbed, her hands prominent and expressive. She is seated in a carved wooden chair beneath a swag of deep red drapery and close to a window framed with climbing greenery. Outside is a rural landscape and a cloudy sky. Completing the country house setting is a well-observed spaniel, which curls around the leg of the chair, at Lady Beaumont's feet.

Lady Beaumont was the mother of Sir George Howland Beaumont (1753–1827), an important collector of art and patron of painters and poets. In particular, he was the lifelong friend of John Constable, the great landscape painter. They first met when Beaumont visited his mother at her Suffolk home of Dunmow, at Dedham.[1] Constable's early painting locations were in the Suffolk countryside, and he included Dedham church as the main focus of several of his most important landscapes. In the present painting, the church tower can be seen in the distance through the window. The backdrop to this portrait is the kind of darkly windswept countryside that so directly inspired Constable – and that Boase referred to as 'the symbol of the new world of landscape'.[2]

Lady Beaumont wears a warm and luxurious robe trimmed with fur; a pair of spectacles hangs around her neck and she holds a small gold snuffbox in her mittened hand. Her sturdy character is described in a contemporary report by the English painter and diarist Joseph Farington:

> August 9 [1808]. – Owen called; Had been at Dunmow with Sir G. Beaumont three weeks, in which time He had nearly finished a whole length of Old Lady Beaumont now in Her ninety-first year. She rises at 7 & associates with the family, & continues up till Half-past 9 at night, is chearful & as Owen sd. *strong*.[3]

Lady Beaumont's intellectual acumen was such that Sir George's achievements could be ascribed to her influence: '[H]is mother observed the progress of her son in learning and taste with no little pleasure; her powers of mind were such that she would direct as well as appreciate his studies'.[4]

Owen's early work was in the manner of Joshua Reynolds – a manner that Owen inflected with a solidity and unromantic quietude in his many portraits of leading members of society. The influence of precedents such as Thomas Lawrence's portrait of Queen Charlotte, 1789 (National Gallery, London),[5] is perhaps evident in the setting, and in the pose and almost regal stature of Lady Beaumont, enhanced by the columnar monumentality of the open portico in which she sits. On 6 March 1808 the painter David Wilkie recorded in his journal: 'Called on Owen and saw his picture of the Dowager Lady Beaumont, which I think much the finest thing Owen has yet done'.[6] The portrait creates a peculiarly English ambience, which includes a respect for the wisdom of longevity, the pleasant security of a country landscape, the loyalty of a silky-haired dog, and the noble stature of a venerable subject.

Vivien Gaston

PROVENANCE

Exhibited by the artist, Royal Academy, London, 1809, no. 78; Sir George Howland Beaumont (1753–1827), Coleorton Hall, Coleorton, Leicestershire, 1825; with Colnaghi, London, 1955; from whom acquired by the Felton Bequest, for the National Gallery of Victoria, 1955.

58. JOHN CONSTABLE
English, 1776–1837

'The Quarters' behind Alresford Hall

Unsigned, undated; painted 1816
Oil on canvas
33.5 x 51.5 cm (13 1/4 x 20 1/4 in.)
Gift of Mrs Ethel Brookman Kirkpatrick, 1958 (78–5)

John Constable was invited to paint this small landscape and a larger companion picture, *Wivenhoe Park, Essex* (National Gallery of Art, Washington DC), by his patron and friend Major General Francis Slater-Rebow, in the late summer of 1816.[1] As the artist wrote to his fiancée, Maria Bicknell:

> My dearest love, I returned from my very pleasant visit at General Rebow's on Monday ... I am going to paint two small Landscapes for the General – views one in the park of the house & a beautifull wood and peice of water – and another a scene in a wood with a beautiful little fishing house – where the young Lady (who is the heroine of all these scenes) goes occasionally to angle.[2]

The 'young Lady' mentioned in the letter was the Major General's daughter, Mary Rebow, whose portrait (now lost) Constable had painted four years earlier, in 1812. That work had marked the beginning of the artist's long association with this local landowning family, with further paintings subsequently commissioned.[3] The request in 1816 for two small 'views' of the Rebow estates was prompted by the Major General's knowledge of Constable's impending marriage; for, as the artist confided to Maria Bicknell, his patron was very aware 'that *we* may soon want a little ready money'.[4]

The Melbourne painting depicts the 'little fishing house' (now known as 'the Quarters') at Alresford Hall.[5] The Quarters had been built for Slater-Rebow's father-in-law during the 1760s, in the fashionable chinoiserie style.[6] During the mid eighteenth century, Chinese garden pavilions were frequently placed beside water, where they were used for informal parties, fishing or boating.[7] Constable's painting at first glance gives little indication of the pastimes associated with the 'Chinese Temple'. Instead, the artist appears more interested in the dramatic contrast between the 'exquisite and enchanting artificiality' of the white oriental pavilion and the rich autumnal tones of the surrounding English woodland.[8] The closely observed details of the scene (the dappled light, the lilies on the still water, the skimming swallows) indicate not only the season but also the time of day: a late summer's afternoon. This careful naturalism reflects one of the principles of Constable's art, a principle that he would later describe in terms of the 'chiar'oscuro of nature', referring to both 'the influence of light and shadow upon Landscape', and the use of light and shadow as an expressive device.[9] The artist also used variations of tone to cause the viewer to experience vagaries of perception comparable to those associated with direct visual experience. Thus some forms (such as the white Chinese Temple against the dark woods) stand out clearly, while other objects (such as the darker roof of the ancient dovecote) require further time and study to bring into focus.[10]

Constable's letters provide some insights into the picture's execution. His comment 'I live in the park and Mrs Rebow says I am very unsociable'[11] suggests that the composition was executed before the motif, in the open air.[12] Nevertheless, the existence of a detailed pencil study (Royal Institution of Cornwall, Truro),[13] as well as a grid of lines in the underdrawing of the finished canvas, testifies to the artist's careful preparation before commencing work. His interest in the fleeting effects of time and weather did not preclude an equal concern for the correct spatial construction of his image.

Alison Inglis

PROVENANCE

Major General Francis Slater-Rebow, Alresford Hall, Colchester, Essex, 1816; Benjamin Brookman (d. 1932), London, 1932; Florence Brookman (d. 1940), London, 1932, 1940; Ethel Kirkpatrick (née Ethel Brookman) (d. 1950), London, 1940, 1950; by whom presented (posthumously) to the National Gallery of Victoria, 1958.

SELECTED EXHIBITIONS

John Constable, Isetan Museum of Art, Fukuoka Prefectural Museum of Art, Fukuoka, Yamanashi Prefectural Museum of Art, Yamanashi, Sogo Museum of Art, 1986, cat. no. 19.

59. JOHN CONSTABLE

Study of a Boat Passing a Lock

Unsigned, undated; painted c.1823
Oil on canvas
102.2 x 128.0 cm (40 1/4 x 50 1/2 in.)
Felton Bequest 1951 (2900–4)

Constable is regarded as one of the foremost landscape painters of the nineteenth century. His powerful and original conception of what he termed 'natural painture' (or the 'pure and unaffected representation' of nature)[1] first came to the attention of his contemporaries in the six great canvases, depicting the Stour valley in the Suffolk countryside, that he exhibited at the Royal Academy between 1819 and 1825.[2] Working on a scale usually reserved for idealized history painting, Constable endowed his images of everyday agricultural Britain with a new dignity and authority. He also redefined the notion of a 'finished' picture by imbuing his grandiose works with something of the spontaneous freedom of a rapidly executed sketch. One of the subjects in his series, *The Lock*, 1824 (Museo Thyssen-Bornemisza, Madrid),[3] was taken up by the artist in a number of versions. The *Study of a Boat Passing a Lock* is one of these.

The Melbourne painting shows the sluice gates of Flatford lock being opened to allow a sailing boat to make its way along the river Stour. The subject had enormous personal significance for Constable, who had been born in nearby East Bergholt and whose father owned and operated the mill beside the lock. Constable was later to acknowledge the formative influence of his childhood surroundings: '[T]he sound of water escaping from Mill dams ... Willows, Old rotten Banks, slimy posts, & brickwork. I love such things ... Painting is but another word for feeling. I associate my 'careless boyhood' to all that lies on the banks of the *Stour*. They made me a painter'.[4]

A number of interpretations have been put forward regarding the relationship of the Melbourne *Lock* to Constable's other depictions of this famous subject. When the present work first appeared on the art market in the 1950s, it was generally accepted as a preliminary oil study for Constable's Diploma picture, *A Boat Passing a Lock* of 1826,[5] the work presented to the Royal Academy by Constable, as was required, upon his election as an Academician in 1829.[6] Both works are horizontal in format and show a sailing boat ascending the river. Another opinion emerged in the 1970s, when the Melbourne painting's highly finished foreground and carefully executed sky led some scholars to reinterpret the picture as a replica of – rather than a study for – the Diploma work, but a replica 'not carried entirely to completion'.[7]

More recently, the *Study of a Boat Passing a Lock* has been proposed as a precocious but 'abandoned' attempt at the subject, predating both the Diploma work and the vertical version of *The Lock* dated 1824 and now in Madrid.[8] According to this theory, the Melbourne *Lock* should in fact be compared with the vertical oil sketch of c.1823 at the Philadelphia Museum of Art,[9] a work that the artist is known to have initially envisaged as a horizontal composition.[10] In support of this conjecture is the fact that the pose of the Melbourne lock-keeper is far closer to that of the Philadelphia figure than to that of the figure in the Diploma work.[11]

The comparison with the Philadelphia study highlights the un-sketchlike treatment in the Melbourne painting. Constable's full-scale sketches are characterized by their expressive handling, but their richly textured surfaces tend to overwhelm all subtleties of atmosphere and depth. The more highly finished brushwork of the Melbourne *Lock* brings a greater definition and coherence to the scene. Thus, the modulating light of the sky creates a real sense of wind and weather, while the detailed observation of plant life on the river bank, and the rich tones of the lock's wooden structure, vividly convey the artist's own engagement with this location.

Alison Inglis

PROVENANCE

Private collection, Exeter; with Arthur Tooth & Sons, London, 1950; from whom acquired by the Felton Bequest, for the National Gallery of Victoria, 1950.

SELECTED EXHIBITIONS

Constable, Tate Gallery, London, 1991, cat. no. 159.

60. THÉODORE ROUSSEAU
(Pierre-Étienne-Théodore Rousseau) French, 1812–1867

Landscape with a Clump of Trees

Unsigned, undated; painted *c.*1844
Oil on wood panel
41.6 x 63.8 cm (16 1/2 x 25 in.)
Felton Bequest 1955 (3260–4)

Théodore Rousseau was the central figure in a group of artists working in France in the mid nineteenth century who were associated with the village of Barbizon in the Forest of Fontainebleau, near Paris. The painters who constituted what came to be known as the Barbizon School shared a love of painting direct from nature. Their interest in landscape painting for its own sake was a relatively recent development in French art and was to some degree a result of the influence of John Constable and other earlier English landscapists.

Although he had settled permanently at Barbizon in 1848, Rousseau also travelled extensively in the French provinces and *Landscape with a Clump of Trees* was probably painted during his time in the Berry and Landes regions in central and southwest France. This painting is characteristic of the objective naturalism that governed Rousseau's approach to landscape in the 1840s.

Here is nature at her most serene, benign and accessible. The sense of nature's permanence and stability that pervades the work is based on the solidity of the composition: an elemental opposition of vertical trees and the wide horizontal land. The middle ground is occupied by a still grove of trees, and the foreground by placid, unmoving animals and their keeper. Occupying two-thirds of the painting, the clear and spacious expanse of sky that joins the earth at the distant horizon confirms the sense that the natural world is tranquil, harmonious and enduring.

The motifs that make up *Landscape with a Clump of Trees* appear in other paintings by Rousseau dating from this period, but any danger of schematic rigidity is averted by the close observation of the specific effects of light and atmosphere over the land. In this painting, the artist's feeling for nature and his fascination with its material reality is also revealed in the meticulous record of the rocks, grasses and undergrowth, which here litter the foreground.

Rousseau received little official recognition until quite late in his career. In a preface to his review of the Salon of 1844, about the time that *Landscape with a Clump of Trees* was executed, the critic Théophile Thoré (1807–1869) addressed his remarks to his friend Rousseau. 'You, dear poet', he wrote, 'have spent your life looking at the great outdoors … at a thousand things imperceptible to the common eye. Nature for you has mystic beauties which escape us, and secret favours that you lovingly reproduce'.[1]

Rousseau is known to have painted very slowly, often reworking his pictures. His naturalism therefore was based on a careful meditation on the data of the natural world and on the uncovering of the 'secret favours' of nature.

The work of Rousseau and the Barbizon School became associated with a specifically nineteenth-century ideal of the relationship between man and nature, an ideal that provided an antidote to the often sordid reality of modern urban life. It has been argued that the modern naturalistic landscape, epitomized by paintings like *Landscape with a Clump of Trees*, in fact came into being as a contrast to the advances of industrialization. By the end of the nineteenth century, Rousseau was seen as one of the few great modern painters of landscape. But his reputation declined in the early years of the twentieth century and it is only relatively recently that his work has been rediscovered.

Rosemary Stone

PROVENANCE

William Schaus, New York, 1881;
Theron R. Butler, 1910; with
Knoedler's, New York; Billings, 1926;
Eli B. Springs; the late Eli B. Springs
sale, Anderson Galleries, New York,
23 November 1934; A. Levinson;
with Hazlitt Gallery, London, 1955;
from whom acquired by the Felton
Bequest, for the National Gallery of
Victoria, 1955.

SELECTED EXHIBITIONS

*Van Gogh: His Sources, Genius
and Influence*, National Gallery of
Victoria, Melbourne, Queensland
Art Gallery, Brisbane, 1993–94,
cat. no. 9; *Narratives, Nudes and
Landscapes: French 19th-Century
Art*, National Gallery of Victoria,
Melbourne, 1995.

62. ARTHUR HUGHES
English, 1832–1915

Fair Rosamund

Signed l.l.: *A. Hughes*, undated; painted 1854
Oil on wood panel
40.3 x 30.5 cm (15 3/4 x 1/2 in.)
Gift of Miss Eva Gilchrist in memory of her uncle P.A. Daniel, 1956 (3334–4)

When Arthur Hughes painted *Fair Rosamund*, which was exhibited in the Winter Exhibition at the French Gallery, Pall Mall, in 1854, he was a follower and close associate of the Pre-Raphaelites. He shared with them a love of medieval subjects and in 1857 worked with Dante Gabriel Rossetti, William Morris and Edward Burne-Jones on Arthurian mural decorations for the Oxford Union, the debating society at Oxford University. As a young artist, Hughes adopted a technique developed by John Everett Millais and William Holman Hunt: meticulously applying the oil medium in a thin layer, section by section, onto a wet white ground, so that the paint was particularly luminous. As a result, Hughes's paintings from this early period are characterized by their translucent jewel-like colour.

Fair Rosamund illustrates an episode from the tragic story of Henry II, the twelfth-century English king, his queen, Eleanor of Aquitaine, and his mistress, Rosamund Clifford. Over time, the tale lost much of its connection with actual events, as it was adapted and embellished in the course of a long literary tradition. The king is said to have hidden his mistress at the palace at Woodstock in Oxfordshire, in a garden bower reached only by a maze, but his estranged wife, Queen Eleanor, discovered the secret location and poisoned her rival. Rosamund's body was then buried at the nunnery at Godstow, near Oxford.

The combination of a medieval setting, beauty, jealousy and violent death captured the imagination of numerous Victorian writers and artists, including Alfred Tennyson, William Bell Scott, Algernon Charles Swinburne, Rossetti and Burne-Jones.[1] Hughes's *Fair Rosamund* has none of the destructive passion of Swinburne's later treatment of the story nor the strange primitivism of Rossetti's or Burne-Jones's painted versions. Instead Hughes relies on the work's small scale and intense colour to create an atmosphere of overheated sweetness.

Hughes's depiction concentrates on the moment of the queen's entry into the secret garden. The portal through which she has passed is inscribed with the initials *HR*, a reference to King Henry. A purple shadow connects Queen Eleanor to the figure of Rosamund, who stands hidden near her namesake, the rose, in the foreground. A contemporary Victorian audience would have been able to read and appreciate the painting's flower symbolism. The broken lilies at Rosamund's feet suggest lost virtue, while the poisonous blue foxgloves that line the queen's path indicate the means by which the murder will be committed. The dove tethered above the ivy-covered arch reappears in embroidered form on the cloth on the table beneath, and may allude to the earlier Rosamund poems of Tennyson and Bell Scott, in which her confinement within the maze is compared to the life of a caged bird.[2]

The painting was included in an important exhibition of British works, held at the National Academy of Design, New York, in 1857, but was not well received by the critics, who were hoping for pictures exemplifying Pre-Raphaelite principles of 'truth to nature', by the leading exponents of the movement.[3]

As well as sustaining a long and successful painting career, Hughes gained considerable fame as an illustrator. The National Gallery of Victoria possesses examples of his graphic work, and also one of his Arthurian paintings, *La Belle Dame sans Merci*, 1863.

Jennifer Long

PROVENANCE

Peter Augustine Daniel, London, 1917;
Eva M. Gilchrist, 1917, 1956; by whom
presented to the National Gallery of
Victoria, 1956.

63. JOHN EVERETT MILLAIS
English, 1829–1896

The Rescue

Signed and dated l.l.: *JEM* [monogram] *1855*
Oil on canvas (arched top)
121.5 x 83.6 cm (47 3/4 x 33 in.)
Felton Bequest 1924 (1302–3)

PROVENANCE

Purchased from the artist by Joseph
Arden, Rickmansworth Park,
Rickmansworth, Hertfordshire, 1855;
the late Joseph Arden sale, Christie's,
London, 26 April 1879, lot 68;
from which purchased by Agnew's,
London; Holbrook Gaskell, Woolton,
Liverpool; the late Holbrook Gaskell
sale, Christie's, London, 24 June
1909, lot 67; from which purchased
by Agnew's, London; Charles Fairfax
Murray, 1917; his sale, Christie's,
London, 14 December 1917, lot 59;
from which purchased by Eugene
Cremetti; with McLean Galleries,
London (Eugene Cremetti), 1923;
Eugene Cremetti sale, Christie's,
London, 1 June 1923, lot 149; from
which purchased by W. W. Sampson;
from whom acquired by the Felton
Bequest, for the National Gallery of
Victoria, 1923.

SELECTED EXHIBITIONS

Fontane und die bildende Kunst, Alte
Nationalgalerie, Staatliche Museen
zu Berlin – Preußischer Kulturbesitz,
Berlin, 1998, cat. no. 53.

John Everett Millais was one of Britain's most popular artists in the later nineteenth century. He was known for the virtuosity of his painting technique, and his works were admired for their richness of colour and engaging subject matter. In 1848, Millais had been a founding member of the Pre-Raphaelite Brotherhood. The group's primary motivation was their rejection of the stale conventions associated with the Royal Academy. In their search for clarity and directness, they looked to the early Italian masters as a source of inspiration and regeneration. Millais and William Holman Hunt, in particular, developed a style based on 'truth to nature' combined with luminous colour and a high degree of finish.

The Rescue presents a boldly modern subject. While there are different accounts of Millais's inspiration for the work, it is clear that the artist's first-hand experience of a local fire was a significant factor.[1] In 1855 he spoke to fellow artist Arthur Hughes of his intention in this picture 'to honour a set of men quietly doing a noble work – firemen'.[2] Another source for the Melbourne composition has been identified as an illustration by William Mulready in the 1843 edition of Oliver Goldsmith's *Vicar of Wakefield*. In the engraving, the vicar is shown rescuing children from a fire.[3]

In his biography of his father, John Guille Millais singled out *The Rescue* as an example of the artist's laborious early painting technique:

> It was his practice then to paint piecemeal, and finish parts of his pictures as he went on. White, mixed with copal, was generally laid on where he intended to work for the day, and was painted into and finished whilst wet, the whole drying together. The night-dresses of the children were executed in this manner. Strontian yellow was mixed with the white, and then rose-madder mingled with copal, floated, as it were, over the solid but wet paint – a difficult process, and so ticklish that as soon as a part was finished the canvas had to be laid on its back till the colour had dried sufficiently to render the usual position on the easel a safe one.[4]

The finished painting received mixed reviews when it was first shown at the Royal Academy in 1855. Ruskin described the picture as a 'very great' work.[5] Other critics, however, found fault with the lack of realism, particularly the strong red glow and the figure of the mother. As the critic in the *Athenaeum* pointed out: '[T]he lady seems to have already suffered much from the flames, having saved a voluminous night-gown, but lost the greater part of her body'.[6]

One aspect of the work that did find approval among commentators was the manliness of the fireman. He was described as 'thoroughly English, cool, determined and self-reliant',[7] with the 'lofty fortitude of a real hero'.[8] These descriptions are curiously similar to those used for Millais himself, who, after his death in 1896, was portrayed as 'Anglo-Saxon from skin to core – vigorous ... full of healthy power of mind and body',[9] and 'typically English in the best sense, with all the physical and mental attributes that have enabled our race to dominate the empire'.[10] The fact that the fireman displays qualities that the artist himself cultivated may account for Millais's assessment of this work as one of his best.[11]

Jennifer Long

64. JEAN-BAPTISTE-CAMILLE COROT
French, 1796–1875

The Bent Tree (Morning) (Ville d'Avray, Bouleau Pond)

Signed l.r.: *COROT*, undated; painted *c*.1855–60
Oil on canvas
44.3 x 58.5 cm (17 1/2 x 23 in.)
Felton Bequest 1907 (338–2)

As a painter of landscape, Jean-Baptiste-Camille Corot is generally regarded as the most significant figure in French painting in the first half of the nineteenth century. Although he executed figure studies and portraits throughout his life, Corot's fame in his own time rested on his later, composed landscapes, of which the Melbourne *Bent Tree (Morning)* is a fine and characteristic example.

Corot's early work was conditioned by the principles of classical landscape painting, the precepts of which he combined with the recording of the actual experience of the eye. The pictorial habits that resulted were arrangements of great formal balance and harmony, which governed even the most spontaneous-seeming studies from nature. The *Bent Tree (Morning)* belongs to a type of landscape that was favoured by Corot in the middle years of his career and that brought him great success. In these paintings he moved away from the direct study of nature, which had been the main base of his work, to landscapes composed to a large degree from memories, from the remembered moods and feelings that belonged to certain places and times. Accordingly, Corot often included the word *souvenir* (memory) in the titles of these landscapes.

If the Melbourne picture is not a direct recording of a particular place at a particular time of day, it is still based on naturalistic motifs and effects. It is this seemingly effortless evocation of landscape through the filter of memory and imagination which gives the work its dreamlike beauty. In his notebooks, Corot wrote that he was affected by any place he saw, and he observed that even in seeking to recreate a specific location: 'I never for a moment lose sight of its first emotional impact on me. Let your feelings be your guide … Reality is part of art, but it is feeling which makes it whole'.[1]

The poetic mood of the *Bent Tree (Morning)* is largely dependent on the effects of the light, which softens all the forms: the small figures, the trees, the earth, the sky and the water. This silvery light appears to emanate from the depths of the painting and to very slowly advance into the foreground. The feathery, silhouetted trees against a soft, luminous sky; a distant sheet of water; indistinct architectural forms against the horizon; and the small, self-absorbed figures in the foreground are all motifs that recur in the composed landscapes of Corot. The composition is a balanced arrangement of light and dark, of horizontal and vertical, animated by the counterbalance of the bent tree of the title. This finely judged harmony of relationships reflects the origins of Corot's style, in the tradition of French classical landscape painters like Claude. But the Arcadian pastoral mood, and the subtle truth of light and of atmosphere expressed with the hallmark delicacy of touch, are purely Corot.

Until the emergence of the composed lyrical landscapes such as the present work, Corot was all but ignored by the critics and dealers. The reasons for the popular success of such works appear to be related to the impact of the social, economic and political changes taking place in contemporary life. In paintings like the *Bent Tree (Morning)*, Corot offered a retreat into nature, an escape from the increasingly materialist reality of nineteenth-century France, back into a simpler and more ideal world. Now the place of Corot in the history of art is secure; his work forms a vital connection between the tradition of French classicism and the nineteenth-century stream of naturalism. Later he exerted a profound influence on the Impressionists and he was generally revered by all the major landscape painters of the latter part of the century.

Rosemary Stone

PROVENANCE

Benoist, 1883; Benoist (dec.) sale, Paris, 9 March 1883; from which purchased by Détrimont; Alexander Young, 1888, 1891; with Agnew's, London, 1907; from whom acquired by the Felton Bequest, for the National Gallery of Victoria, 1907.

SELECTED EXHIBITIONS

Narratives, Nudes and Landscapes: French 19th-Century Art, National Gallery of Victoria, Melbourne, 1995.

66. ÉDOUARD MANET

The House at Rueil

Signed and dated l.l.: *Manet / 1882*
Oil on canvas
92.8 x 73.5 cm (36 1/2 x 29 in.)
Felton Bequest 1926 (2050–3)

While *The Ship's Deck* (cat. no. 65) stands at the threshold of Manet's career, this painting belongs among his late works. In 1882 Manet rented this house at Rueil, where he was to spend his last summer. By now he was much affected by illness but during his stay in this Restoration-style villa he was still able to sit outside under a tree and to paint a number of views of the garden and the sunlit facade of the house. There is another version of this view of the house at Rueil, a work also painted in 1882 (Alte Nationalgalerie, Staatliche Museen zu Berlin – Preußischer Kulturbesitz).[1] The Berlin painting is similar in its dimensions, but uses a horizontal format rather than the vertical.

The composition of the Melbourne picture is characteristic of Manet's preferred structure. This comprises a central form (in this case the tree), combined with strong vertical and horizontal elements (such as the architectural features of the villa's facade). The same pictorial structure was used by Manet in his images of modern life – for example, the late masterpiece *A Bar at the Folies-Bergère* (Courtauld Institute Galleries, London), completed in the same year as *The House at Rueil*.[2]

The garden of *The House at Rueil* provides an organic frame for the view of the villa: the centrally placed tree rises up from a bed of lush grasses and flowers, which frame the lower part of the building, and the lower edges of the tree's canopy extend across the upper edge of the canvas. Within this natural framework, the facade of the villa glows with the warm light of summer, and so an intimate connection is established between the work of nature and that of man. This sense of intimacy is enhanced by the cropping of the composition at the top and sides so that we see only the face of the villa, as it were, with roof and sky omitted from our view. At the same time, however, the spectator is denied visual access into the villa, as the doorway is obscured by the tree. We are therefore detained in the shady garden. As in many of Manet's paintings, the controlling element here is his choice of viewpoint, which to a large degree determines our experience of the work. Aligned with other factors, it is this compositional vision which creates a sense of the random and the immediate, giving paintings such as this their vivid sense of actuality. Yet the number of preparatory sketches made for *The House at Rueil* reveals the careful calculations required to achieve this casual effect.

Manet's handling of colour in this painting is close to that of his Impressionist friends and contemporaries, such as Monet and Renoir. Manet was an important early influence on the Impressionists, and shared many of their interests. But he never joined the Impressionists in their exhibitions, and within the context of the avant-garde of his day he remained an independent. In this painting, the Impressionist characteristic is the luminosity of the colour, achieved to some degree by the use of a system of complementary contrasts: red against green; blue against an orange-red; and the garden path is a blue-violet dappled with patches of yellow light, a colour arrangement that is repeated on the house facade.

In exploiting the principle that complementary colours heighten each other when juxtaposed, Manet has evoked the dazzling effects of bright summer light and air. These effects are reinforced by his playing off of the more sombre-toned tree foliage against the clear, light colour harmonies of the facade. In *The House at Rueil*, the unexpected viewpoint, the compositional structure, the virtuoso freeness of the paint application, and the masterful handling of colour operate together to create what Manet's friend the poet Stéphane Mallarmé called his 'living reality'.[3]

Rosemary Stone

PROVENANCE

Purchased from the artist by Jean-Baptiste Faure (1830–1913), Paris, 1883; Jean-Baptiste Faure, 1884, 1906; Théodore Behrens, Hamburg; with Knoedler's, Paris, 1924; with Knoedler's, London, 1926; from whom acquired by the Felton Bequest, for the National Gallery of Victoria, 1926.

SELECTED EXHIBITIONS

Van Gogh: His Sources, Genius and Influence, National Gallery of Victoria, Melbourne, Queensland Art Gallery, Brisbane, 1993–94, cat. no. 19; *Narratives, Nudes and Landscapes: French 19th-Century Art*, National Gallery of Victoria, Melbourne, 1995; *Manet*, Fondation Pierre Gianadda, Martigny, 1996, cat. no. 88.

153

67. HONORÉ DAUMIER
French, 1808–1879

Don Quixote Reading

Unsigned, undated; painted c.1867
Oil on wood panel
33.6 x 26.0 cm (13 1/4 x 10 1/4 in.)
Felton Bequest 1923 (1276–3)

Don Quixote Reading is one of a series of nearly thirty paintings by Honoré Daumier that are based on episodes from Miguel de Cervantes's novel *Don Quixote de la Mancha* (1605–15). From 1850 onward, the adventures of Don Quixote and his squire, Sancho Panza, were a subject Daumier returned to on numerous occasions over a period of some twenty years. He also made many drawings of the same characters, and the large number of images devoted to the one subject suggests that it had a particular significance for him. However, painting was only a relatively small part of Daumier's artistic output, and in his lifetime he was most famous as France's greatest social and political satirist, using mainly the medium of lithography. Daumier's stature as one of the most important painters and sculptors of his time has only very gradually been recognized.

Daumier's satirical work began with political caricatures, but from 1835 his graphic works became more focused on social-satirical themes. In these works, he satirized the vast, variable and often ridiculous range of human behaviour and social mores. A republican all his life, Daumier was a partisan of the poor and the dispossessed. In his satirical work, side by side with his often devastating denunciations of human stupidity and vanity, there is a deeply felt sense of sympathy for those subjected to poverty and injustice. But although his brilliant style of caricature always had an appreciative popular audience, Daumier saw his graphic work as journalism and as something that kept him away from the higher art of painting.

The subjects of Daumier's paintings range from images of daily life to images from literature, such as *Don Quixote Reading*. Cervantes, like Daumier, was a satirist and his *Don Quixote* sets out as a satire of the romances of chivalry. Cervantes's hero, the idealistic Don Quixote, is an impecunious gentleman whose mind has been turned by reading too many romances, as a consequence of which he sets out on a series of absurd adventures with his servant Sancho. Here Daumier shows the knight alone in his study, absorbed in those very romances that will set events in motion. Through the doorway two figures observe the reader. As with much of Daumier's work in oils, colour plays a minor role, and most of the essentials lie in the drawing. Daumier's style here – the use of paint to mould the forms, and the very broad, summary treatment of the figure and his surroundings – in some respects marks him as a precursor of the Impressionists.

In the eighteenth century, the misfortunes of Don Quixote were seen as comedy but, by the mid nineteenth century, Cervantes's character had undergone a reinterpretation. Instead of a figure of fun, he became the man of imagination and a symbol of the artist, misunderstood and often persecuted by society. Don Quixote joined other historical and fictional figures, such as Tasso, Dante and Hamlet, with whom the Romantic artists identified themselves. He became 'the sublime child, the noblest, the worthiest, the wisest of men',[1] and the subject of countless paintings and drawings. Furthermore, the idealistic knight and his materialistic squire came to be seen as two aspects of the one creative personality. This duality would have been understood by Daumier, the idealistic satirist whose art was a vehicle both for moral ideas and for a critique of the excesses of human behaviour. The eccentric character of Don Quixote would have corresponded to his own fondness for eccentricity, at the same time serving as a metaphor for idealism, always at odds with the pettiness, vulgarity and meanness of the world.

Rosemary Stone

PROVENANCE

Lemaire, 1878; Jungers; Bernheim, Paris; with Reid & Lefevre, London, 1922; from whom acquired by the Felton Bequest, for the National Gallery of Victoria, 1922.

SELECTED EXHIBITIONS

Daumier 1808–1879, National Gallery of Canada, Ottawa, Galeries Nationales du Grand Palais, Paris, Phillips Collection, Washington DC, 1999, cat. no. 368.

68. JULES BASTIEN-LEPAGE
French, 1848–1884

Season of October: The Potato Gatherers

Signed and dated l.l.: *1878 DAMVILLERS / J. BASTIEN-LEPAGE*
Oil on canvas
180.7 x 196.0 cm (71 1/4 x 77 1/4 in.)
Felton Bequest 1928 (3678–3)

Season of October, exhibited at the Paris Salon of 1879, is one of a pair of harvest scenes that marked a new direction in Jules Bastien-Lepage's career as a painter. The earlier work, *The Haymakers* (Musée d'Orsay, Paris), exhibited in 1878, shows two weary haymakers resting in the summer heat;[1] by contrast, *Season of October* is an account of the bleak autumnal potato harvest, set in a bare, featureless landscape.

In 1875 Bastien-Lepage had been expected to win the coveted Prix de Rome with the set piece *The Annunciation to the Shepherds* (also at the National Gallery of Victoria), but his failure to do so, on a technicality, led to his decision to leave Paris and to abandon his intended career as an establishment painter. He returned to his native village of Damvillers, in the Meuse valley to the northeast of Paris, where, inspired by the example of Millet and Courbet, he planned to paint rural life as he knew it, celebrating its hardships as well as the inherent dignity of the peasants themselves. He particularly despised those city painters whose sentimental views of rustic life confirmed their ignorance of it, but whose paintings continued to fill the annual Salons.

Despite Bastien-Lepage's intentions there is something unconvincing about these potato gatherers. The pose of the stooping foreground figure is reminiscent of one of Millet's gleaners but, unlike Millet's peasants, this woman has a strangely selfconscious air and seems frozen in mid-movement. The static poses of both foreground figures, and the dramatic difference in scale between these figures and the distant workers, suggest the strong influence of contemporary photography.[2]

In his review of the 1879 Salon, the critic and novelist Joris Karl Huysmans wrote that 'the wonderfully real aspect of Millet's peasants in the countryside does not come through in Lepage's work'.[3] The model was the artist's fifteen-year-old cousin, Marie-Adèle Robert. Huysmans noted perceptively that this figure was no peasant: '[Her] hands are not the hands of a woman who works with the soil – they are like the hands of my maid who dusts as little as possible'.[4]

The choice of large-scale canvases for his two harvest scenes demonstrates not only Bastien-Lepage's ambitious artistic program, but also his confidence in his own technical virtuosity. It was perhaps this latter element which was most noticed by Salon audiences. The public was pleased by the painter's ability to combine both the high 'finish' expected of an Academic picture and elements of the Impressionists' technique. However, Bastien-Lepage's flirtation with Impressionism caused the critics to be wary – they had recognized that the artist's technique aimed to be all things to all people. Though he noted that the Melbourne picture seemed painted without effort, Huysmans detected in it 'the affection of sham treatment, a step forward which has been interrupted and then skillfully halted in order not to displease the public'.[5]

Bastien-Lepage's widely admired style was still imitated internationally long after the painter's early death. A change in fashion was already apparent, however, by the time the painting was purchased by the Felton Bequest for the National Gallery of Victoria in 1927: the picture was purchased for only a third of the price asked for it when it had first been offered to the Melbourne Gallery, in 1910.

Sonia Dean

PROVENANCE

Exhibited by the artist, Salon, Paris, 1879, no. 164; collection of the artist, 1884; the late Jules Bastien-Lepage sale, Hôtel Drouot, Paris, 11 May 1885, lot 13; Émile Bastien-Lepage, 1897; from whom purchased by Arthur Tooth, London; George McCulloch, 1897; Mrs Coutts Richie (widow of George McCulloch), 1927; from whom acquired by the Felton Bequest, for the National Gallery of Victoria, 1927.

SELECTED EXHIBITIONS

Van Gogh: His Sources, Genius and Influence, National Gallery of Victoria, Melbourne, Queensland Art Gallery, Brisbane, 1993–94, cat. no. 17; *Narratives, Nudes and Landscapes: French 19th-Century Art*, National Gallery of Victoria, Melbourne, 1995.

69. CLAUDE MONET
French, 1840–1926

Vétheuil

Signed l.r.: *Claude Monet*, undated; painted 1879
Oil on canvas
60.0 x 81.0 cm (23 1/2 x 32 in.)
Felton Bequest 1937 (406–4)

In 1878 a financially straitened Claude Monet returned to Paris from the semi-rural district of Argenteuil, where he and fellow Impressionists had frequently painted. In August that year, after only a short time in the French capital, Monet moved further still from Paris – to Vétheuil, a country town bordering the Seine between Paris and Rouen. Home to only 622 inhabitants at this time, and some ten kilometres from the nearest railway station, Vétheuil was a small farming village noted principally for its thirteenth-century Gothic church of Notre-Dame.[1] Monet was soon joined in Vétheuil by his wife, Camille, and their two children, and also by Alice Hoschedé, wife of Monet's friend the collector Ernest Hoschedé, with the six Hoschedé children. Initially a summer rental-share arrangement designed to cut costs for both families, this merging of households developed into a permanent ménage.

Throughout 1878 and 1879 Monet painted many views in and around Vétheuil, observing the town's aspects across the changing months and virtually 'mapping' the differing effects of seasonal light upon its forms. He also painted the small village of Lavacourt, which faced Vétheuil on the opposite bank of the Seine. Since the two towns had no bridge across the river and communicated by means of a local ferry service, it was no doubt advantageous for Monet's freedom of movement that he had brought with him the houseboat he had enjoyed at Argenteuil. This boat served as a floating studio, which he could ply up and down the river, and moor before a motif he wished to paint. *Vétheuil* was probably painted from Monet's studio-boat, if not from one of the islands that dot the stretch of the Seine between Vétheuil and Lavacourt.

In the late summer of 1879, after a long illness, Camille Monet died; but, while this was a year of great turmoil in Monet's life, there is no sign of personal distress in the idyllic and sunny calm of *Vétheuil*. Similarly, it seems clear that Monet framed this and other views of Vétheuil quite selectively, to eliminate physical aspects of the town that he presumably found visually unappealing. Not only did he remove the Lavacourt–Vétheuil ferry from his composition, but he also excluded all signs of quite heavy commercial river traffic from what was then one of the busiest tradeways of western France. The effect, shared by all Monet's paintings of these twin towns, was to make them appear more peacefully rural than was actually the case.[2]

Coupled with this vision of rural 'innocence', it is Monet's virtuoso manipulation of shimmering, iridescent hues which imparts such a lyrical feel to *Vétheuil*. The strident coloration of Monet's palette perplexed some critics at the time. Paul Sébillot, for example, had 'trouble understanding a number of his newer canvases where all the colours of the rainbow have been juxtaposed'.[3] Spate has linked Monet's use of a high-hued palette, in certain of the Vétheuil paintings, to the artist's appreciation of the 'transparent tints of [Japanese] wood-block prints', which he avidly collected.[4] This association was certainly noted upon the first unveiling of Monet's Vétheuil canvases. In June 1880, when the artist showed a number of these paintings at the gallery of the Paris journal *La Vie moderne*, Théodore Duret wrote that Monet now possessed 'the audacity to push his colorations as far as them [the Japanese]'.[5]

Ted Gott

PROVENANCE

With Durand-Ruel, Paris, 1899, 1935; with Arthur Tooth & Sons, London, 1936, 1937; from whom acquired by the Felton Bequest, for the National Gallery of Victoria, 1937.

SELECTED EXHIBITIONS

Claude Monet: Painter of Light, Auckland City Art Gallery, Auckland, Art Gallery of New South Wales, Sydney, National Gallery of Victoria, Melbourne, 1985, cat. no. 5; *Van Gogh: His Sources, Genius and Influence*, National Gallery of Victoria, Melbourne, Queensland Art Gallery, Brisbane, 1993–94, cat. no. 18; *Narratives, Nudes and Landscapes: French 19th-Century Art*, National Gallery of Victoria, Melbourne, 1995.

159

70. CLAUDE MONET

Rough Weather at Étretat

Signed l.r.: *Claude Monet*, undated; painted 1883
Oil on canvas
65.0 x 81.0 cm (25 1/2 x 32 in.)
Felton Bequest 1913 (582–2)

Claude Monet's choice of the popular seaside resort of Étretat for a working holiday in late January 1883 was perhaps prompted by the region's fame as a recreational location, and was in keeping with 'the impressionists' interest in subject matter reflecting modern life, especially the leisure activities of the bourgeoisie'.[1] A popular haven since the 1830s for artists and writers, Étretat, on the Normandy coast, had by 1883 developed into a thriving tourist resort, celebrated for its views of three enormous natural stone arches (the Porte d'Aval, Porte d'Amont and Manneporte) and a spectacular rocky 'needle' carved from the surrounding cliffs by the ferocious action of the sea. In three short weeks, Monet painted some twenty canvases, which recorded all three arches and the spiky 'needle' under varying climatic conditions.

Parisians holidaying in Étretat could party in the town's lavish casino or retire to the many luxury villas scattered nearby. Monet stayed in the Hôtel Blanquet, whose advertisements not only announced 'family suites' and six classes of horse-and-carriage for transporting luggage, but boasted that 'every public and private room looks directly onto the ocean'. The hotel was situated extremely close to the beach, and the high viewpoint of many of the canvases produced during this trip shows that Monet often sheltered indoors from the inclement weather, painting 'nature' from the establishment's windows. Certain canvases, including *Rough Weather*, nonetheless seem to have been partly painted on the beach, directly in front of the motif. A single grain of sand still embedded in the paint surface of the Melbourne picture hints at the chill wind and salt spray swirling around Monet as he painted outdoors on a winter's day at the ocean's rim.[2]

Étretat was positioned directly on the beach immediately to the right of the view depicted in Monet's composition, but no indication is given here of the bustling presence of the town. The painting has been framed instead to focus upon the awesome power of nature (whose majesty is underscored by the tiny scale of the waving figures at the water's edge) – although signs of the relentless tourist paths beaten around Étretat remain in the heavy zigzags of the numerous walking trails that surmount the Porte d'Amont in the distance. Rough surf was not uncommon at Étretat, where the pebbled beach dropped away very steeply, close to the shore.[3]

Close technical analysis of *Rough Weather* reveals that the underlayer of paint in the lower half of the composition seems to have had its oil content removed, so that the area of the sea has a stiff texture with considerable body.[4] Monet has applied a complex veil of flicks and whirls of paint over this dry sea 'bed', and it would therefore appear that the picture was worked to completion in a number of sessions (it was probably started on the beach, and later finished indoors). While the painting obviously records a distinct atmospheric effect, it also shows Monet delighting – when he came to the finishing surface layer of the composition – in a magical play of calligraphic licks and coils of paint. Affinities with his appreciation of Japanese calligraphy, which we know he could have seen demonstrated first-hand in Paris on several occasions in 1878,[5] seem evident, and a number of his friends at this time owned Japanese ink paintings.

It is intriguing to note that, when *Rough Weather* was recommended for purchase by the National Gallery of Victoria's London adviser in 1913, Monet was a second-tier choice. Sir Sidney Colvin had originally visited Monet's Paris dealer, Paul Durand-Ruel, in search of Barbizon School paintings by Jean-François Millet or Charles-François Daubigny; it was only after Colvin found no Barbizon works for sale that 'it became necessary to consider only the painters of the younger generation'.[6]

Ted Gott

PROVENANCE

Purchased from the artist by Durand-Ruel, Paris, 1883; Jean-Baptiste Faure (1830–1913), Paris; with Durand-Ruel, Paris, 1901, 1908, 1910, 1913; from whom acquired by the Felton Bequest, for the National Gallery of Victoria, 1913.

SELECTED EXHIBITIONS

Claude Monet: Painter of Light, Auckland City Art Gallery, Auckland, Art Gallery of New South Wales, Sydney, National Gallery of Victoria, Melbourne, 1985, cat. no. 13; *Monet: A Retrospective*, Bridgestone Museum of Art, Tokyo, Nagoya City Art Museum, Nagoya, Hiroshima Museum of Art, Hiroshima, 1994; *Narratives, Nudes and Landscapes: French 19th-Century Art*, National Gallery of Victoria, Melbourne, 1995.

161

71. PAUL CÉZANNE
French, 1839–1906

The Uphill Road

Unsigned, undated; painted 1881
Oil on canvas
58.9 x 71.6 cm (23 1/4 x 28 1/4 in.)
Felton Bequest 1938 (543–4)

> I do not remember ever having seen Cézanne at the Nouvelle-Athènes; he was too rough, too
> savage a creature, and appeared in Paris only rarely. We used to hear about him – he used to be
> met on the outskirts of Paris wandering about the hillsides in jack-boots … His work may be
> described as the anarchy of painting, as art in delirium.[1]

George Moore's colourful description of Paul Cézanne may exaggerate the wildness of one of the nineteenth century's most important painters, but does suggest the radical nature of his art and the passion
with which he undertook it. For his own part Cézanne probably cared little for how Moore viewed him:
by the late 1870s his search for creative expression saw him reject the Impressionists, with whom he had
previously exhibited, in his desire to find a stylistically new way of depicting nature.

Cézanne's intense process of artistic realization is reflected in a letter of 1879 to childhood friend Émile
Zola. As Cézanne wrote: 'I am still striving to discover my right way as a painter. Nature puts the greatest
obstacles in my way'.[2] This 'striving' is evident in *The Uphill Road*, a painting that can be considered a
transitional work in the artist's career as he moved away from the Impressionist interest in capturing
transitory effects, towards a more solid and structured approach to nature. Recent research indicates
that Cézanne painted this work in May 1881, when he was staying in Pontoise near his friend and
mentor, Camille Pissarro.[3] *The Uphill Road* was one of a series Cézanne made that showed the small
villages of the area set in their natural surroundings: a subject that attracted the artist less for its
picturesque qualities than for the challenge of representing the geometric relationships between the
landscape and buildings.

The Uphill Road appears, at first glance, to be a simple enough painting: a group of carefully articulated
buildings with their distinctive grey roof tiles are separated from a grassy hill and country road by a
low stone fence. However, this scene is given complexity through a carefully conceived composition in
which Cézanne divides the picture space into four bands, comprising sky, houses, grass and road.

Despite this formal arrangement the painting is sketchy in parts, especially in the foreground where the
grassed area is comprised of blocks of light colour. The thinness of Cézanne's paint and his use of rapid
diagonal brushstrokes, particularly in the sky, give this canvas a spontaneity that suggests it was not
completed. This impression is reinforced by the fact that, when he returned to Paris from Pontoise,
Cézanne left *The Uphill Road* with Pissarro, probably working on it again many years later. That, even
then, he still does not appear to have finished it, suggests the demanding temperament of an artist who
was always searching for more complete ways to depict nature.

Isobel Crombie

72. CAMILLE PISSARRO
French, 1830–1903

The Banks of the Viosne at Osny in Grey Weather, Winter

Signed and dated l.l.: *C. Pissarro / 83*
Oil on canvas
65.3 x 54.5 cm (25 3/4 x 21 1/2 in.)
Felton Bequest 1927 (3466–3)

PROVENANCE

With Durand-Ruel, Paris, 1892;
Bonin; with Knoedler's, London,
1923; Sir James Murray, London,
1927; his sale, Christie's, London,
29 April 1927, lot 80; from which
acquired by the Felton Bequest, for
the National Gallery of Victoria, 1927.

SELECTED EXHIBITIONS

*Van Gogh: His Sources, Genius
and Influence*, National Gallery of
Victoria, Melbourne, Queensland
Art Gallery, Brisbane, 1993–94,
cat. no. 20; *Narratives, Nudes and
Landscapes: French 19th-Century
Art*, National Gallery of Victoria,
Melbourne, 1995.

Camille Pissarro like many of the Impressionists spent much of his working life based in an area northwest of Paris, mostly in or around the old town of Pontoise, and within easy reach of the capital. The landscape of the surrounding villages and small towns offered the artist numerous motifs, though not of the dramatic kind – low, bare hills, stone buildings with red or blue roofs, and screens of slender trees seem to characterize the areas he chose to paint. Charles-François Daubigny had lived not far away from here, but, unlike the Barbizon painter, Pissarro did not make the river Oise his particular subject.

In 1882 Pissarro and his family moved from Pontoise to a nearby village called Osny. Situated on the banks of the river Viosne, a tributary of the Oise, Osny was in a region already well known to the artist. It was the intimate aspects of the rural landscape that he chose as his Osny subjects, painting intimate views of the village, the inlet in the river, the local farm, or the road leading to the village. While still at Pontoise in the late 1870s, Pissarro had painted several local features, including the area known as l'Hermitage and the hillside referred to as La Côte des Boeufs, through a trellis-like pattern of trees, which sometimes threatens to hide the view completely. Here in this corner of the village of Osny, the screen of trees remains, but less intrusively, and rather it is the density of the paint layer and the complexity of the brushstrokes which most clearly distinguish this work from the earlier paintings.

The 1870s had been a period of struggle and experiment for Pissarro. He had made a number of dramatic changes of style during the decade, driven in particular by the constant battle between representing 'sensations' of nature and finding a means of doing so while at the same time achieving a more finished and tougher facture or surface. During this period Pissarro again worked for a time with Cézanne, the two often painting the same subjects.

The critic Théodore Duret noted that Pissarro's particular and distinctive strength was what Duret termed 'the power of the brush'.[1] By the 1880s Pissarro's canvases are often densely built up with small brushstrokes layered almost like a woven blanket. The *Banks of the Viosne at Osny in Grey Weather, Winter* has a highly complex paint surface. A dense pattern of directional brushstrokes is marshalled across the canvas, delineating the embankment, the water and the stone walls. The paint surface is layered in some areas and in others scraped back but not uniformly. The sharp green of the foreground seems in some instances to have been applied direct from the tube, and is scattered with occasional dots of red. The palette is strongly green and indigo and violet.

At the time it was acquired for the National Gallery of Victoria, this picture was described by the painter Sir D. Y. Cameron, who wrote: 'This is the new world of observation of the intimacies of nature as contrasted with the great and weighty design of the old. Here is the flicker – the sparkle – the broken jewel colour sought after to-day and revealed in one small canvas'.[2]

Sonia Dean

165

73. CAMILLE PISSARRO

Boulevard Montmartre, Morning, Cloudy Weather

Signed and dated l.r.: *C. Pissarro, 97*
Oil on canvas
73.0 x 92.0 cm (28 3/4 x 36 1/4 in.)
Felton Bequest 1905 (204–2)

In February 1897, Pissarro began a series of paintings of the great boulevards of Paris. On 8 February he wrote to his son Lucien, who was in London: 'I have booked a spacious room at the Grand Hôtel de Russie … from which I can see the whole sweep of the boulevards almost as far as the Porte Saint-Denis, anyway as far as the boulevard Bonne-Nouvelle'.[1] Between 10 February and 17 April, Pissarro painted fourteen views of the boulevard Montmartre from the window of his hotel room on the corner of rue Drouot, and two further canvases from the same vantage point looking to the right to the boulevard des Italiens.

Brettell has noted that Pissarro painted more cityscapes than did any other Impressionist painter, though neither the urban streetscape nor series paintings were his invention. Both Monet and Caillebotte, among others, had painted bird's-eye views of Paris streets, and Monet in particular had painted views in series, though not of Paris.[2]

Pissarro's canvases of Paris are less concerned with topography than with observing and capturing the constantly changing effects of light, weather and season. Writing to another son, Georges, on 13 February 1897, the artist recorded having 'begun my series of boulevards … I have a splendid motif which I must explore under all possible effects'.[3] The fixed viewpoint afforded by the upper-storey window allowed him to observe not only the effects of weather patterns and light on the boulevard, but also, and just as importantly, the ever-changing configurations of the crowds and traffic below. Thus, by observing the motif from a fixed vantage point, he was able to produce his series of canvases, each work capturing a precise moment in the kaleidoscope of light and movement of Paris. Pissarro described being at his post from early morning until afternoon, recording the same scene every day through winter into early spring.[4] These paintings include one night scene (National Gallery, London) and views of a procession celebrating Mardi Gras, which his family came up from the country to watch from his window.[5]

This was not Pissarro's first sortie into painting urban views: he had already completed a group of Paris street scenes in snow. These works had been well received – and sold – by his dealer, Paul Durand-Ruel, who had then encouraged him to embark on a new series of boulevards, but had recommended larger scale canvases. Of the fourteen views of the boulevard Montmartre, two – the Melbourne painting and a sunny afternoon view (Hermitage, St Petersburg) – are larger in format than the rest. Pissarro's choice of the boulevards, and, later, the avenue de l'Opéra, as subject matter reveals his preference for depicting modern Paris rather than the picturesque medieval city, though the boulevard Montmartre was in fact an eighteenth-century thoroughfare, which was connected with the more recent urban developments overseen by Baron Haussmann.

Work on the canvases painted at the Grand Hôtel de Russie was completed by 17 April, when Pissarro, in a letter to Lucien, reported that he had packed his things and sent sixteen canvases to Éragny.[6] On the same day he wrote also to his son Georges: 'I have finished my campaign here'.[7]

This painting, the first Impressionist work to be acquired for the National Gallery of Victoria, came into the collection in 1905, only two years after Pissarro's death, as one of the first purchases made through the Felton Bequest.

Sonia Dean

PROVENANCE

With Durand-Ruel, Paris, 1897, 1899; at Grafton Gallery, London, 1905; from whom acquired by the Felton Bequest, for the National Gallery of Victoria, 1905.

SELECTED EXHIBITIONS

The Impressionist and the City: Pissarro's Series Paintings, Dallas Museum of Art, Dallas, Philadelphia Museum of Art, Philadelphia, Royal Academy of Arts, London, 1992–93, cat. no. 45; *Narratives, Nudes and Landscapes: French 19th-Century Art*, National Gallery of Victoria, Melbourne, 1995; *Paris in the Late 19th Century*, National Gallery of Australia, Canberra, Queensland Art Gallery, Brisbane, 1996–97.

74. EDWARD BURNE-JONES

English, 1833–1898

The Garden of Pan

Signed l.r.: *EB-J*, undated; painted *c*.1886–87
Oil on canvas
152.5 x 186.9 cm (60 x 73 1/2 in.)
Felton Bequest 1919 (961–3)

In the summer of 1855, Edward Burne-Jones and his friend William Morris (1834–1896) were so inspired by their tour of the cathedrals of northern France that they abandoned their studies at Oxford for a life of art.[1] The young Burne-Jones soon made his name as a painter of oils and watercolours and as a designer for the firm of Morris and Company. He often combined a number of sources, interweaving medieval and classical or Renaissance imagery to create subjects located in an indeterminate time and space. Burne-Jones's paintings are known for their rich, sombre colour scheme and for the uneasy, dreamlike state that characterizes his figures.

The *Garden of Pan* was conceived at a time when Burne-Jones was deeply influenced by his travels in Italy. Returning home to London in 1872, he was inspired to set out a program of ambitious new works. Writing in 1904, his widow, Georgiana Burne-Jones, described how the Melbourne painting had its origins in one such scheme: ' "The Garden of Pan" … is a fulfilment of part of Edward's intention to paint the Beginning of the World. He first called it "The Youth of Pan" '.[2]

Burne-Jones's original idea was more complex and grand in scale than this painting would suggest. The artist initially planned to include 'the beginning of the world, with Pan and Echo and sylvan gods, and a forest full of centaurs, and a wild background of woods, mountains, and rivers'.[3] In the finished work there are just three figures in a twilight setting. The image is coloured by the artist's love of the Italian Renaissance. Although Burne-Jones did not travel to Italy after 1872, he saw numerous Renaissance pictures in public and private collections in Britain. He also collected prints and photographic reproductions. In his analysis of the *Garden of Pan*, Christian has drawn attention to Burne-Jones's possible debt to several works by Dosso Dossi and Piero di Cosimo that belonged to William Graham, one of the artist's principal patrons [4] (at one time the owner of the Paolo Veneziano *Crucifixion* in the present exhibition (cat. no. 1)). Burne-Jones's interest in the Renaissance was not only visual, however, for he was also a scholar of literature and mythography. During the 1860s and 1870s both he and Morris became interested in the transformation of stories that had filtered down from Persian and Greek sources to reappear in the Middle Ages and the Renaissance.[5] The deity Pan was the type of migratory figure that appealed to these artists. Pan had appeared in various forms throughout the centuries, ranging from 'the good shepherd' to demonic goat-legged creatures.[6]

In this image, Pan is a beautiful, slender youth; as he plays, the kingfisher and dragonflies – creatures known for their darting speed – stop to listen to the sweet sound. Another characteristic of Burne-Jones's work is his inclusion of elements such as doorways, rock portals or water, which act as boundaries between different states of being. In the *Garden of Pan* a bend in the river divides the young god from his listeners, separating the natural and supernatural worlds.

The painting was first exhibited at the Grosvenor Gallery, London, in 1887 and was enthusiastically received. The critic for the *Athenaeum* wrote at the time: 'In poetic suggestiveness "The Garden of Pan" is second to none of his works'.[7]

Jennifer Long

PROVENANCE

Duchess of Marlborough, 1892, 1899; her sale, Christie's, London, 10 May 1918, lot 95; from which acquired by the Felton Bequest, for the National Gallery of Victoria, 1918.

SELECTED EXHIBITIONS

Burne-Jones: Dal preraffaellismo al simbolismo, Galleria Nazionale d'Arte Moderna, Rome, 1986, cat. no. 64; *Victorian Dreamers: Masterpieces of Neo-Classical and Aesthetic Movements in Britain*, Yamanashi Prefectural Museum of Art, Kofu, Daimaru Museum, Osaka, Yamaguchi Prefectural Museum of Art, Yamaguchi, Ishibashi Museum of Art, Kurume, Isetan Museum of Art, Tokyo, 1989, cat. no. 30; *Edward Burne-Jones: Victorian Artist-Dreamer*, Metropolitan Museum of Art, New York, Birmingham Museums and Art Gallery, Birmingham, Musée d'Orsay, Paris, 1998–99, cat. no. 120.

75. ALFRED SISLEY
English (active in France), 1839–1899

The Loing and the Slopes of Saint-Nicaise – February Afternoon

Signed and dated l.l.: *Sisley. 90.*
Oil on canvas
60.0 x 73.0 cm (23 1/2 x 28 3/4 in.)
Felton Bequest 1938 (453–4)

'Every picture', wrote Alfred Sisley in 1893, 'shows a spot with which the artist himself has fallen in love'.[1] The subject of this painting is a calm stretch of the Loing River outside the historic township of Moret-sur-Loing, where Sisley spent the last decade of his life. It was the artist's practice to draw the landscape scenery for his paintings from the area in which he lived. Sisley had returned to live in this region on the edge of the Forest of Fontainebleau in 1880, and wrote to Monet the following year, praising the area's 'picturesque views'.[2] From the early 1880s until Sisley's death in 1899, the Loing and the towns and hamlets along its banks were a major source of subject matter for his paintings.

This particular spot, with its gently sloping hills, limestone embankment and simple buildings facing each other across the river, was painted by the artist four times in 1890. Sisley often executed multiple paintings of a single location, varying the viewing angle slightly so that the individual canvases present different perspectives on the one scene. These works were not necessarily intended to be viewed together in a sequence, but rather exemplify the artist's programmatic approach to visually plotting the distinctive features of a given location and exploring how they fit together.[3]

All four paintings of Saint-Nicaise were painted from the one location on the left bank of the river; two of the works depict views along the left bank, and two focus upon the view across the river to the right bank.[4] *The Loing and the Slopes of Saint-Nicaise – February Afternoon* provides the most visually harmonious perspective on this scene, balancing a cropped view of the left bank with the view across the river to the buildings and gently sloping hills of the right bank. The strong pictorial harmony of this composition – attained through the formal balance of land and sky elements, the buildings echoing each other, and the receding line of the river, which is balanced by the line of the hills – contributes to the sense of stillness and deep calm that pervades this winter scene.

Sisley and his fellow Impressionists chose the multiple format not only because of the different perspectives it afforded, but also because it enabled the exploration of the effects of changing light, weather and atmospheric conditions, upon a particular subject. In his paintings of Saint-Nicaise, Sisley investigates the seasonal changes in the light upon this riverside landscape. Two of his four canvases are specifically titled with the time of day and month of execution, revealing that the artist returned to the same spot in February and again in March. The National Gallery of Victoria's painting was executed on a chilly afternoon in February, when the winter sun illuminated the dormant landscape with a crisp, clean light. The painting executed in March already shows the softening and brightening of the light of early spring.[5]

In his efforts at painting specific effects of light, Sisley emphasized the importance of the sky, which, he claimed, 'can never be merely a background'.[6] In his paintings the sky provides the key note that resonates throughout the entire landscape. In the Melbourne picture, the sense of winter chill is conveyed through a high-keyed colour scheme that is established by the translucent hues of the sky. Ranging from soft blue in the upper reaches to an intense green-blue above the hills, the tonality of the sky is echoed throughout the landscape, in the pink hills, the lilac and blue water, and the transparent green and blue shadows cast by the bare trees.

Cathy Leahy

PROVENANCE

Purchased from the artist by Charles Ephrussi (1849–1905), Paris; Théodore Reinach (1860–1928), Paris; Gabrielle Reinach; with Wildenstein, London, 1937; from whom acquired by the Felton Bequest, for the National Gallery of Victoria, 1937.

SELECTED EXHIBITIONS

Narratives, Nudes and Landscapes: French 19th-Century Art, National Gallery of Victoria, Melbourne, 1995.

76. ALFRED SISLEY

Haystacks at Moret – Morning Light

Signed and dated l.l.: *Sisley .91*
Oil on canvas
73.8 x 93.1 cm (29 x 36 3/4 in.)
Felton Bequest 1913 (583–2)

Sisley executed two paintings of haystacks in the summer of 1891, a few months after Monet's famous series had been exhibited to critical acclaim in Paris. While haystacks had occasionally appeared as incidental elements in Sisley's landscapes from the mid 1880s onward, the prominence of the motif in his two paintings from 1891 – the Melbourne picture and a painting at the Musée de Douai[1] – points to his awareness of Monet's works. Although he adopted Monet's subject, however, Sisley's treatment of the haystacks is very much his own. While similarly concerned with rendering a particular effect of light, Sisley eschewed Monet's abstraction of the landscape context and his transformation of the fleeting moment into a universal statement. In *Haystacks at Moret – Morning Light* Sisley locates his haystacks in the middle of a mown field that is lined by a row of densely foliated poplars, a few wooden buildings and a dusty path. Alongside the haystacks, a worker is shown raking and stacking the mown hay. Sisley's depiction remains a record of a particular location seen in the sparkling sunlight of a summer's morning.

This painting is an outstanding example of Sisley's late style, in its intensity of colour and its pronounced brushwork and surface texture. When he painted a landscape, Sisley's main concern was with conveying to the spectator the sensation that the natural scene had excited in him. He ascribed particular importance in this process to the painting's surface, which he felt should be varied in accordance with the play of light across the individual parts of the landscape. He explained this aspect of his practice to the critic Adolphe Tavernier:

> You see that I am in favor of a variation of surface within the same picture. This does not correspond to customary opinion, but I believe it to be correct, particularly when it is a question of rendering a light effect. Because when the sun lets certain parts of a landscape appear soft, it lifts others into sharp relief. These effects of light, which have an almost material expression in nature, must be rendered in material fashion on the canvas.[2]

PROVENANCE

François Depeaux (1853–1920), Rouen, 1897, 1901; his sale, Hôtel Drouot, Paris, 25 April 1901; from which purchased by Lehman, Paris; François Depeaux, Rouen; his sale, Galerie Georges Petit, Paris, 31 May 1906, lot 233; from which purchased by Durand-Ruel, Paris; with Durand-Ruel, Paris, 1910; from whom acquired by the Felton Bequest, for the National Gallery of Victoria, 1913.

SELECTED EXHIBITIONS

Sisley, Royal Academy of Arts, London, Musée d'Orsay, Paris, Walters Art Gallery, Baltimore, 1992–93, cat. no. 63; *Narratives, Nudes and Landscapes: French 19th-Century Art*, National Gallery of Victoria, Melbourne, 1995.

The varied handling of the paint to suggest material substance and different light effects makes *Haystacks at Moret* an excellent example of the application of this tenet. Staccato brushstrokes are employed on the foremost haystack and in the foreground to evoke the spiky texture of mown hay, while longer, smoother strokes along the sides of the stacks suggest their recession into the distance as well as the shadow cast along their flank. In the background, short dabs of paint are used to create the shimmering leaves of the poplars, and in the sky the chalky white brushstrokes convey the sparkling, refractive light of a summer's morning. Through this vigorous handling of paint and use of bright colour, Sisley succeeds in conveying the smiling mood of nature on a brilliant summer's day.

This painting has long been recognized as a significant work in Sisley's oeuvre. The artist himself accorded the picture this status when he selected it for inclusion in the 1892 exhibition of the Société Nationale des Beaux-Arts in Paris. This society had formed in 1890, following a split from the official Salon, and had invited Sisley to participate in its first exhibition in May of that year. He eagerly accepted the invitation, sending six to eight paintings for exhibition every year between 1890 and 1898, with the exceptions of 1896 and 1897. The artist had hoped that these exhibitions would improve his opportunities for gaining sales of his work and would thus help to ease his financially straitened circumstances. This outcome, however, did not eventuate. Sisley was never to achieve critical success or financial reward during his lifetime and died almost penniless, of cancer of the throat, in 1899.

Cathy Leahy

77. JOHN WILLIAM WATERHOUSE
English, 1849–1917

Ulysses and the Sirens

Signed and dated l.r.: *J. W. WATERHOUSE. / 1891*
Oil on canvas
100.6 x 202.0 cm (39 1/2 x 79 1/2 in.)
Purchased 1891 (p.396.3–1)

John Waterhouse established his career in the 1870s and 1880s with paintings of subjects from ancient Greek and Roman history, in a style strongly influenced by Lawrence Alma-Tadema (1836–1912). From 1886, Waterhouse increasingly turned to poetry and mythology as sources for his work.

The story of Ulysses and the Sirens, as told by Homer, was well known to Victorian audiences. The mythological hero Ulysses (Odysseus) had to sail past the cliffs where the sirens used the irresistible beauty of their song to lure sailors to their death. Ulysses was warned of the sirens' power, and instructed his crew to block their ears with wax. He had himself tied to the mast, with his ears unprotected, so that he could listen to the fatal music without throwing himself overboard.

According to nineteenth-century artistic convention, sirens were usually painted as mermaids or nymphs reclining on the seashore. Waterhouse, however, chose to depict them as bird-women. He was apparently inspired by a design on a well-known Greek vase (5th century BC) in the British Museum.[1] The vase had been illustrated in William Smith's *A Smaller Classical Mythology* (1867),[2] as well as in an article in the *Magazine of Art*, by the classical scholar Jane Harrison in 1887.[3] Texts such as Harrison's *Mythology and Monuments of Ancient Athens* (1890) began to replace the idea of serene Olympian gods with a view of archaic Greek religion as darker and more complex than previously recognized.[4] Waterhouse's sharp-taloned sirens reflect this changing interpretation.

Waterhouse's use of an antique vase as a starting point for an imaginative treatment of Greek legend represents a change in the way that Victorian artists used archaeology. The artefact is no longer simply a background detail that sets the scene; rather, it is the catalyst for a poetic meditation on the spirit of an ancient myth. Waterhouse uses a second archaeological reference in an equally suggestive way. Elizabeth Pemberton has identified the painting on the interior of Ulysses' ship as a depiction of Heracles wrestling with Triton. The image is taken from an Athenian black-figure cup, which Waterhouse either would have seen during his regular travels in Italy or would have encountered in publications.[5] The vase was located at Tarquinia (near Rome) and published in *Notizie degli scavi* in 1880. Pemberton argues that Heracles' defeat of Triton, the son of the sea god Poseidon, was an image of hope for Ulysses. Ulysses, like Heracles, had been in conflict with a son of Poseidon and needed to appease or outwit the sea god in order to return home.[6]

Ulysses and the Sirens attracted considerable attention when first exhibited at the Royal Academy in 1891. Some commentators were disturbed by the interpretation of sirens as birds rather than nymphs.[7] However, the painting was generally well received, both in London and in Melbourne. Sir Hubert Herkomer, who purchased the work on behalf of the National Gallery of Victoria, found in this picture 'a curious regard for Japanese art',[8] referring perhaps to the peacock blue of the sea and to the dramatic diagonal thrust of the ship across the picture plane.

Jennifer Long

PROVENANCE

Exhibited by the artist, Royal Academy, London, 1891, no. 475; acquired from the artist by the National Gallery of Victoria, 1891.

SELECTED EXHIBITIONS

Queens and Sirens: Archaeology in 19th Century Art and Design, Geelong Art Gallery, Geelong, Victoria, 1998, cat. no. 9.

78. PIERRE PUVIS DE CHAVANNES
French, 1824–1898

Winter

Signed and dated l.r.: *P. Puvis de Chavannes / 96*
Oil on canvas
96.2 x 147.2 cm (37 3/4 x 58 in.)
Felton Bequest 1910 (487–2)

PROVENANCE

Prince Alexandre de Wagram
(1883–1918), Paris, 1896, 1910;
from whom acquired by the Felton
Bequest, for the National Gallery of
Victoria, 1910.

SELECTED EXHIBITIONS

*Narratives, Nudes and Landscapes:
French 19th-Century Art*, National
Gallery of Victoria, Melbourne, 1995;
The 1890s, National Gallery of
Australia, Canberra, Queensland Art
Gallery, Brisbane, 1996–97.

The Hôtel de Ville (City Hall) was one of the many buildings burned down during the period of the Paris Commune in 1871. The massive rebuilding program that followed was put in the hands of the Paris architects Ballu and Deperthes, who, after lengthy deliberations, commissioned Pierre Puvis de Chavannes in December 1888 to decorate the so-called Salon du Zodiaque with friezes representing the seasons Summer and Winter.

This foyer-like space was badly lit and narrow, and there was an intrusive doorway: problems that caused Puvis to describe the Salon as 'indécorable'.[1] Nevertheless, he accepted these challenges, and his two paintings were completed in 1891 and 1892 respectively. Still unhappy with the space upon the completion of the pictures, however, he asked to remove them and offered to refund the commission.[2]

There is no attempt at narrative in either of these works, and period and location are undefined; the paintings are, rather, poetic evocations of the seasons. *Summer*, with classically inspired figures and gentle landscape, suggests a calm and peaceful existence, while cruel *Winter* reduces its inhabitants to subsistence living through the unrelenting cold. Indeed, Puvis eschewed any idea of naturalism and spoke of such works as 'poems' or 'symphonies'. The two compositions were painted on large canvases that could then be attached to the wall, the oil paint imitating the chalky, dry effect of fresco.

It was four years later that Puvis received a commission to paint a reduced version of *Winter* for a private client, Prince Alexandre de Wagram.[3] No longer inhibited by problems of space and light, Puvis was able to produce an easel painting that was perhaps closer in spirit to his original idea. The scale is now more compact, and the figures have become more dominant in the landscape.

The essential character of fresco, however, is retained in the Melbourne picture in the overall flatness of design. The effect is essentially a poetic evocation of the winter cold. The palette is strongly pink, violet and white but the paint is applied in a surprisingly sketchy fashion, the strong drawing carrying the composition, while the application of paint seems almost perfunctory. The trees have been drawn strongly in chalk over an aggressively pink winter sky, the branches reinforced with blue paint applied with a thin brush. The three men who strain on a rope to bring down one of the trees are drawn in black chalk, and only lightly painted in, yet they remain, with the two collectors of firewood in the foreground, the strongest figure group in the composition.

It was precisely the sketchiness of this painting that caused the then Director of the National Gallery of Victoria, himself a painter trained in the academic manner, to dismiss the work as 'this frankly primitive picture'.[4] The painting was acquired for the National Gallery of Victoria from the Prince de Wagram in 1910, through the Felton Bequest and against the recommendation of the Director. At the time of acquisition it was noted in the correspondence that the frame for the picture had been specially commissioned by the Prince de Wagram.

Sonia Dean

79. PIERRE BONNARD
French, 1867–1947

Siesta – The Artist's Studio

Signed l.r.: *Bonnard*, undated; painted 1900
Oil on canvas
109.0 x 132.0 cm (43 x 52 in.)
Felton Bequest 1949 (2053–4)
© Pierre Bonnard, 1900/ADAGP
Licensed by VISCOPY, Sydney, 2000

This painting of a naked woman, stretched out asleep on a dishevelled bed in a contemporary boudoir, is remarkable within Pierre Bonnard's oeuvre for its pronounced sensuality. It is not only the details referring to sexual activity – discarded clothing, tousled sheets – which give this painting its erotic charge, but also, primarily, the artist's presentation of his voluptuous nude. The languorous pose of the nude was derived by Bonnard from a famous classical sculpture at the Louvre, a work that was renowned for its eroticism. The Borghese *Hermaphrodite* had such a reputation that visitors to the Villa Borghese in Rome, where the sculpture was first displayed in the seventeenth century, were advised 'not to look at it if they did not want to blush with pleasure and shame simultaneously'.[1] By employing the pose of this sculpture, Bonnard presents the nude in an attitude that accentuates the sinuous curves of her back, while allowing a simultaneous view of her full bottom and rounded breast. Her position on the bed, while suggestive of a heavy-limbed satiety, offers up her body to the viewer for a lingering appraisal. Furthermore, the heightened viewing angle implicates viewers in the scene, making them feel as if they are standing within the room and looking across the nude and the expanse of bed to the patterned wallpaper.

Bonnard used his model and mistress, Marthe Boursin, as the subject for this painting and posed her on the bed in their apartment.[2] This highly personal aspect to the work was not unusual for the artist, who always drew his subjects from the domestic and daily scenes around him. It was with the onset of his relationship with Marthe in 1893, however, that a new, intimate subject matter began to appear in his art. Marthe is posed on the bed, pulling on her stockings; is shown washing in a tub; and from 1897 was the subject of a series of sensually charged paintings and drawings that were to culminate in the artist's lithographs for *Parallèlement* (1900), a collection of poems by Paul Verlaine. *Siesta*, painted in 1900,[3] is one of the major paintings in this group of works, and is closely related to another, even more overtly erotic, picture, *Indolence*, 1898/99 (private collection).[4] In this work, Marthe is the very picture of sexual availability – she lies on the bed on her back, with her legs parted and breasts supported by one arm, and looks knowingly at the viewer.

While these works obviously relate to the personal life of the artist, they should also be viewed in the context of contemporary cultural discourse. Newman has argued that in Paris in this period the role and place of women in society was under discussion and also that there was intense interest in issues of eroticism and sexuality.[5] Issues such as prostitution, and sex outside marriage, engendered debates fuelled by feminism and the increasingly visible 'modern woman'. This series of works in which the sexual activity of woman is a central motif announces Bonnard's opposition to middle-class values that saw sex outside marriage as dangerous to the established order. Although himself born into the bourgeoisie, Bonnard recognized the inherent hypocrisies of a class that sanctioned prostitution while upholding the virtues of marriage. He not only voiced his opposition in his art, but also lived it in his personal life, as he and Marthe were not to marry until 1925, nearly thirty years after they began living together.

Cathy Leahy

80. MARK GERTLER
English, 1891–1939

The Apple Woman and Her Husband

Signed and dated u.l.: *Mark. Gertler. / May. 1912*
Oil on canvas
66.0 x 56.0 cm (26 x 22 in.)
Purchased 1953 (3002–4)
© Luke Gertler

While his immense talent should have marked him out as one of the leading lights of early British modernism, Mark Gertler is not particularly well known. He is often overshadowed by other English painters of his generation, such as Stanley Spencer, David Bomberg, Harold Gilman, Duncan Grant and Augustus John. This relative obscurity may be due, in part, to the fact that Gertler's career ended abruptly when, dogged by depression and ill health and frustrated by his recent lack of success, he took his own life. Or it may be due to the fact that Gertler was something of an artistic loner; he had no imitators and formed no school.

Due to his immigrant parents' financial hardship, Gertler came to art later than most: he began attending the Regent Street Polytechnic, London, in 1906, at age fifteen. His time at the Polytechnic was brief – only one year – but his fortunes changed when, in 1908, he won a prize in a national art competition. The resulting exposure brought him to the attention of the influential artist William Rothenstein (1872–1945), who was instrumental in helping Gertler to win a scholarship to the Slade School of Fine Art in 1908.[1] Gertler proved an outstanding student, winning several prizes and scholarships and developing friendships with fellow students Paul Nash (who is represented in this exhibition by *Landscape of the Summer Solstice*, 1943 (cat. no. 85)), C. R. Nevinson and Edward Wadsworth.

The Apple Woman and Her Husband, dated May 1912, belongs to the period immediately following Gertler's heady successes at the Slade. The sitters are the artist's parents, Louis and Golda, who were patient models for a number of portraits and family groups executed by Gertler while he was a student.[2] The best known of these works are *The Artist's Mother*, 1911 (Tate Gallery, London), and *The Artist's Parents*, 1909–10 (Luke Gertler Collection), which shows Louis and Golda in reverse positions to those they occupy in the Melbourne picture. The main difference between these portraits and the present work is that *The Apple Woman and Her Husband* is not a portrait as such, but a study of costumed figures – perhaps because apple gatherers were a subject for the Slade Sketch Club in 1912 (in 1912–13 fellow student Stanley Spencer made a painting of the same theme, a work now at the Tate Gallery, London).

The Apple Woman and Her Husband received positive reviews when it was first shown at the New English Art Club in the summer of 1912. The critic for the *Observer* praised the painting's 'sureness of purpose, clear fine colour [and] … strong sense of pattern without loss of plastic roundness'.[3] The critic for the *Star* newspaper was more effusive, asserting that the picture was 'a triumph of artistic skill, won by a thoroughness of workmanship governed by a sense of style, disciplined and developed by an intimate knowledge of the best work of the past'.[4]

On the strength of these reviews and his distinction at the Slade, Gertler appeared set to enjoy a long and prosperous career. However, his sporadic exhibition success over the next twenty years wreaked havoc upon his intense and anxious mental state. In 1916, his friend D. H. Lawrence, sensing Gertler's emotional fragility, cautioned: 'Take care, or you will burn your flame so fast, it will suddenly go out … try to save yourself'.[5] Sadly, in the end, Gertler did not heed this advice, committing suicide in his studio in 1939 at the age of forty-eight.

Tracey Judd

PROVENANCE

Sir Augustus Daniel; with Leicester Galleries, London, 1953; from whom acquired by the National Gallery of Victoria, 1953.

SELECTED EXHIBITIONS

Mark Gertler Centenary Exhibition, Camden Arts Centre, London, 1991–92.

183

81. ROBERT DELAUNAY
French, 1885–1941

Nude Woman Reading

Unsigned, undated; painted 1915
Oil on canvas
86.2 x 72.4 cm (34 x 28 1/2 in.)
Felton Bequest 1966 (1665–5)

This painting of a woman reading is one of Robert Delaunay's nine versions of this theme. Delaunay rarely painted the nude figure, and a series devoted to the subject is most unusual in his work. The element that connects *Nude Woman Reading* with the broader scope of Delaunay's art is colour. According to Delaunay, colour is the central language of the artist. 'Colour', he said, 'is form and subject'.[1] In contrast to this intimate interior, the subjects of Delaunay's earlier work tended to be centred around the dynamic character of modern city life. The nude, on the other hand, was a traditional subject with a history stretching back to the distant past.

During the early years Delaunay was absorbing the principal colour theories of the time, which he applied in a synthesized form in his *Windows* series of 1910–13. These images have only a tenuous relationship to visual reality. By 1912, in the *Circular Forms*, colour is released from any association with reality and is used abstractly to create effects of movement and depth. The *Circular Forms* are seen as the first non-representational paintings by a French artist. Unlike many other early-twentieth-century abstractionists, however, Delaunay also continued to paint figurative works. In this category is the *Nude Woman Reading*, where the same colour principles used in the abstract paintings are now applied to the human figure.

This boudoir scene of a woman seated reading at a dressing table is a finely tuned orchestration of colour and form. The oval format of the image echoes and accentuates the soft, leaning curve of the woman's body, and the curve of the oval is repeated in the lines of her hip and left leg. The curvilinear shapes of the body are present in miniature form in the pattern of the cloth on the dressing table.

The colour in *Nude Woman Reading* is a similarly balanced yet dynamic arrangement, based on the principles of complementary contrast, which were the foundation of Delaunay's colour theories. These derived from the great body of nineteenth-century colour science and especially from Michel-Eugène Chevreul (1786–1889) and his famous *De la loi du contraste simultané des couleurs et ses applications* (On the Law of Simultaneous Contrast of Colours) (1839). Delaunay gives the shadows of the red hair, for example, in green, a contrast that fades to pinks and light green-blues on the body. The blue background in the upper part of the painting is contrasted and balanced by the complementary orange highlights of the hair and by the near complementary reds to the left and right of the figure. The blue-black stocking responds to the background and also forms a contrast with the red cloth and the rose pink of the flesh on either side.

But, appropriately, it is the nude which is the centre of colouristic interest. The woman's body is a repository of all the colours found in the image, but in a less saturated, more luminescent, form. As a whole the painting is made from all the colours of the spectrum – from red through to violet – and in the hands of Delaunay these the colours of light create an image of great decorative elegance. Delaunay himself seems to have been very satisfied with the *Nude Woman Reading* series. Writing at the time, he said that his *Nude* was 'born transparent, iridescent, almost a rainbow, but firm and vigorous in its realistic construction'.[2] That he painted this subject so many times also suggests that it held a particular significance for him. The reason perhaps was that the nude was a time-honoured subject for all artists but one that could become emphatically modern through an autonomous system of colour, emancipated from its traditional descriptive role. Here, as Delaunay claimed, colour is the subject and the form.

Rosemary Stone

PROVENANCE

With Galerie Fricker, Paris; from whom purchased by Arthur Tooth & Sons, London; from whom acquired by the Felton Bequest, for the National Gallery of Victoria, 1966.

82. AMEDEO MODIGLIANI
Italian (active in France), 1884–1920

Portrait of the Painter Manuel Humbert

Signed u.r.: *MODIGLIANI*, undated; painted 1916
Oil on canvas
100.2 x 65.5 cm (39 1/2 x 25 3/4 in.)
Felton Bequest 1948 (1854–4)

The restrained elegance of Amedeo Modigliani's painting style has always seemed at odds with his notoriously turbulent private life. Addicted to drugs and alcohol, struggling with ill health, poverty and tempestuous personal relationships, Modigliani, living in Paris in the early decades of the twentieth century, was set on a destructive course. However, in 1916 – the year he painted this portrait of his friend the Spanish artist Manuel Humbert (1890–1975) – there was a rare shift in his fortunes. He had just met Leopold Zborowski, a Polish intellectual who would become his sole dealer and would support him with a studio and a small monthly allowance.

With his domestic situation eased for a time, Modigliani was able to concentrate more effectively on his art and he worked to refine an already distinctive personal style influenced by African art and by Cubism. Modigliani was especially attracted to portraiture and produced many drawings, paintings and sculptures based on the human body. In 1916, the sculptor Jacques Lipchitz and his wife asked him to paint their portraits, and Lipchitz's description of the sittings provides an interesting insight into the artist's working methods:

> [Modigliani] came the next day and made a lot of preliminary drawings, one right after the other, with tremendous speed and precision … The following day at one o'clock, Modigliani came with an old canvas and his box of painting material, and we began to pose. I can see him so clearly even now – sitting in front of his canvas which he had put on a chair, working quietly, interrupting only now and then to take a gulp of alcohol from a bottle standing nearby. From time to time he would get up and glance critically over his work and look at his models. By the end of the day he said, 'Well, I guess it's finished'.[1]

Modigliani had a reputation for generosity towards his friends and they, in turn, often acted as his models. Manuel Humbert, for instance, was part of the so-called School of Paris: an assemblage of artists, including Modigliani, who had immigrated to the cultural Mecca of Paris. Humbert, born in Barcelona, was president of the Salon de Monjuic, a group of young Catalan painters. He was twenty-six at the time that Modigliani painted this portrait, which is one of two related works made in 1916; the other, a head-and-shoulders portrait, is at the Los Angeles County Museum of Art.[2]

Portrait of the Painter Manuel Humbert is a rather solemn painting of the young man, posed wearing a suit, his slightly skewed tie the only deviation from his serious demeanour. The darkness of both the suit and the background acts to draw the viewer's attention to the sitter's neatly placed hands and his pale, elongated face. Humbert's delicate features are arresting, but more remarkable are his almond-shaped eyes. Modigliani's paintings often focus on the eyes of his subjects, frequently depicting them as strange, blank spaces, but here they are still realistically presented. However, despite Humbert's gaze being fixed on the viewer, the impression is less one of lively engagement than of his self-reflective nature: the model's manifest composure barely hides the sense of an inner life of spiritual isolation and melancholy.

Isobel Crombie

PROVENANCE

Leopold Zborowski, Paris; Netter, Paris; J.-C. Girard, Paris; Étienne Bignou, Paris; with Reid & Lefevre, London, 1948; from whom acquired by the Felton Bequest, for the National Gallery of Victoria, 1948.

187

83. RENÉ MAGRITTE
Belgian, 1898–1967

In Praise of Dialectics

Signed l.r.: *magritte*, undated; painted 1937
Oil on canvas
65.5 x 54.0 cm (25 3/4 x 21 1/4 in.)
Felton Bequest 1971 (EA2–1971)
© René Magritte, 1937/ADAGP
Licensed by VISCOPY, Sydney, 2000

With their strange juxtapositions and memorable images, the paintings of René Magritte are based upon the conviction that depictions of mental ideas are as valid as the recording of external events. This ideational perspective drew the praise of the leading Surrealist writer André Breton (1896–1966) and prompted him to purchase four of Magritte's paintings in 1928. Thereafter, Magritte's much reproduced works became pictorial hallmarks of Surrealism's intellectual and psychological concerns. Magritte himself became a prominent and respected Surrealist, and his works commanded the highest regard among an artistic group not known for its ready praise.

Few artists have given us so many clear depictions of the life of the inner self. Magritte's works are both confronting in their vivid realism and comforting in their recognition of familiar urban realities. In making the familiar so unfamiliar, however, Magritte stops us short and reminds us of life as lived in the mind. His thematic concerns fully address Marcel Duchamp's injunction that art should register as a 'brain fact' – it should appeal more to the mind than the eye. Magritte's intellectual and thematic complexities owe much to his consistent incorporation of semantic and conceptual conundrums and his study of personal interactions between poetic insight and philosophical thought – as he put it: 'The painter's art, as I see it, is about making poetic images visible'.[1]

In Praise of Dialectics, 1937, shows images typical of the enigmatic compositions of the Surrealists and is a characteristic example of the artist's meditations on the world of everyday objects and external events. The objects in Magritte's paintings are imbued with meaning through the process of human intellection – the artist acts as a human divining rod, locating meaning in the mundane. Lautréamont's metaphorical evocation of beauty as 'the fortuitous encounter between a sewing machine and an umbrella upon a dissecting table'[2] was the impetus for this divining rod, and Breton outlined its purpose: 'Let us not mince words, the marvellous is always beautiful, anything marvellous is beautiful; in fact, only the marvellous is beautiful!'.[3] In this schema the artist, 'antennae' extended, wanders on a 'blind date' with the 'marvellous', ever ready to pick up a signal, to transfigure the world that we take so for granted.

In Praise of Dialectics reminds us of the evocative power of chance observations. In this painting a building is represented with a window that seems to open out to the view of a doll's house, a model of a building, or a reflection of another building. This enigmatic painting, no doubt inspired by a chance observation of a building reflected in the windows of another, sets up an optical puzzle that is as perplexing as it is compelling. This visual paradox of a house within a house seduces us into a childlike appreciation of the wonder of the everyday. We pause to reflect upon the mysteries of such images and thus share in Magritte's view of the Surrealist 'marvellous'. We treasure such chance events because of their private associations and because of their redolent emotional residues. These souvenirs of sensation all find their place upon the mantelpiece of our minds.

Magritte's paintings with their oneiric substance and concatenated imagery stand as intellectually constructed attempts to forge insightful and artistic links between dream and reality, between the voice within and the given without, and between form and feeling – in short, between the things around us and the thoughts within us.

Kenneth Wach

PROVENANCE

Robert Giron (d. 1967), Brussels, 1937, 1967; with Hanover Gallery, London, 1968; from whom purchased by Gabrielle Keiller, Kingston-upon-Thames; with Mayor Gallery, London; sale, Sotheby's, London, 2 December 1970, lot 56; from which acquired by the Felton Bequest, for the National Gallery of Victoria, 1970.

SELECTED EXHIBITIONS

From Ensor to Delvaux, Provinciaal Museum voor Moderne Kunst, Ostend, 1996–97; *René Magritte 1898–1967*, Royal Museums of Fine Arts of Belgium, Brussels, 1998, cat. no. 116.

189

84. PABLO PICASSO
Spanish (active in France), 1881–1973

Weeping Woman

Unsigned, undated; painted 1937
Oil on canvas
55.2 x 46.2 cm (21 3/4 x 18 1/4 in.)
Purchased by donors of The Art Foundation of Victoria with the assistance
of the Jack and Genia Liberman family, Founder Benefactor, 1986 (1C2–1986)
© Pablo Picasso, 1937/Succession Pablo Picasso
Licensed by VISCOPY, Sydney, 2000

PROVENANCE

Collection of the artist; Marina
Picasso (the artist's daughter), 1973;
with Galerie Jan Krugier, Geneva;
from whom purchased by E. V. Thaw,
New York; from whom acquired by
the National Gallery of Victoria, 1986.

SELECTED EXHIBITIONS

*From the Southern Cross: A View of
World Art c.1940–88 (1988 Australian
Biennale)*, Art Gallery of New South
Wales, Sydney, National Gallery of
Victoria, Melbourne, 1988; *Pablo
Picasso: The Artist before Nature*,
Auckland City Art Gallery, Auckland,
1989, cat. no. 38; *Picasso: Die
Zeit nach Guernica 1937–1973*,
Nationalgalerie, Staatliche
Museen zu Berlin – Preußischer
Kulturbesitz, Berlin, Kunsthalle der
Hypo-Kulturstiftung, Munich,
Hamburger Kunsthalle, Hamburg,
1992–93, cat. no. 14; *Picasso and the
Weeping Woman: The Years of
Marie-Thérèse Walter and Dora Maar*,
Los Angeles County Museum of Art,
Los Angeles, Metropolitan Museum of
Art, New York, Art Institute of
Chicago, Chicago, 1994–95; *Beyond
Belief: Modern Art and the Religious
Imagination*, National Gallery of
Victoria, Melbourne, 1998; *Picasso and
the War Years 1937–1945*, Fine Arts
Museums of San Francisco, California
Palace of the Legion of Honor, San
Francisco, Solomon R. Guggenheim
Museum, New York, 1998–99,
cat. no. 14.

By 1937, when Picasso painted *Weeping Woman*, his Cubist period was over. His new responses were conditioned by his fourteen-year association with Surrealism and occasioned by his recent personal traumas, and his anxieties flood the painting. All of this was caught up in the uneasiness that characterized the penumbral period in Europe between the outbreak of the Spanish Civil War and the advent of the Second World War. Created mid-point during this fateful period, *Weeping Woman* presents us with a condensed apprehensiveness and reflects some of Picasso's identification with universal human suffering.

Weeping Woman also bears witness to Picasso's personal interest in the concept of *amour fou* (mad love), as espoused by André Breton (1896–1966), the leader of the Surrealist movement. Picasso never joined the Surrealists but he was persuaded to show with them in their first exhibition in Paris in 1925. Thereafter, he often exhibited with them and took a supportive interest in their theories, which run through many of his major works in the 1930s, like the threads of a recurrent dream. Breton's concept of 'mad love' was propounded in the very year in which *Weeping Woman* was painted. Breton recommended a surrender to emotional attachments in order to achieve an energizing regeneration – the muse-like female was seen as a font of the creative unconscious. Given Picasso's priapic motivations, Breton's theory must have seemed like an intellectual validation of, and convenient rationalization for, the fifty-six-year-old artist's recurrent urges.

When the idealized peaks of *amour fou* are considered in conjunction with the reality of the troughs of hysteria, we get an insight into Surrealism's interest in the graph of human emotions. The frenzied features of hysterics provided the Surrealists with a manifestation of passion gone awry and of supposedly inspirational mental states. The significance of the Surrealists' observations of mental agitation was not lost on Picasso. *Weeping Woman* gives us an empathetic depiction of romantic passion come undone and confronts us with the emotionally negative underside of Picasso's libidinous attractions. Breton's concept is interpreted by Picasso in self-referential terms. *Weeping Woman* reeks of the actual observation of the psychological effects of rejection. The painting refers to real events, such as the anxieties of Dora Maar, one of Picasso's many mistresses. Maar met Picasso in 1936 and their relationship was so fraught with despair that she suffered a breakdown and was treated by the psychoanalyst Jacques Lacan in 1945.

The painting's vivid colours – its lime green and jealous tones, its flushed pinks – the contorted features, the rolling eyes and the two cascades of tears are all caught within a remarkable imagist knot of emotion. This intensity is magnified by the contrast between the woman's face and the painting's comparatively plain background, which shows a small room with a dark archway looming. The archway, culled from Giorgio de Chirico, also surfaces in other of Picasso's darkly emotional works. Significantly, the weeping figure in this bracing painting faces this dark archway as though recently banished to its ominous depths.

Weeping Woman is enlivened by its personal resonance, formed by its grasp of human emotion, and informed by its adoption of Surrealist pictorial fracture. Picasso's remarkable skills are subsumed within an almost expiatory desire to present the handwringing realities of his personal life in ways that are psychologically vivid and emotionally searing.

Kenneth Wach

85. PAUL NASH
English, 1889–1946

Landscape of the Summer Solstice

Signed l.l.: *Paul Nash,* undated; painted 1943
Oil on canvas
71.8 x 91.6 cm (28 1/4 x 36 in.)
Felton Bequest 1952 (2948–4)
© Tate, London, 2000

In 1942 Paul Nash visited his friend Hilda Harrison at her house, 'Sandlands', at Boar's Hill, near Oxford. This painting represents the view that Nash admired to the south, out over the gardens and towards the Berkshire Downs. Nash would have experienced the view through his binoculars, of which he is reported to have said: 'Through field-glasses one sees a landscape that one can see in no other way'.[1] The locale surrounding Sandlands, an area dominated by the mysterious twin hills known as the Wittenham Clumps, proved deeply inspiring to Nash. So much so that he spent the final years of his life painting a group of evocative, semi-abstract landscapes in which he explored the cosmic drama of the changing seasons. These pictures, known as the Boar's Hill series, represent the pinnacle of Nash's oeuvre and testify to the many stylistic influences that he had absorbed in his long career: Paul Cézanne; Dante Gabriel Rossetti and the Pre-Raphaelites; the Bloomsbury Group; Pittura Metafisica; and, above all, the Surrealists.

Landscape of the Summer Solstice is permeated with the strange, dreamlike quality commonly associated with Surrealism. The flowering plants, which dance across the very front of the pictorial stage, resonate with the strangeness of the surreal in their weird colouring and overly precise treatment. However, in a meticulous note made at the time, Nash went to great lengths to stress the formal – as opposed to symbolic – properties that prompted his choice of compositional elements. He described, for example, how the tall, straight stem of St John's wort 'makes a significant division where it is absolutely needed'.[2] Yet Nash's seemingly direct approach to the formal arrangement of a painting is belied by his admission that 'the presence of these magic flowers somehow influences the atmosphere of the picture. That is a mystery, but I believe in it without question and without being able to explain'.[3]

Our eye is led from the colourful, vertical procession of the flowers in the immediate foreground to the weighty forms of the Wittenham Clumps in the middle distance. The impressive, grove-covered hills, which were once thought to have been a Neolithic burial site,[4] had strong symbolic significance for Nash. It was as a young boy that he had first seen the Wittenham Clumps, and even then they had made a powerful impression on him. 'They were', he said, 'the Pyramids of my small world'.[5] The sight of these ancient hills, topped by their twin coronets of trees, would surely have stirred the artist's memory, connecting past to present, a reminder to Nash, who had suffered from asthma and chronic bronchitis since 1930, that his journey through life had almost reached its conclusion.

Perhaps, then, this painting suggests something deeper and far more personal than the surreal surface elements indicate. The visual clues are there for us to ponder. Nash's depiction of the exact, suspended moment at which the sun reaches its solstitial zenith, pausing before returning to the equator, may allude to his acute awareness of the passing of time. The eternal, timeless forms of the Wittenham Clumps may have heightened his sense of his own mortality, for he knew that his life's work was sweeping back, full circle, to its close.

Landscape of the Summer Solstice is perhaps one of the most deeply complex and extraordinarily powerful paintings in the collection of the National Gallery of Victoria. It is an image which leaves one feeling uplifted and yet strangely melancholy, an image that is both an exploration of the inexplicable, humble beauty of nature and a metaphor for the awesome threshold that marks the transition from living to dying.

Tracey Judd

86. FRANCIS BACON
English, 1909–1992

Study from the Human Body

Unsigned, undated; painted 1949
Oil on canvas
147.0 x 134.2 cm (57 3/4 x 52 3/4 in.)
Purchased 1953 (2992–4)
© Francis Bacon, 1949/ARS
Licensed by VISCOPY, Sydney, 2000

Study from the Human Body is the earliest surviving of Francis Bacon's nudes. By 1949 he was painting prolifically and would destroy or abandon canvases once he felt that an image had been lost through excessive work. Bacon believed that the process through which his imagery emerged was reliant initially on accident and subsequently on instinct. It was not until the 1960s that he felt he could work for lengthy periods on a canvas, bringing the 'thing that has happened by accident to a much further point by will'.[1]

The Melbourne painting belongs to an important period of exploratory work in Bacon's oeuvre – one marked by an intense focus on the human body and the problems of its configuration in paint. From about 1948 to 1956, Bacon generally restricted his palette to a range of dark tones, feeling that he could 'make these images much more poignant in the darkness and without colour'.[2] When shown at the Hanover Gallery, London, in 1949, in what is regarded as the artist's first solo exhibition, *Study from the Human Body* was accompanied predominantly by studies for portraits and by a number of other works in grisaille, among them *Head II*, 1949 (Ulster Museum, Belfast). It is in this earlier work – uncharacteristically dense, due to several months' painting to arrive at the image – that Bacon composed the first version of a partially drawn curtain with a safety pin attached to the right drape.[3]

What characterizes *Study from the Human Body*, and in fact most of the paintings of this 'dark' period, is its sketch-like and tentative rendering, a treatment that makes this enigmatic picture appear effortless in its crossing of what Bacon called the 'tightrope walk between … figurative painting and abstraction'.[4]

> Does this work take us by the throat chiefly because of its lyrical beauty or because of the elegiac poignancy of its sense of farewell?[5]

In its indistinct yet sensuous modelling, this male figure has a quiet, erotic intensity by comparison with Bacon's images of couples or some of the isolated occupants of his triptychs. *Study from the Human Body* probably has its source in Eadweard Muybridge's 1870s photographic sequence of a bald boxer striking a blow. Most of Bacon's male figures correspond to this heavily muscled masculine type, although the figure in the Melbourne picture could be a composite of several of Muybridge's studies, or could derive from the sporting magazines to which Bacon referred, or from the works of Michelangelo, whom Bacon considered to be the greatest draughtsman.

Bacon stated that he loved rooms hung with curtains, and he reconfigured the motif of the curtain in numerous paintings between 1948 and 1957, exploring also at this time the textural and absorptive qualities of the unprimed surface of the canvas. The curtain operated alternately as a diaphanous veil or to delineate an architectural space – as is suggested by the paint lines at the lower left of the Melbourne picture. The poignancy for which Bacon strove in his images relied on formal devices in the construction of a picture: here the containing space, safety pin and arrows all serve his purpose – to 'anchor' the paint and image to the canvas, and to direct the eye to the central figure.

In its allusive density and enduring freshness as a painting, *Study from the Human Body* realizes one of Bacon's primary aims, to 'unlock the areas of feeling which lead to a deeper sense of the reality of the image, where you attempt to make the construction by which this thing will be caught raw and alive and left there'.[6]

Jason Smith

PROVENANCE

With Hanover Gallery, London, 1949, 1950, 1953; from whom acquired by the National Gallery of Victoria, 1953.

SELECTED EXHIBITIONS

Francis Bacon, Tate Gallery, London, 1985, cat. no. 10; *From the Southern Cross: A View of World Art c.1940–88 (1988 Australian Biennale)*, Art Gallery of New South Wales, Sydney, National Gallery of Victoria, Melbourne, 1988; *Francis Bacon*, Centre National d'Art et de Culture, Georges Pompidou, Paris, Haus der Kunst, Munich, 1996–97, cat. no. 1; *Francis Bacon: The Human Body*, Hayward Gallery, London, 1998, cat. no. 3.

87. BALTHUS

(Balthazar Klossowski de Rola) French, born 1908

Nude with Cat

Signed and dated c.l.: *Balthus / 1949*
Oil on canvas
65.1 x 80.5 cm (25 1/2 x 31 3/4 in.)
Felton Bequest 1952 (2949–4)
© Balthus, 1949/ADAGP
Licensed by VISCOPY, Sydney, 2000

Balthus assiduously cultivated a mysterious aura in his life and art. He was raised in a family with considerable cultural riches that lived within an aristocratic ambience. The poet Rainer Maria Rilke was a constant visitor, and friends such as the writer André Gide and the artist Pierre Bonnard contributed to a multilingual artistic sensibility. Rilke's influence was considerable and some of his neurasthenic temper and rectitude remains with Balthus to this day. Balthus developed an individualistic vision, without formal training, by copying the works of Nicolas Poussin and studying Renaissance art. Rilke's credo that art should base itself upon affirmations of life – which must be renounced – encapsulates the equivocal content of Balthus's paintings. What is said of Rilke's poetry – that it is easier to love than to understand – may well be applied to the work of Balthus. Thus, his painted world of stagelike interiors is like our dreams: realms in which we know everything has meaning but where meaning eludes us.

Nude with Cat of 1949 is related to *Nude in an Armchair*, 1950,[1] and *The Room*, 1952–54[2] (private collections). The Melbourne painting is also similar to striking earlier compositions such as the *Week of Four Thursdays* of 1949 (Frances Lehman Loeb Art Center, Vassar College, Poughkeepsie).[3] All of these paintings are languorous depictions, with young girls as their subject. When we realize that, in France, Thursdays were traditionally set aside for holidays from school, we get a hint of the origin of the indolent atmosphere of these lubricious pictures, which show schoolgirls in moments of reverie and revealing a budding sexuality. The forbidden quality of these scenes is heightened by the presence of a curtain or sheet, in deference to historical paintings of female bodies being revealed as though in a private viewing. Balthus's depictions of these private moments lend to his works a keyhole aesthetic, which is voyeuristic and faintly disturbing. His paintings, especially *Nude with Cat*, are carefully constructed to exacerbate these disturbing feelings. The central figures in the paintings are presented with deliberate erotic inflections, as the artist employs technical restraint so as to emphasize the body and its torpid gestures.

This deliberate eroticism may be appreciated through a comparison with the 1949 drawing for *Nude with Cat*, in the Museum of Modern Art, New York.[4] This Boucher-like drawing shows the naked schoolgirl with the cat perched on the high back of the chair – she raises her arm in a playful gesture while the cat seems to respond. The background figure is posed nonchalantly at the window; the space is recessive and furniture is arranged in ways that delineate the room's dimensions. However, in the less innocuous painting the background is skewed around so that the scene is presented as a stage, emphasizing the central figure; the cat rests on the sideboard and lolls about with the same replete contentment as its young owner. The girl has finished washing, had her hair brushed, got out of bed or is simply enjoying the light that streams in from the right. Her hands are imprecise, yet the body and the face are more detailed and the play of light is given careful attention. Significantly, the compositional diagonal is more pronounced than in the drawing, and stresses the schoolgirl's languid repose in a way that positions her genital area centrally in the painting. *Nude with Cat* is neither pornography nor an intimation of paedophiliac desire: its suggestive power is drawn from smoking jacket fantasies and drawing room dreams. Balthus's painting remains as vapid as smoke-filled rooms and has more in common with the transgressive writings of Georges Bataille and André Pieyre de Mandiargues, with the *femme-enfant* of the Surrealists, with Nabokovian confections and with contemporary awareness of Freud's ideas of childhood sexuality.

Kenneth Wach

PROVENANCE

With Reid & Lefevre, London, 1952; from whom acquired by the Felton Bequest, for the National Gallery of Victoria, 1952.

SELECTED EXHIBITIONS

Balthus, Musée National d'Art Moderne, Centre Georges Pompidou, Paris, Metropolitan Museum of Art, New York, 1984, cat. no. 36/31; *From the Southern Cross: A View of World Art c.1940–88 (1988 Australian Biennale)*, Art Gallery of New South Wales, Sydney, National Gallery of Victoria, Melbourne, 1988; *Balthus*, Museo Nacional Centro de Arte Reina Sofía, Madrid, 1996; *Omaggio a Balthus*, Accademia Valentino, Rome, 1996; *Body*, Art Gallery of New South Wales, Sydney, 1997, cat. no. 8.

88. DAVID HOCKNEY
English (active in USA), born 1937

The Second Marriage

Signed on reverse: DAVID HOCKNEY, undated; painted 1963
Oil, gouache and collage on canvas
197.8 x 228.7 cm (77 3/4 x 90 in.) (irreg.)
Presented by the Contemporary Art Society of London 1965 (1525–5)
© David Hockney, 1963

> Richard [Hamilton] had come along to the College and seen what people were really doing, and recognized it instantly as something interesting. The staff didn't even recognize it as a kind of movement where the ideas were similar; they didn't even see it. Richard was quite a boost for students; we felt … it *is* an interesting thing and I should do it … And also, suddenly, at last there were paintings you could talk about again, instead of just abstract pictures. There was subject matter, and the idea of painting things from ordinary life, and that was when everything was called 'pop art'.[1]

The early 1960s was a period of rapid development in David Hockney's work, particularly in the introduction of narrative, text and the figure into his compositions, at a time when the figure was considered particularly 'anti-modern'. He was certainly one of the most inventive and technically adept artists in his milieu, loving 'formal impurity as long as it was clearly underwritten by formal skill'.[2]

After leaving the Royal College of Art in 1962, Hockney travelled through Europe with an American friend named Jeff Goodman. On his return to London the same year, Hockney began to produce a series of paintings inspired mainly by his observations and imaginative remembrances of Berlin. An experience in the Pergamon Museum was the catalyst for *The First Marriage*, 1962 (Tate Gallery, London), the precursor to the Melbourne picture. Hockney had become separated from Goodman in the museum and finally caught sight of him standing in profile beside a sculpture of an Egyptian female figure. Both figures were momentarily facing the same direction. Hockney became focused on the humorous aspect of the unlikely, coincidental coupling of Goodman with the culturally and historically distant sculpture, and used the incident to explore the theme of marriage.[3]

Livingstone has noted that *The First Marriage* is 'the first of Hockney's two-figure compositions in which one of the figures can be seen to have a specific identity'.[4] For Hockney, *The Second Marriage* was a more 'complex' version of the first picture and evolved in the studio in early 1963[5] after a series of preparatory drawings that focus in particular on the bridegroom, who bears a striking resemblance to the main protagonist of Hockney's 1961–63 series of etchings, *A Rake's Progress*. Given the increasingly overt references in Hockney's work around this period to sexuality and domestic intimacy, the bridegroom in *The Second Marriage* could be seen to be a tongue-in-cheek self-portrait. The figure of the bride derives from a photograph of an Egyptian princess of the Armana period, to which image Hockney was drawn by both the quality of the reproduction and the beauty of the head.[6]

The Second Marriage synthesizes various painterly and decorative styles, corresponding to Hockney's experimental approach to picture making at the time: 'style is something you can use … taking what you want. The idea of the rigid style seemed to me then something you needn't concern yourself with, it would trap you'.[7]

The cubic geometry of the canvas and the inclusion of wallpaper as part of the support emphasize the domestic setting of *The Second Marriage*. It has a tableau vivant quality that Hockney continued to develop in other works of the same year, repeating leitmotifs like the curtain, patterning and an unconventional organization of perspective and pictorial space.

Jason Smith

PROVENANCE

With Kasmin, London, 1963; presented by the Contemporary Art Society, London, to the National Gallery of Victoria, 1965.

SELECTED EXHIBITIONS

David Hockney: A Retrospective, Los Angeles County Museum of Art, Los Angeles, Metropolitan Museum of Art, New York, Tate Gallery, London, 1988–89, cat. no. 19.

NOTES

ABBREVIATIONS

Dean = S. Dean, *European Paintings of the 19th and Early 20th Centuries in the National Gallery of Victoria*, Melbourne, 1995
Hoff = U. Hoff, with contributions by E. Devapriam, *European Paintings before 1800 in the National Gallery of Victoria*, 4th edn, Melbourne, 1995

Cat. no. 1 (Hoff, pp. 208–9)

1 For a brief biography of Paolo, see R. Gibbs, Paolo Veneziano entry, in *The Dictionary of Art*, ed. J. Turner, vol. 24, London, 1996, pp. 29–34.
2 R. van Marle, *The Development of the Italian Schools of Painting* (1925), vol. V, New York, 1970, pp. 482–3.
3 R. Fry, 'Notes on the Italian Exhibition at Burlington House – I', *Burlington Magazine*, vol. LVI, no. 323, February 1930, p. 83.
4 E. Sandberg Vavalà, 'Maestro Paolo Veneziano', *Burlington Magazine*, vol. LVII, no. 331, October 1930, p. 177, no. 21.
5 ibid., pp. 177–8.
6 ibid., p. 177, no. 9, pl. V.A.
7 ibid., pp. 171, 177, no. 10, pl. IV.B.
8 ibid., p. 177, no. 22; see also van Marle, vol. IV (1924), p. 95, fig. 47.
9 Sandberg Vavalà, 'Maestro Paolo', p. 178, no. 24, pl. VII.A.
10 G. Fiocco, 'Le primizie di Maestro Paolo Veneziano', *Dedalo*, vol. XI, June 1931, pp. 889–90, repr. p. 888 (detail).
11 ibid., p. 888.
12 See G. Millet, *Recherches sur l'iconographie de l'Évangile aux XIVe, XVe et XVIe siècles d'après les monuments de Mistra, de la Macédoine et du Mont-Athos* (1916), Paris, 1960, pp. 418–22; see also E. Sandberg Vavalà, *La croce dipinta italiana e l'iconografia della Passione*, Verona, 1929, p. 148 ff.
13 V. Lasareff, 'Two Newly-Discovered Pictures of the Lucca School', *Burlington Magazine*, vol. LI, no. 293, August 1927, p. 62, pls IV.C (Gospel, *c.*1259–84, fol. 88a, Gulbenkian Library, Armenian Patriarchate, Jerusalem, no. 2568/13), and IV.D (Gospel, 1272, fol. 362b, Gulbenkian Library, no. 2563/8).
14 See F. R. Shapley, *Catalogue of the Italian Paintings*, vol. I, Washington DC, 1979, p. 354, no. 254; vol. II, pl. 256.
15 See *The Lee Collection*, London, 1960, no. 8; see also Shapley, vol. I, p. 355 n. 3.
16 Sandberg Vavalà, 'Maestro Paolo', p. 165.
17 ibid., p. 177.

Cat. no. 2 (Hoff (Devapriam), pp. 268–9)

1 J. J. Jarves, *Art Studies*, New York, 1861; see also J. Pope-Hennessy, *Sassetta*, London, 1939, pp. 1–2.
2 See M. Torriti, Sassetta entry, in *The Dictionary of Art*, ed. J. Turner, vol. 27, London, 1996, pp. 859–63.
3 Pope-Hennessy, p. 3.
4 See G. Moran, 'The Original Provenance of the Predella Panel by Stefano di Giovanni (Sassetta) in the National Gallery of Victoria: A Hypothesis', *Art Bulletin of Victoria*, vol. 21, 1980, pp. 33–6.

5 See F. Zeri, 'Ricerche sul Sassetta: La pala dell'Arte della Lana (1423–26)', *Quaderni di emblema*, vol. 2, 1973, pp. 22–34; K. Christiansen, 'Three Dates for Sassetta', *Gazette des beaux-arts*, vol. CXIV, 1989, pp. 263–4. For a possible completion date of 1426, see K. Christiansen, 'Sassetta', in *Painting in Renaissance Siena 1420–1500* (exh. cat.), by K. Christiansen, L. B. Kanter & C. B. Strehlke, Metropolitan Museum of Art, New York, 1988, p. 64.
6 For the predella panels, see Christiansen, in Christiansen, Kanter & Strehlke, cat. nos 1a–1f, reprs.
7 P. Scapecchi, *La pala dell'Arte della Lana del Sassetta*, Siena, 1979, p. 11 ff. Cf. M. Rubin, *Corpus Christi: The Eucharist in Late Medieval Culture*, Cambridge, 1991, p. 34 ff.
8 Christiansen, in Christiansen, Kanter & Strehlke, cat. no. 1e.
9 C. Gilbert, 'Some Special Images for Carmelites, circa 1330–1430', in *Christianity and the Renaissance: Image and Religious Imagination in the Quattrocento*, eds T. Verdon & J. Henderson, Syracuse, New York, 1990, pp. 190–2.
10 See E. Cohen, *The Crossroads of Justice: Law and Culture in Late Medieval France*, Leiden, 1993; L. Puppi, *Torment in Art: Pain, Violence and Martyrdom*, trans. J. Scott, New York, 1991; M. B. Merback, *The Thief, the Cross and the Wheel: Pain and the Spectacle of Punishment in Medieval and Renaissance Europe*, Chicago, 1998.
11 See Christiansen, in Christiansen, Kanter & Strehlke, cat. no. 1e.

Cat. no. 3 (Hoff, pp. 189–90)

1 The original painted surface measured 36.0 x 25.3 cm (14 1/4 x 10 in.).
2 See M. Martens, 'La Clientèle du peintre', in *Les Primitifs flamands et leur temps*, eds R. van Schoute & B. de Patoul, Brussels, 1995, pp. 174–8.
3 The panel was with Galerie F. Kleinberger, Paris, in 1927.
4 See E. Michel, 'A propos de Simon Marmion', *Gazette des beaux-arts*, vol. XVI, 1927, repr. p. 142.
5 See D. De Vos, *Rogier van der Weyden: The Complete Works*, trans. T. Alkins, Antwerp, 1999, pp. 323–7, no. 33, repr. p. 324.
6 ibid., pp. 298–301, no. 25, repr. p. 300.
7 See M. Ainsworth, 'New Observations on the Working Techniques in Simon Marmion's Panel Paintings', in *Margaret of York, Simon Marmion, and the Visions of Tondal*, ed. T. Kren, Malibu, 1992, pp. 243–56.

Cat. no. 4 (Hoff, pp. 192–4)

1 The date on the column at the left of the composition, especially the last numeral, is badly abraded. Hoff and Davies suggested that this date should be read as 1475 (U. Hoff & M. Davies, *The National Gallery of Victoria, Melbourne*, Les Primitifs flamands, I: Corpus de la peinture des anciens Pays-Bas méridionaux au quinzième siècle, vol. 12, Brussels, 1971, pp. 60, 63, no. 134); more recently, De Vos has argued for 1479 (D. De Vos, *Hans Memling: The Complete Works*, London, 1994, p. 62, no. 24).
2 Inventory of Margaret of Austria, [1516], Archive du Nord, Lille, B 3507; see also J. Finot, *Inventaire sommaire des archives départementales antérieures à 1790*, vol. VIII, Série B, Chambre des Comptes, Lille, 1895, p. 210.
3 See P. Lorentz, 'Un Ange de Hans Memling (v. 1435–1494) au Louvre', *La Revue du Louvre et des Musées de France*, 1994, pp. 10–18.
4 See M. J. Friedländer, *Early Netherlandish Painting*, rev. N. Veronee-Verhaegen, trans. H. Norden, rev. edn, vol. VI, part I, *Hans Memlinc and Gerard David*, Leiden, 1971, no. 37a, pl. 89.

Cat. no. 5 (Hoff, pp. 167–8)

1 The painting has been extended on the top and at the left side by approximately 3.0 cm (1 1/4 in.) and on the right side by up to 1.0 cm (1/2 in.).
2 P. Simons, 'A Profile Portrait of a Renaissance Woman in the National Gallery of Victoria', *Art Bulletin of Victoria*, no. 28, 1987, pp. 34–52.
3 Domenico Ghirlandaio (Florentine, 1448/49–1494), *Portrait of Giovanna Tornabuoni (née Albizzi)*, 1488, tempera on wood panel, 77.0 x 49.0 cm (30 1/4 x 19 1/4 in.), Museo Thyssen-Bornemisza, Madrid (see P. Hendy, *Some Italian Renaissance Pictures in the Thyssen-Bornemisza Collection*, Lugano, 1964, p. 45, repr.).
4 Antonio Pollaiuolo (Florentine, *c.*1432–1498), *Portrait of a Young Woman*, 1475, tempera on wood panel, 55.0 x 34.0 cm (21 3/4 x 13 1/2 in.), Galleria degli Uffizi, Florence (see Simons, 'A Profile Portrait', fig. 6).
5 Piero Pollaiuolo (Florentine, *c.*1441–*c.*1496), *Portrait of a Woman*, tempera on wood panel, 48.9 x 35.2 cm (19 1/4 x 13 3/4 in.), Metropolitan Museum of Art, New York (see K. Baetjer, *European Paintings in the Metropolitan Museum of Art by Artists Born in or before 1865: A Summary Catalogue*, vol. II, New York, 1980, repr. p. 32).
6 Simons, 'A Profile Portrait', p. 44.
7 ibid.; and P. Simons, 'Women in Frames: The

Gaze, the Eye, the Profile in Renaissance Portraiture', in *Expanding Discourse: Feminism and Art History*, eds N. Broude & M. D. Garrard, New York, 1992, pp. 38–57.

8   Simons, 'A Profile Portrait', p. 38.

9   R. Hatfield, 'Five Early Renaissance Portraits', *Art Bulletin*, vol. XLVII, no. 3, September 1965, p. 328.

10 ibid., p. 327.

11 Simons, 'A Profile Portrait', p. 43, observes: 'The cherub's golden head above rubies and pearls in the Melbourne portrait may also connote the woman's spiritual well-being or, if the portrait is posthumous, her blessed state in paradise'.

12 See Hoff, p. 168 n. 4.

13 See Simons, 'A Profile Portrait', p. 43.

14 L. Ettlinger, *Antonio and Piero Pollaiuolo: Complete Edition with a Critical Catalogue*, Oxford, 1978, p. 170.

Cat. no. 6 (Hoff, pp. 210–11)

1   G. Vasari, *Le opere di Giorgio Vasari*, ed. G. Milanesi, rev. edn, vol. V, Florence, 1906, pp. 587–632.

2   See B. F. Davidson, 'Drawings by Perino del Vaga for the Palazzo Doria, Genoa', *Art Bulletin*, vol. XLI, no. 4, December 1959, pp. 315–26; M. B. Hall, *After Raphael: Painting in Central Italy in the Sixteenth Century*, Cambridge, 1999, p. 107 ff.

3   See B. F. Davidson, 'The Decoration of the Sala Regia under Pope Paul III', *Art Bulletin*, vol. LVIII, no. 3, September 1976, pp. 395–423.

4   See E. Gaudioso, F. M. Aliberti Gaudioso, R. Einaudi, A. Ghidoli Tomei & C. Carocci, *Gli affreschi di Paolo III a Castel Sant'Angelo: Progeteto ed esecuzione 1543–1548*, 2 vols, Rome, 1981.

5   I am grateful to Laurie Benson, Assistant Curator, International Art, and John Payne, Senior Conservator of Paintings, National Gallery of Victoria, for giving me access to digitized infrared photographs.

6   See Hoff, p. 210.

7   See D. Jaffé, 'La "Sacra Famiglia" di Melbourne nella cronologia dei dipinti religiosi di Perino del Vaga', in *Raffaello e l'Europa: Atti del IV Coro Internazionale di Alta Cultura*, eds M. L. Madonna & M. Fagiolo, Rome, 1990, pp. 211–28. Cf. E. Parma Armani, *Perin del Vaga: L'anello mancante*, Genoa, 1986, pp. 317–18.

8   See E. de Boissard, in *Chantilly, Musée Condé: Peintures de l'École italienne*, Inventaire des collections publiques françaises, vol. 34, Paris, 1988, pp. 113–15, no. 59, repr., as by an assistant.

9   ibid., p. 115, as autograph.

10 See D. Jaffé, 'La "Sacra Famiglia" di Melbourne'; D. Jaffé, in *Rubens and the Italian Renaissance* (exh. cat.), by M. Chiarini et al., Australian National Gallery, Canberra, 1992, cat. no. 7.

Cat. no. 7 (Hoff, pp. 120–1)

1   For Vasari's biographies of Innocenzo da Imola, Taddeo Zuccaro and Francesco Primaticcio, see G. Vasari, *Le opere di Giorgio Vasari*, ed. G. Milanesi, rev. edn, vol. V, Florence, 1906, p. 188; vol. VII, pp. 82, 410; for the redating of Prospero's birth from 1512 to 1509/10, see A. Nova, in *Rubens and the Italian Renaissance* (exh. cat.), by M. Chiarini et al., Australian National Gallery, Canberra, 1992, cat. no. 9.

2   C. C. Malvasia, *La felsina pittrice*, vol. II, Bologna, 1678, pp. 215–19; see also V. Fortunati Pietrantonio, in *The Age of Correggio and the Carracci: Emilian Painting of the Sixteenth and Seventeenth Centuries* (exh. cat.), National Gallery of Art, Washington DC, 1986, pp. 136–40.

3   See B. Davidson, *Mostra di disegni di Perino del Vaga e la sua cerchia* (exh. cat.), Florence, 1968, p. 28.

4   See J. A. Gere, 'The Decoration of the Villa Giulia', *Burlington Magazine*, vol. CVII, no. 745, 1965, pp. 201–2.

5   See R. W. Gaston, 'Prospero Fontana's *Holy Family with Saints*', Art Bulletin of Victoria, vol. 19, 1978, pp. 28–45.

6   For the iconography, see Gaston, 'Prospero Fontana's *Holy Family with Saints*'; see also D. Ekserdjian, *Correggio*, New Haven, 1997, p. 146 ff.

7   See I. Zdanowicz (ed.), *Albrecht Dürer in the Collection of the National Gallery of Victoria*, The Robert Raynor Publications in Prints and Drawings, no. 5, Melbourne, 1994, repr. p. 140.

8   See Gaston, 'Prospero Fontana's *Holy Family with Saints*', fig. 3.

9   See Ekserdjian, fig. 163.

10 ibid., fig. 207.

11 See R. W. Gaston, 'Attention and Inattention in Religious Painting of the Renaissance: Some Preliminary Observations', in *Renaissance Studies in Honor of Craig Hugh Smyth*, eds A. Morrogh et al., vol. II, Florence, 1985, pp. 253–76; R. W. Gaston, 'Sacred Erotica: The Classical *Figura* in Religious Painting of the Early Cinquecento', *International Journal of the Classical Tradition*, vol. 2, no. 2, 1996, pp. 238–64.

12 Carl Villis, examination report, 9 February 2000, National Gallery of Victoria (Conservation Department) files.

Cat. no. 8 (Hoff, pp. 195–6)

1   The Melbourne portrait has not been published in the Mor literature.

2   For Mor's relations with the Spanish Hapsburgs, see T. Coppens, *Antonius Mor: Hofschilder van Karel V*, Baarn, 1999.

3   For details of Mor's life and work, see H. Hymans, *Antonio Mor: Son oeuvre et son temps*, Brussels, 1910; L. C. J. Freichs, *Antonio Moro*, Amsterdam, 1947.

4   For Mor's use of this format in a number of portraits known mainly through copies, see Coppens, pp. 232–6, reprs.

5   For other portraits by Mor, see M. J. Friedländer, *Antonis Mor and His Contemporaries*, trans. H. Norden, vol. XIII, Leyden, 1975, nos 343–405, reprs.

6   ibid., vol. XIII, no. 352, pl. 175.

Cat. no. 9 (Hoff, pp. 290–1)

1   See J. Payne, 'Tintoretto's *Doge Pietro Loredano* at the National Gallery of Victoria: The Earlier Version', *Art Bulletin of Victoria*, no. 33, 1993, fig. 3.

2   See E. Pillsbury & W. Jordan, 'Recent Acquisitions – III: The Kimbell Art Museum', *Burlington Magazine*, vol. CXXIX, no. 1016, November 1987, pp. 771–3, fig. 6.

Cat. no. 10 (Hoff, pp. 302–3)

1   See S. Marinelli (ed.), *Veronese e Verona* (exh. cat.), Museo di Castelvecchio, Verona, 1988, pp. 31–51.

2   See P. Fehl & M. Perry, 'Painting and the Inquisition at Venice: Three Forgotten Files', in *Interpretazioni veneziane*, ed. D. Rosand, Venice, 1983, pp. 371–83; R. Cocke, 'Venice, Decorum and Veronese', in *Nuovi studi su Paolo Veronese*, ed. M. Gemin, Venice, 1990, pp. 241–55.

3   T. Borenius, *A Catalogue of the Paintings at Doughty House, Richmond, and Elsewhere in the Collection of Sir F. Cook*, ed. H. Cook, vol. I, London, 1913, p. 197, no. 174.

4   B. Berenson, *Pitture italiane del Rinascimento: Catalogo dei principali artisti e delle loro opere con un indice dei luoghi*, trans. E. Cecchi, Milan, 1936, p. 365.

5   T. Pignatti, *Veronese*, vol. 1, Venice, 1976, no. A179.

6   F. Pedrocco, in *Veronese: Catalogo completo dei dipinti*, by T. Pignatti & F. Pedrocco, Florence, 1991, p. 19.

7   F. Pedrocco, in *Veronese*, by T. Pignatti & F. Pedrocco, 2 vols, Milan, 1995.

8   E. Tietze-Conrat, 'Due componimenti morali di Paolo Veronese', *Arte veneta*, vol. VII, 1953, p. 98 n. 2.

9   See J. G. Caldwell, 'Mantegna's St. Sebastian's Stabilitas in a Pagan World', *Journal of the Warburg and Courtauld Institutes*, vol. 36, 1973, pp. 373–7.

10 See E. Wind, *Pagan Mysteries in the Renaissance*, rev. edn, London, 1968, p. 102.

11 See S. Béguin, *L'École de Fontainebleau* (exh. cat.), Grand Palais, Paris, 1972, cat. no. 235.

12 See C. Scailliérez, *François I*er *et ses artistes dans les collections du Louvre*, Paris, 1992, p. 116.

13 See F. Hartt, *The Drawings of Michelangelo*, London, 1971, p. 252, fig. 361.

14 See R. Smith, 'A Matter of Choice: Veronese, Palladio, and Barbaro', *Arte veneta*, vol. 31, 1977, pp. 60–71.

15 J. Payne, 'Veronese and Friends: A Technical Examination of *Nobleman between Active and Contemplative Life*', Art Bulletin of Victoria, no. 32, 1991, pp. 64–5.

16 ibid., p. 65.

17 ibid., p. 68.

18 ibid.

19 B. L. Brown, 'Replication and the Art of Veronese', in *Retaining the Original: Multiple Originals, Copies, and Reproductions*, Studies in the History of Art, vol. 20, Washington DC, 1989, pp. 111–24.

Cat. no. 11 (Hoff (Devapriam), pp. 311–12)

1   J. Vander Auwera, 'Sebastiaen Vrancx's "Crossing of the Red Sea"', *Art Bulletin of Victoria*, no. 30, 1989, pp. 4–7.

2   ibid., pp. 12–13.

Cat. no. 12 (Hoff, pp. 137–8)

1   A. Palomino de Castro y Velasco, *Lives of the Eminent Spanish Painters and Sculptors* (1724), trans. N. Ayala Mallory, Cambridge, 1987, p. 83.

2 See M. B. Cossío, *El Greco*, vol. II, Madrid, 1908, pp. 572–3, no. 122; H. Wethey, *El Greco and His School*, vol. II, Princeton, New Jersey, 1962, p. 216, no. X-243.

3 See T. Frati, *La obra pictórica completa de El Greco*, Clásicos del Arte, vol. 16, Madrid, 1970, pp. 112–13, 116, nos 116a–i, 117a–k, 131a–m, reprs.

4 See F. Marías, *El Greco: Biografía de un pintor extravagante*, Madrid, 1997, pp. 260–75.

5 For El Greco's studio and assistants, see Wethey, vol. I, pp. 114–19; J. Brown, 'El Greco and Toledo', in *El Greco of Toledo* (exh. cat.), Toledo Museum of Art, Toledo, Ohio, 1982, pp. 103–9.

6 See Cossío, vol. II, p. 572.

7 See R. G. Mann, *El Greco and His Patrons: Three Major Projects*, Cambridge Studies in the History of Art, Cambridge, 1989.

8 See D. Davies, *El Greco*, Oxford, 1976, pp. 4–6.

9 See Marías, pp. 62–72.

Cat. no. 13 (Hoff, pp. 227–8)

1 For Régnier's biography, see P. L. Fantelli, 'Nicolò Renieri: "Pittor fiamengo" ', *Saggi e memorie di storia dell'arte*, vol. 9, 1974, pp. 77–115. See also H. Voss, 'Die Caravaggeske Frühzeit von Simon Vouet und Nicolas Régnier', *Zeitschrift für bildende Kunst*, vol. 58, 1924, pp. 121–8; N. Ivanoff, 'Nicolas Régnier', *Arte antica e moderna*, vol. 29, 1965, pp. 12–24; A. Skliar-Piguet, Régnier entry, in *The Dictionary of Art*, ed. J. Turner, vol. 26, London, 1996, pp. 94–5; B. Nicolson, *The International Caravaggesque Movement: Lists of Pictures by Caravaggio and His Followers throughout Europe from 1590 to 1650*, Oxford, 1979.

2 See Fantelli, p. 105, no. 108.

3 Fantelli cited in particular the *Death of Sophonisba* (formerly Colnaghi, London (present whereabouts unknown)), which he dated to the late 1650s (Fantelli, p. 97, no. 44, fig. 22), and the *Madonna and St Bruno* (parish church, Aviano), which he dated to after 1661 (p. 91, no. 3, pl. 1). In the latter case, the similarities in landscape are real, as far as one can tell from the reproduction, but are not necessarily sufficient to establish the dating.

4 A. Cottino, 'Michele Desubleo', in *La scuola di Guido Reni*, eds E. Negro & M. Pirondini, Modena, 1992, p. 209, repr.

5 ibid., pp. 252–3, fig. 211.

6 Dr Hermann Voss, Felton Bequest correspondence, 1955, cited in Hoff, pp. 227–8.

7 Ivanoff, p. 16.

8 Fantelli dated the Rouen picture towards 1626 (Fantelli, p. 104, no. 99, fig. 41); Skliar-Piguet, more convincingly, advances this date to *c*.1624 (Skliar-Piguet, p. 94).

9 Fantelli, p. 96, no. 40, fig. 20.

10 See D. S. Pepper, *Guido Reni: A Complete Catalogue of the Works with an Introductory Text*, Oxford, 1984, pp. 252–3, no. 104, fig. 134. The landscape in the *Hero and Leander* may be compared with the landscapes in earlier works by Reni, for example his *Samson* of *c*.1618–19 (Pinacoteca Nazionale, Bologna) (Pepper, pp. 236–7, no. 60, fig. 86).

11 See H. Hibbard, *Caravaggio*, London, 1983, fig. 28.

12 Hoff, p. 228.

Cat. no. 14 (Hoff, pp. 94–5)

1 See O. Millar, *Van Dyck in England* (exh. cat.), National Portrait Gallery, London, 1982, cat. no. 12. Millar dates the portrait to *c*.1634.

2 See G. Parry, 'Van Dyck and the Caroline Court Poets', in *Van Dyck 350*, eds S. J. Barnes & A. K. Wheelock Jr, Washington DC, 1994.

3 The king himself chose to pose on occasion as a knight of the Order of the Garter (see A. K. Wheelock Jr, S. J. Barnes & J. S. Held, *Van Dyck Paintings* (exh. cat.), National Gallery of Art, Washington DC, 1991, cat. no. 66).

4 C. Brown, 'Van Dyck's Pembroke Family Portrait: An Inquiry into Its Italian Sources', in Wheelock, Barnes & Held, pp. 37–44.

5 See J. Summerson, *Architecture in Britain 1530 to 1830*, The Pelican History of Art, Harmondsworth, Middlesex, 1953, pp. 89–90.

Cat. no. 15 (Hoff, pp. 96–8)

1 Knowler, *Strafforde's Letters* (1739), cited in R. W. Goulding, 'Wriothesley Portraits: Authentic and Reputed', *Walpole Society*, vol. VII, 1919–20, p. 39.

2 For a brief account of the life of the Countess of Southampton, see Goulding, p. 39.

3 For the portrait, see U. Hoff, 'Rachel de Ruvigny, Countess of Southampton by Sir Anthony van Dyck', *Annual Bulletin of the National Gallery of Victoria*, vol. II, 1960, pp. 1–4.

4 For van Dyck as an enthusiastic collector of Titian (his inventory included nineteen works by the sixteenth-century master), see O. Millar, *Van Dyck in England* (exh. cat.), National Portrait Gallery, London, 1982–83, pp. 23, 36 n. 24.

5 In 1999, a gathering of scholars, including Oliver Millar and David Scrase, at the Royal Academy, London, agreed that the Melbourne painting is the primary version. Much evidence for the primacy of the Melbourne painting has been marshalled by Dr Emma Devapriam (Emma Devapriam, letter to Oliver Millar, 4 January 1985, National Gallery of Victoria files). For an argument for the primacy of the Fitzwilliam version, see M. Jaffé, 'Van Dyck Studies II: La Belle & Vertueuse Huguenotte', *Burlington Magazine*, vol. CXXVI, no. 979, October 1984, pp. 603–11, fig. 1; see also A. Wilton, *The Swagger Portrait: Grand Manner Portraiture in Britain from Van Dyck to Augustus John 1630–1930* (exh. cat.), Tate Gallery, London, 1992, cat. no. 7.

6 See J. Egerton, in C. Brown & H. Vlieghe, *Van Dyck 1599–1641* (exh. cat.), Koninklijk Museum voor Schone Kunsten, Antwerp, 1999, cat. no. 104.

7 See Jaffé, fig. 3.

8 See Hoff, 'Rachel de Ruvigny', p. 4 n. 22.

9 See J. S. Held, *The Oil Sketches of Peter Paul Rubens: A Critical Catalogue*, vol. I, Princeton, New Jersey, 1980, pp. 199–201, no. 133; vol. II, pl. 16.

10 For skulls added to images after death (James I and family), see H. M. Latham, 'Some Altered Line Portraits of the Seventeenth Century', *Connoisseur*, vol. LXXX, no. 319, March 1928, pp. 134–6.

11 Hoff, 'Rachel de Ruvigny', p. 4.

12 Devapriam letter to Oliver Millar.

13 G. P. Bellori, *Le vite de' pittori, scultori e architetti* (1672), ed. E. Brea, Turin, 1976, pp. 279–80 (my translation). Bellori's stated source for van Dyck's London years was Sir Kenelm Digby.

14 For a seventeenth-century emblem relating to the glass-like fragility of Fortune, see J. Cats, *Proteus* (1627), in A. Henkel & A. Schöne (eds), *Emblemata: Handbuch zur Sinnbildkunst des XVI. und XVII. Jahrhunderts*, Stuttgart, 1978, col. 531 ('Fortuna vitrea est, cum splendet frangitur' (Fortune is glass-like, although it shines it is broken)).

15 See Goulding, p. 35.

16 ibid.

17 See Jaffé, fig. 4.

18 See G. du Choul, *Discours de la religion des anciens romains illustré* (1556), New York, 1976, pp. 66–7.

Cat. no. 16 (Hoff, pp. 55–6)

1 M. Roethlisberger, 'Additions to Claude', *Burlington Magazine*, vol. CX, no. 780, March 1968, p. 119; M. Roethlisberger, 'Claude Gelée à Nancy', *Revue du Louvre et des Musées de France*, vol. 31, no. 1, 1981, p. 52 n 4.

Cat. no. 17

1 Ovid, *Metamorphoses*, trans. F. J. Miller, vol. 1, London, 1960, pp. 42–53.

2 For other works in which the old man used as the model for Argus appears, see *The Satyr and the Peasant* (Staatliche Gemäldegalerie, Kassel), *Satyr Playing the Flute* (Muzeum Narodowe, Warsaw) and *St Peter Finding the Tribute Money in the Fish's Mouth* (Statens Museum for Kunst, Copenhagen).

3 For another picture that shows Jordaens's ability to depict cows directly from life, see his spontaneously painted *Five Studies of Cows* (Musée des Beaux-Arts, Lille) of the early 1620s (see R.-A. d'Hulst, in *Jacob Jordaens (1593–1678): Tableaux et tapisseries* (exh. cat.), by R.-A. d'Hulst, N. De Poorter & M. Vandenven, Koninklijk Museum voor Schone Kunsten, Antwerp, 1993, pp. 114–15, repr.).

4 See d'Hulst, in d'Hulst, De Poorter & Vandenven, cat. no. A26, repr. p. 109. The Lyon picture measures 195.0 x 235.0 cm (76 3/4 x 92 1/2 in.)

5 See S. Dean, 'An Important Gift: Jacob Jordaens' *Mercury and Argus*', *Gallery: Members Magazine of the National Gallery Society of Victoria*, November 1996, p. 24.

6 See R.-A. d'Hulst, *Jacob Jordaens*, trans. P. S. Falla, London, 1982, pp. 218–20, repr.

7 ibid., repr. (without caption).

8 For the Latin caption, which appears below the engraving, see H. Buijs & M. van Berge-Gerbaud, *Tableaux flamands et hollandais du Musée des Beaux-Arts de Lyon*, Paris, 1991, p. 76 n. 10.

9 C. van Mander, *Wtlegghingh op den Metamorphosis Pub. Ovidij Nasonis* (1604), cited in d'Hulst, in d'Hulst, De Poorter & Vandenven, cat. no. A26.

Cat. no. 18 (Hoff (Devapriam), pp. 177–8)

1 See D. R. Smith, *Masks of Wedlock: Seventeenth-Century Dutch Marriage Portraiture*, Michigan, 1982, p. 2.

2   See E. Devapriam, in Hoff, p. 177.
3   See D. Haynes, 'The Arundel "Homerus" Rediscovered', *J. Paul Getty Museum Journal*, vol. I, 1974, pp. 73–80.
4   See E. Devapriam, 'A Double Portrait by Thomas de Keyser in the National Gallery of Victoria', *Burlington Magazine*, vol. CXXXII, no. 1051, October 1990, fig. 40.

Cat. no. 19 (Hoff, pp. 76–7)
1   Horst Gerson, letter to Ursula Hoff, 24 April 1959, cited in Hoff, p. 76.
2   See S. Reiss, *Aelbert Cuyp*, Boston, 1975, no. 60, repr.
3   See T. Ingram, 'Cuyp's Cow a Compromise to Appease the Refined', *Financial Review*, 4 December 1986, p. 24.

Cat. no. 20 (Hoff (Devapriam), pp. 16–17)
1   See Clohsmann, inventory of Elector Palatinate Gallery, Mannheim, 1780, p. 31, no. 137, Bayerische Staatsgemäldesammlungen archives.
2   For a fuller account of this painting, see my article in *Art Bulletin of Victoria*, no. 41, 2000 (forthcoming).
3   P. Tomory & R. Gaston, *Summary Catalogue: European Paintings before 1800 in Australian and New Zealand Public Collections*, Sydney, 1989, p. 72, no. 205.
4   For Bernini's self-portraits, see A. Weston-Lewis, 'Portraits of Bernini: Portrait Drawings and Caricatures', in *Effigies and Ecstasies: Roman Baroque Sculpture and Design in the Age of Bernini* (exh. cat.), ed. A. Weston-Lewis, National Gallery of Scotland, Edinburgh, 1998, pp. 47–63; K. H. Fiore, 'Tre ritratti dipinti da Gian Lorenzo Bernini nella Galleria Borghese', in *Bernini scultore* (exh. cat.), eds A. Coliva & S. Schütze, Galleria Borghese, Rome, 1998, cat. nos 19–24, pp. 233–9; M. G. Bernardini & M. Fagiolo dell'Arco, *Gian Lorenzo Bernini: Regista del Barocco* (exh. cat.), section 1, Museo Nazionale del Palazzo Venezia, Rome, 1999, pp. 38–61, cat. nos 1–21. See also R. Wittkower, 'Works by Bernini at the Royal Academy', *Burlington Magazine*, vol. XCIII, no. 575, February 1951, pp. 51–5; M. Marini, 'Un contributo a Gianlorenzo Bernini al dipingere ... molto inclinato', *FIMA antiquari*, 1992, pp. 41–50.
5   See Bernardini & Fagiolo dell'Arco, fig. 3.
6   ibid., fig. 2.
7   ibid., fig. 6.
8   ibid., fig. 11.

Cat. no. 21 (Hoff (Devapriam), pp. 304–5)
1   Here we refer in particular to the work of the Rembrandt Research Project, a team of scholars analysing all of the paintings that to date have been attributed to Rembrandt (see J. Bruyn, B. Haak, S. H. Levie, P. J. J. van Thiel & E. van de Wetering, *A Corpus of Rembrandt Paintings*, trans. D. Cook-Radmore, 3 vols to date, Stichting Foundation Rembrandt Research Project, The Hague, 1982–).
2   Exhibitions on the paintings of Rembrandt and his school include *Rembrandt: The Master and His Workshop – Paintings*, Gemäldegalerie, Staatliche Museen zu Berlin – Preußischer Kulturbesitz, Rijkmuseum, Amsterdam, National Gallery, London, 1991–92; *Rembrandt/ Not Rembrandt in the Metropolitan Museum of Art: Aspects of Connoisseurship*, Metropolitan Museum of Art, New York, 1995–96; *Rembrandt: A Genius and His Impact*, National Gallery of Victoria, Melbourne, National Gallery of Australia, Canberra, 1997–98.
3   The catalogue is located in the Rijksbureau voor Kunsthistorische Documentatie, The Hague.
4   For a succinct analysis of various scholars' opinions, see V. Manuth, in *Rembrandt: A Genius and His Impact* (exh. cat.), by A. Blankert, National Gallery of Victoria, Melbourne, 1997, cat. no. 52. For a tentative attribution to Backer, see D. Miller, 'Jan Victors (1619–76)', PhD diss., vol. I, University of Delaware, 1985, no. R19. This attribution is dismissed by Manuth.
5   See Manuth, cat. nos 50, 51, reprs.
6   W. Sumowski, *Gemälde der Rembrandt-Schüler*, vol. V, Landau/Pfalz, 1990, no. 2086.
7   Sale, George A. Hearn, New York, 25 February – 4 March 1918, lot 416 (from which purchased by Henry Mack) (see Manuth, cat. no. 52, fig. 52a).

Cat. no. 22 (Hoff, pp. 145–6)
1   J. von Sandrart, *Academie der edlen Bau-, Bild- und Mahlerey-Künste* (1675), cited in I. Bergström, *Dutch Still-Life Painting in the Seventeenth Century*, trans. C. Hedström & G. Taylor, London, 1956, p. 196.

Cat. no. 23 (Hoff, pp. 265–6)
1   See Hoff, p. 266.
2   See J. Giltaij & J. Kelch, *Lof der Zeevaart: De Hollandse zeechilders van de 17e eeuw* (exh. cat.), Museum Boijmans Van Beuningen, Rotterdam, 1997, p. 29.

Cat. no. 24 (Hoff, p. 54)
1   This dating follows that assigned by Lurie and Percy, who place the *Virgin Annunciate* with a group of related works that they locate, in sequence, after the signed and dated *St Cecilia in Ecstasy* of 1645, in the Palazzo Vecchio, Florence (A. T. Lurie & A. Percy, in *Bernardo Cavallino of Naples 1616–1656* (exh. cat.), Cleveland Museum of Art, Cleveland, 1984, cat. nos 44–50). Percy and Lurie's dating is preferable to the date of *c.*1640 reported, without comment, by Hoff (Hoff, p. 54).
2   See A. Lurie, in *Bernardo Cavallino of Naples*, fig. 49a.
3   For the five states of the Virgin during the Annunciation, see M. Baxandall, *Painting and Experience in Fifteenth-Century Italy: A Primer in the Social History of Pictorial Style*, 2nd edn, Oxford, 1988, pp. 49–56; for seventeenth-century interpretations of the Virgin's gesture of submission (which for the contemporary critic and theorist Giovanni Pietro Bellori denoted obedience and humility), see R. E. Spear, *The 'Divine' Guido: Religion, Sex, Money and Art in the World of Guido Reni*, New Haven, 1997, pp. 152–5.
4   For related paintings by Stanzione, see S. Schütze & T. Willette, *Massimo Stanzione: L'opera completa*, Naples, 1992, nos A17–A20 and passim; for related paintings by Artemisia Gentileschi, see R. Ward Bissell, *Artemisia Gentileschi and the Authority of Art*, University Park, Pennsylvania, 1999, nos 33a, 43.
5   The analysis was undertaken 22 May 2000 by John Payne, Senior Conservator of Paintings, and Carl Villis, Conservator of Paintings, National Gallery of Victoria, in the company of the author and Laurie Benson, Assistant Curator, International Art. I would like to thank John Payne, Carl Villis and Laurie Benson for their assistance and advice.
6   See A. Percy, introduction to *Bernardo Cavallino of Naples*, p. 9; N. Spinosa, in *Bernardo Cavallino of Naples*, cat. no. 29 (with technical note by G. Kopelman); see also Ward Bissell, p. 267.
7   See A. Lurie, in *Bernardo Cavallino of Naples*, cat. no. 73, repr.
8   See A. Percy, in *Bernardo Cavallino of Naples*, cat. nos 30, 31, reprs (formerly on the London art market).
9   For the inventory of Pompilio Gagliano, dated 10 October 1699, see G. Labrot, *Collections of Paintings in Naples 1600–1780*, Munich, 1992, pp. 108–9, nos 45, 69; for the inventory of Francesco de Palma, duca di Sant'Elia, of 1716, see F. Strazzullo, 'Le collezioni artistiche del duca di S. Elia (1716)', *Napoli Nobilissima*, vol. XXIX, nos 1–4, 1990, p. 30, no. 39.
10 For a painting by Michele Regolia of a Neapolitan palace interior, a work that has been dated to the third quarter of the seventeenth century and that demonstrates the usefulness of pendant paintings, see *Civiltà del Seicento a Napoli* (exh. cat.), vol. II, Museo di Capodimonte, Naples, 1984, cat. no. 5.111, repr.

Cat. no. 25 (Hoff, pp. 252–3)
1   Ovid, *Metamorphoses*, trans. A. D. Melville, The World's Classics, Oxford, 1986, pp. 18–23.
2   The second picture was formerly in the Lyndon G. Harris collection (see Hoff, p. 253). For these two versions of the Mercury and Argus subject, see B. B. Fredericksen, 'A Pair of Pendant Pictures by Claude Lorrain and Salvator Rosa from the Chigi Collection', *Burlington Magazine*, vol. CXXXIII, no. 1061, August 1991, pp. 543–6, figs 61, 62; J. Scott, *Salvator Rosa: His Life and Times*, New Haven, 1995, p. 126.
3   F. Baldinucci, *Notizie dei professori del disegno da Cimabue in qua* (1681–1728), cited in Scott, p. 128.
4   See L. Salerno, *La pittura di Salvator Rosa*, Milan, 1963, p. 125.

Cat. no. 26 (Hoff, pp. 262–3)
1   See S. Slive, introduction to *Jacob van Ruisdael* (exh. cat.), by S. Slive & H. R. Hoetink, Mauritshuis, The Hague, 1981, p. 16.
2   See E. J. Walford, *Jacob van Ruisdael and the Perception of Landscape*, New Haven, 1991, p. 123.
3   See S. Slive, *Dutch Painting 1600–1800*, New Haven, 1995, p. 199.

Cat. no. 27 (Hoff, pp. 275–6)
1   See Hoff, p. 275. The photograph is located in the Rijksbureau voor Kunsthistorische Documentatie, The Hague.
2   For the symbolism of owls in Dutch art, see S. Slive, *Frans Hals*, vol. 1, London, 1970, pp. 147–52.

3 For the sexual symbolism of mussels, see S. Schama, *The Embarrassment of Riches: An Interpretation of Dutch Culture in the Golden Age*, London, 1987, pp. 204–7. For the cat as a symbol of sensual love, see M. F. Durantini, *The Child in Seventeenth-Century Dutch Painting*, Ann Arbor, Michigan, 1983, p. 36. For kitchen utensils and stockings as sexual symbols, see E. de Jongh, 'Jan Steen, So Near and Yet So Far', in *Jan Steen: Painter and Storyteller* (exh. cat.), by H. P. Chapman, W. T. Kloek & A. K. Wheelock Jr, National Gallery of Art, Washington DC, 1996, pp. 45–9.

4 See H. P. Chapman, in Chapman, Kloek & Wheelock, cat. no. 25, repr.

Cat. no. 28 (Hoff (Devapriam), pp. 276–7)

1 For customs associated with the marriage party, which often lasted several days and was traditionally celebrated at the groom's house or at an inn, see H. P. Chapman, in *Jan Steen: Painter and Storyteller* (exh. cat.), by H. P. Chapman, W. T. Kloek & A. K. Wheelock Jr, National Gallery of Art, Washington DC, 1996, cat. no. 6.

2 I would like to thank Laurie Benson, Assistant Curator, International Art, at the National Gallery of Victoria, for pointing out to me the roundfaced figure to the right of the bride.

3 For brides in seventeenth-century Holland wearing their hair loose as a symbol of chastity, see Chapman, cat. no. 6.

4 For an innkeeper similar to the man in the Melbourne picture, and also wearing a white apron, see Steen's *A Peasant Wedding*, 1672 (Rijksmuseum, Amsterdam) (see C. Brown, *Scenes of Everyday Life: Dutch Genre Painting of the Seventeenth Century*, London, 1984, p. 172, repr.); see also Brown, p. 159.

5 For the influence of these two commedia dell'arte characters on Steen's paintings, see S. J. Gudlaugsson, *The Comedians in the Work of Jan Steen and His Contemporaries*, trans. J. Brockway, Soest, 1975, pp. 23–9, 38–40.

6 See E. Devapriam, 'The Wedding Party by Jan Steen', *Gallery: Monthly Magazine of the National Gallery Society of Victoria*, July 1992, p. 11 (her translation). For the emblem (no. 96 in *Le Théâtre des bons engins*), see A. Henkel & A. Schöne (eds), *Emblemata: Handbuch zur Sinnbildkunst des XVI. und XVII. Jahrhunderts*, vol. 1, Stuttgart, 1967, p. 685.

7 For a discussion of the relationship of this painting to Bredero's poems, see M. Westermann, *The Amusements of Jan Steen: Comic Painting in the Seventeenth Century*, Zwolle, 1997, pp. 218–20.

Cat. no. 29 (Hoff, pp. 157–8)

1 See S. Slive, *Dutch Painting 1600–1800*, New Haven, 1995, p. 205.

2 ibid.; see also S. Slive, in *Jacob van Ruisdael* (exh. cat.), by S. Slive & H. R. Hoetink, Mauritshuis, The Hague, 1981, cat. no. 108, repr.

3 See Slive, in Slive & Hoetink, cat. nos 108A–108C, reprs.

4 W. Stechow, *Dutch Landscape Painting of the Seventeenth Century*, Oxford, 1966, p. 76.

Cat. no. 30 (Hoff, pp. 232–4)

1 See A. Bredius, *Rembrandt: The Complete*

Edition of the Paintings*, rev. H. Gerson, 3rd edn, London, 1969, p. 575, no. 323.

2 ibid., p. 575, no. 321, repr. p. 247.

3 See J. Gregory, '*Portrait of a Fair-Headed Man*, the "*Self-Portrait*", and Problems Relating to Rembrandt's Late Period', in *Rembrandt in the Collections of the National Gallery of Victoria*, by J. Gregory & I. Zdanowicz, The Robert Raynor Publications in Prints and Drawings, no. 2, Melbourne, 1988, p. 54.

4 See Bredius, p. 575, no. 323A, repr. p. 251.

5 See C. Brown, in *Rembrandt: The Master and His Workshop – Paintings* (exh. cat.), by C. Brown, J. Kelch & P. van Thiel, trans. E. Clegg, M. Hoyle & P. Vincent, Gemäldegalerie, Staatliche Museen zu Berlin – Preußischer Kulturbesitz, Berlin, 1991, cat. no. 50.

6 See E. van de Wetering, *Rembrandt: The Painter at Work*, Amsterdam, 1997, p. 164.

7 ibid., pp. 281, 291.

8 See Bredius, p. 552, no. 60, repr. p. 53.

Cat. no. 31 (Hoff, pp. 131–2)

1 See I. M. Veldman, *Maarten van Heemskerck*, part 1, *The New Hollstein: Dutch and Flemish Etchings, Engravings and Woodcuts 1450–1700*, ed. G. Luitjen, Roosendaal, 1993, p. 138, no. 158, repr. p. 137.

2 See C. White & K. G. Boon (eds), *Hollstein's Dutch and Flemish Etchings, Engravings and Woodcuts*, vol. XVIII, Amsterdam, 1969, p. 20, no. B.40; vol. XIX, repr. p. 26.

3 For further discussion of this picture, see *Arent de Gelder (1645–1727), Rembrandts laatste leering* (exh. cat.), Dordrechts Museum, Dordrecht, 1998, p. 90.

Cat. no. 32 (Hoff, pp. 181–2)

1 See M. N. Rosenfeld, *Largillierre and the Eighteenth-Century Portrait* (exh. cat.), Montreal Museum of Fine Arts, Montreal, 1982, cat. no. 61, repr.

2 ibid., pp. 292, 294, figs 61a, 61e.

3 For the wider social significance of wigs, see M. Pointon, *Hanging the Head: Portraiture and Social Formation in Eighteenth-Century England*, New Haven, 1993, pp. 107–40.

4 See P. Rosenberg, foreword to Rosenfeld, p. 15.

Cat. no. 33 (Hoff (Devapriam), pp. 43–4)

1 See M. Liversidge & J. Farrington (eds), *Canaletto and England*, Birmingham, 1993.

2 See E. Devapriam, 'Bacino di San Marco: From the Piazzetta', *Art Bulletin of Victoria*, no. 25, 1985, p. 35.

3 See W. G. Constable, *Canaletto: Giovanni Antonio Canal 1697–1768*, rev. J. G. Links, 2nd edn, vol. II, Oxford, 1989, pp. 248–9, no. 128.

4 For further discussion, see Devapriam, pp. 33–41.

5 See V. Pemberton-Pigott, 'The Development of Canaletto's Painting Technique', in *Canaletto* (exh. cat.), by K. Baetjer & J. G. Links, Metropolitan Museum of Art, New York, 1989, pp. 53–62.

Cat. no. 34 (Hoff, pp. 12–13)

1 For these seven views and for the dating of the present picture, see C. Villis, 'Bernardo Bellotto's

Seven Large Views of Rome, c.1743', *Burlington Magazine*, vol. CXLII, no. 1163, February 2000, pp. 76–81, figs 1, 3, 4, 6, 7, 9, 10.

2 See W. G. Constable, *Canaletto: Giovanni Antonio Canal 1697–1768*, rev. J. G. Links, 2nd edn, vol. II, Oxford, 1989, pl. 131.

3 See M. Levey, *The Later Italian Paintings in the Collection of Her Majesty the Queen*, 2nd edn, Cambridge, 1991, pl. 17.

Cat. nos 35 & 36 (Hoff (Devapriam), pp. 143–4)

1 James Brockman, cash book entry, 20 July 1744, cited in E. Devapriam, 'Two Conversation Pieces by Edward Haytley', *Apollo*, vol. CXIV, no. 234, August 1981, p. 87.

2 Brockman cash book, 9 August 1744, cited in Devapriam, p. 87.

3 Elizabeth Robinson, letter to Elizabeth Montagu, 28 December 1743, Montagu Papers, MO4682, Henry E. Huntington Library, San Marino, California. The authorship, date and subjects of these two paintings were first established by Devapriam (Devapriam, pp. 85–7).

4 Elizabeth Robinson, letter to Elizabeth Montagu, 8 May 1745, cited in *English Eighteenth Century Paintings* (exh. cat.), Leger Galleries, London, 1978, cat. no. 7.

5 Elizabeth Robinson, letter to William Friend, 10 September 1754, cited in *English Eighteenth Century Paintings*, cat. no. 7.

6 For the payment for two paintings (presumably the Melbourne pictures) on 6 May 1746, see Devapriam, p. 87.

7 See J. Hayes, introduction to *Polite Society by Arthur Devis 1712–1787: Portraits of the English Country Gentleman and His Family* (exh. cat.), Harris Museum and Art Gallery, Preston, Lancashire, 1983, p. 10; E. Einberg, in *Manners and Morals: Hogarth and British Painting 1700–1760* (exh. cat.), Tate Gallery, London, 1987. A pair of portraits (in identical frames), one work by Haytley and the other by Devis, have been recorded by Leger Galleries in London (National Gallery of Victoria files).

Cat. no. 37 (Hoff, p. 156)

1 George Vertue, notebook entry, in 'Vertue Note Books: Volume III', *Walpole Society*, vol. XXII, 1933–34, p. 29.

2 Samuel Richardson, letter to Lady Bradshaigh, in A. L. Barbauld (ed.), *The Correspondence of Samuel Richardson*, vol. IV, London, 1804, p. 255.

3 See Hoff, pp. 152–4, reprs.

4 J. Duncombe, in *Gentleman's Magazine* (1780), cited in A. S. Lewis, 'Joseph Highmore: 1692–1780', PhD diss., Harvard University, 1975, p. 286.

5 See Hoff, pp. 151–2, repr.

6 ibid., pp. 154–5, repr.

7 J. Highmore, in *Gentleman's Magazine*, no. 34, November 1764.

8 W. Mild, 'Susanna Highmore's Literary Reputation', *Proceedings of the American Philosophical Society*, vol. 122, no. 6, December 1978, p. 378.

9 Duncombe, cited in Lewis, p. 286.

Cat. nos 38 & 39 (Hoff (Devapriam), pp. 21–3)

a See A. Ananoff & D. Wildenstein, *François Boucher*, vol. II, Lausanne, 1976, pp. 6–7, 14–15, nos 311, 320. It was against the rules for a painting to be exhibited at the Salon twice, but in the case of *The Enjoyable Lesson* Boucher may have wanted to exhibit the whole set when it was completed (see A. Laing, 'Boucher et la pastorale peinte', *Revue de l'art*, vol. LXXIII, 1986, p. 63 n. 73). The first owner of the two pictures is unknown.

b The pictures, which were recorded in the boudoir at Mentmore, were probably acquired in the nineteenth century by Mayer Amschel de Rothschild (1818–1874), from whom they would have passed to his daughter, the Countess of Rosebery, with the contents of Mentmore.

c I would like to thank Alastair Laing for providing the information that has enabled the provenances to be revised (Alastair Laing, letter to the author, 27 May 2000). The National Gallery of Victoria also thanks Gerald G. Stiebel, of Stiebel, Ltd, New York, for his assistance with additional information.

1 See Ananoff & Wildenstein, vol. II, p. 13, no. 319, repr.

2 Laing letter, 27 May 2000.

3 Ananoff & Wildenstein, vol. II, pp. 6–7, 14–15, nos 311, 320.

4 See L. Soullié & C. Masson, 'Catalogue raisonné de l'oeuvre peint et dessiné de François Boucher', in *François Boucher*, by André Michel, rev. edn, Paris, 1906, no. 1379.

5 See A. Laing, 'Boucher: The Search for an Idiom', in *François Boucher 1703–1770* (exh. cat.), Metropolitan Museum of Art, New York, 1986, pp. 67–72, cat. no. 53; Laing, 'Boucher et la pastorale peinte'.

6 F. Parfaict & C. Parfaict, *Dictionnaire des théâtres de Paris*, vol. VI, Paris, 1756, pp. 69–84.

7 See Laing, 'Boucher et la pastorale peinte', p. 56.

8 ibid., pp. 55–64.

9 Cf. J. Clark & P. McCaughey, 'Love among the Ruins: Two Pastorals by François Boucher', *Art Bulletin of Victoria*, no. 23, 1982, pp. 5–12.

10 Laing, 'Boucher et la pastorale peinte'.

Cat. no. 40 (Hoff, pp. 1–3)

1 See J. Clark, *The Great Eighteenth Century Exhibition in the National Gallery of Victoria* (exh. cat.), National Gallery of Victoria, Melbourne, 1983, p. 122. For the similar attire worn by Paolo de' Matteis in his *Self-Portrait with Allegory of the Peace of Utrecht and of Rastatt*, after 1714 (Sarah Campbell Blaffer Foundation, Houston), see *Settecento napoletano: Sulle ali dell'aquila imperiale, 1707–1734* (exh. cat.), Kunstforum Wien, Vienna, 1993, cat. no. 12.

2 For further references to *Las Meninas* in this context, see L. G. Hennessey, 'Friends Serving Itinerant Muses: Jacopo Amigoni and Farinelli in Europe', in *Italian Culture in Northern Europe in the Eighteenth Century*, ed. S. West, Cambridge, 1999, pp. 41–2.

3 See D. Heartz, 'Farinelli and Metastasio: Rival Twins of Public Favour', *Early Music*, vol. XII, 1984, pp. 361–3.

4 ibid., p. 362.

5 See A. Scarpa Sonino, *Jacopo Amigoni*, Soncino, 1994, p. 160.

6 C. Burney, *The Present State of Music in France and Italy*, London, 1771, p. 220.

Cat. no. 41 (Hoff (Devapriam), pp. 84–5)

1 George Vertue, notebook entry, October 1737, in 'Vertue Note Books: Volume III', *Walpole Society*, vol. XXII, 1933–34, p. 81; see also J. Burke, 'The Clavey Family by Arthur Devis', *Art Bulletin of Victoria*, no. 18, 1977, pp. 20–4. For an excellent general discussion of the conversation piece, see J. Burke, *English Art 1714–1800*, Oxford, 1976.

2 See E. Einberg, in *Manners and Morals: Hogarth and British Painting 1700–1760* (exh. cat.), Tate Gallery, London, 1987.

3 See S. V. Sartin, 'Arthur Devis: His Life and Art', in *Polite Society by Arthur Devis 1712–1787: Portraits of the English Country Gentleman and His Family* (exh. cat.), Harris Museum and Art Gallery, Preston, Lancashire, 1983, pp. 22–3.

4 See F. Haskell & N. Penny, *Taste and the Antique: The Lure of Classical Sculpture 1500–1900*, New Haven, 1981, fig. 138.

Cat. no. 42 (Hoff, pp. 327–8)

1 See W. L. Pressly, 'Johan Zoffany as "David the Anointed One"', *Apollo*, vol. CXLI, no. 397, March 1995, p. 53; see also M. Watson, 'Zoffany as Punster and Prankster: Some Comments on His *David with the Head of Goliath*', *Art Bulletin of Victoria*, no. 36, 1995, p. 10.

2 See Pressly, pp. 53, 54.

Cat. no. 43 (Hoff, pp. 329–30)

1 W. Hazlitt, *Criticism and Dramatic Essays*, London, 1851, p. 49.

2 See E. K. Waterhouse, *Reynolds*, English Master Painters, ed. H. Read, London, 1941, pl. 100.

3 See S. Bloxam, *Walpole's Queen of Comedy: Elizabeth Farren, Countess of Derby*, Ashford, Kent, 1988, p. 49.

Cat. no. 44 (Hoff, pp. 319–20)

1 H. Fuseli, 'Invention' (1801), in J. Knowles (ed.), *The Life and Writings of Henry Fuseli, Esq. M.A. R.A.*, vol. I, London, 1831, p. 217.

2 ibid.

Cat. no. 45 (Hoff, pp. 225–6)

1 For the portrait, see A. Smart, *Allan Ramsay: A Complete Catalogue of His Paintings*, New Haven, 1999, p. 188, no. 509; A. Smart, *Allan Ramsay 1713–1784* (exh. cat.), Scottish National Portrait Gallery, Edinburgh, 1992, cat. no. 77.

Cat. no. 46 (Hoff, pp. 87–8)

1 There is some evidence to suggest that this portrait may in fact depict Sophie's sister Louise (Laurent Hugues, letter to Patrick McCaughey, 7 July 1987, National Gallery of Victoria files).

2 Jeanne-Antoinette Poisson Le Normand d'Étiolles, Marquise de Pompadour, letter, 19 October 1750, cited in C. Stryienski, *The Daughters of Louis XV*, London, 1915, p. 62.

3 ibid., p. 173.

4 See A. Ribeiro, *The Art of Dress: Fashion in England and France 1750 to 1820*, New Haven, 1995, p. 59; for depictions of aristocratic women in this period, see E. Goodman, *The Portraits of Madame de Pompadour: Celebrating the Femme Savante*, Berkeley, 2000.

Cat. no. 47 (Hoff, pp. 238–9)

1 J. Clark, *The Great Eighteenth Century Exhibition in the National Gallery of Victoria* (exh. cat.), National Gallery of Victoria, Melbourne, 1983, p. 146.

2 Joshua Reynolds, letter to Daniel Daulby, 9 September 1777, in F. W. Hilles (ed.), *Letters of Joshua Reynolds*, Cambridge, 1929, p. 56.

3 See N. Penny, 'An Ambitious Man: The Career and the Achievement of Sir Joshua Reynolds', in *Reynolds* (exh. cat.), ed. N. Penny, Royal Academy of Arts, London, 1986, p. 22.

4 See D. Mannings, in Penny, cat. no. 51, repr.

5 See A. K. Wheelock Jr, S. J. Barnes & J. S. Held, *Van Dyck Paintings* (exh. cat.), National Gallery of Art, Washington DC, 1991, cat. no. 36, repr.

6 See Hoff, p. 238.

Cat. no. 48 (Hoff, p. 240)

1 See J. Clark, *The Great Eighteenth Century Exhibition in the National Gallery of Victoria* (exh. cat.), National Gallery of Victoria, Melbourne, 1983, p. 161.

2 D. Shawe-Taylor, *The Georgians: Eighteenth Century Portraiture and Society*, London, 1990, p. 133.

3 J. Thomson, preface to *Winter: A Poem*, 3rd edn, London, 1726, p. 15.

4 ibid.

5 See Clark, p. 161.

6 D. Webb, *An Inquiry into the Beauties of Painting, and the Merits of the Most Celebrated Painters, Ancient and Modern*, London, 1760, p. 73.

Cat. no. 49 (Hoff, pp. 7–8)

1 For the painting, see A. M. Clark, *Pompeo Batoni: A Complete Catalogue of His Works with an Introductory Text*, New York, 1985, pp. 306–7, no. 305.

2 For Batoni and the Grand Tour, see E. P. Bowron, *Pompeo Batoni and His British Patrons* (exh. cat.), Kenwood House, London, 1982; A. Wilton & I. Bignamini (eds), *Grand Tour: The Lure of Italy in the Eighteenth Century* (exh. cat.), Tate Gallery, London, 1996, pp. 51–62, 77; E. P. Bowron & J. J. Rishel (eds), *Art in Rome in the Eighteenth Century* (exh. cat.), Philadelphia Museum of Art, Philadelphia, 2000, pp. 305–20.

3 See Clark, pp. 399–402.

4 For Sir Sampson, see *Dictionary of National Biography*, vol. VII, Oxford, pp. 1168–9; J. Ingamells, *Dictionary of British and Irish Travellers in Italy, 1701–1800*, New Haven, 1997, p. 399.

5 It is interesting to note that in a letter from Rome dated 24 March 1770, to Sir Sampson's father-in-law, Sir John Eardley-Wilmot, the dealer Thomas Jenkins wrote: 'I hope Sir Sampson will receive his Portrait Safe, and to his Satisfaction' (Osborn files, Beinecke Library, Yale University, New Haven). If Jenkins is referring to the Batoni, it is clear that there was a very considerable gap between the first sitting in Rome in 1766 and the picture's completion and despatch to England in early 1770; such a delay is entirely consistent with many other complaints recorded in the eighteenth century about the dilatoriness of Batoni's studio (see Bowron, p. 15).

Cat. no. 50 (Hoff, pp. 249–50)

1 See H. Walpole, 'Notes by Horace Walpole, Fourth Earl of Orford, on the Exhibition of the Society of Artists and the Free Society of Artists, 1760–1791', ed. H. Gatty, *Walpole Society*, vol. XXVII, 1938–39, p. 77.

2 David Garrick, 1768, quoted in J. Romney, *Memoirs of the Life and Works of George Romney*, London, 1830, p. 56.

3 George Romney, letter to William Hayley, February 1787, cited in W. Hayley, *The Life of George Romney, Esq.*, London, 1809, p. 123.

4 Walpole, p. 77.

5 ibid.

6 For the formation of the modern family, see L. Stone, *The Family, Sex and Marriage in England, 1500–1800*, London, 1977.

7 See J. Burke, 'Romney's "Leigh Family" (1768): A Link between the Conversation Piece and the Neo-Classical Portrait Group', *Annual Bulletin of the National Gallery of Victoria*, vol. II, 1960, pp. 5–14.

8 ibid.; see also J. Jones-O'Neill, 'George Romney's Sketchbook in the National Gallery of Victoria: The Development of a New Expressive Vocabulary', *Art Bulletin of Victoria*, no. 39, 1998, pp. 45–52.

Cat. no. 51 (Hoff, pp. 126–7)

1 See Hoff, p. 126.

2 See W. M. Nolan, 'An Officer of the 4th Regiment of Foot', *Cavalcade*, August 1979.

3 This work was on the London art market in 1987.

4 See E. Waterhouse, *Gainsborough*, rev. edn, London, 1966, p. 56, no. 95, pl. 139.

5 M. Cormack, *The Paintings of Thomas Gainsborough*, Cambridge, 1991, p. 84.

Cat. no. 52 (Hoff, pp. 128–9)

1 The work was exhibited at the Royal Academy in 1878 as *View at the Mouth of the Thames* (see Hoff, p. 128).

2 For Gainsborough's relationship to Dutch art, see J. Hayes, *The Landscape Paintings of Thomas Gainsborough: A Critical Text and Catalogue Raisonné*, vol. 1, London, 1982, pp. 44–54.

3 E. Waterhouse, *Gainsborough*, rev. edn, London, 1966, p. 31.

4 See Hoff, p. 128; Hayes, vol. 2, p. 509, no. 141.

5 See J. Mayne, 'Thomas Gainsborough's Exhibition Box', *Victoria and Albert Museum Bulletin*, vol. 1, no. 3, 1965, pp. 17–24.

6 J. Reynolds, *Discourses on Art* (1797), ed. R. R. Wark, New Haven, 1975, p. 249.

7 ibid., p. 253.

8 Hayes, vol. 2, p. 509, no. 141.

Cat. no. 53 (Hoff (Devapriam), pp. 324–5)

1 See E. Devapriam, '"The Synnot Children" by Joseph Wright of Derby', *Art Bulletin of Victoria*, no. 26, 1985, pp. 15–21.

2 See J. Egerton, *Wright of Derby* (exh. cat.), Tate Gallery, London, 1990, cat. no. 21, repr.

3 ibid., cat. no. 126, repr.

4 B. Nicolson, *Joseph Wright of Derby*, vol. I, London, 1968, p. 71.

Cat. no. 54 (Hoff (Devapriam), pp. 123–4)

1 In August 1796, Fuseli wrote to his friend William Roscoe, informing him that about half the pictures for the Milton exhibition were finished and that nearly all were 'Sketched' (Henry Fuseli, letter to William Roscoe, 9 August 1796, in D. H. Weinglass (ed.), *The Collected English Letters of Henry Fuseli*, London, 1982, p. 156).

2 R. Burton, *Anatomy of Melancholy* (1621–52), eds F. Dell & P. Jordan-Smith, New York, 1927, p. 139.

3 H. Fuseli, 'Aphorism 231', in J. Knowles (ed.), *The Life and Writings of Henry Fuseli, Esq. M.A. R.A.*, vol. III, London, 1831, p. 145.

4 For further discussion of this picture, see P. Tomory, 'Henry Fuseli's "Milton when a Youth"', *Art Bulletin of Victoria*, no. 27, 1986, pp. 26–35.

Cat. no. 55 (Hoff, pp. 300–01)

1 J. M. W. Turner, 'Hesperides (2)' sketchbook, 1805, fols 5a–6, Tate Gallery, London, T.B.XCIV (see D. Hill, *Turner on the Thames: River Journeys in the Year 1805*, New Haven, 1993, p. 86).

2 See L. McNaught, 'Thirty Years a Model: Old Walton Bridge and the Picturesque', *Country Life*, vol. CLXVI, 6 March 1980, p. 656.

3 Hill, pp. 120, 126.

4 See M. Butlin, in *Turner 1775–1851* (exh. cat.), Tate Gallery, London, 1974, cat. no. 132.

5 D. B. Brown, 'Rule, Britannia? Patriotism, Progress and the Picturesque in Turner's Britain', in *Turner* (exh. cat.), ed. M. Lloyd, National Gallery of Australia, Canberra, 1996, p. 64.

Cat. no. 56 (Hoff, p. 301)

1 For the dating of this picture, see M. Butlin, 'Turner's Late Unfinished Oils: Some New Evidence for Their Late Date', *Turner Studies: His Art and Epoch 1775–1851*, vol. I, no. 2, 1981, pp. 43–5; see also M. Lloyd (ed.), *Turner* (exh. cat.), National Gallery of Australia, Canberra, 1996, cat. no. 33.

2 M. Butlin, 'A Newly-Discovered Masterpiece by J. M. W. Turner', *Art Bulletin of Victoria*, no. 16, 1975, pp. 2–10.

3 E. V. Rippingille, 'Personal Recollections of Great Artists: No. 8 – Sir Augustus W. Callcott, R.A.' (1860), cited in Butlin, pp. 4–5.

4 J. Eagles, in *Blackwood Magazine* (1836), cited in A. J. Finberg, *The Life of J. M. W. Turner, R.A.*, London, 1967, p. 363.

5 J. Ruskin, 'The Truth of Clouds', in *The Works of John Ruskin*, eds E. T. Cook & A. Wedderburn, vol. III, London, 1905, p. 377.

6 W. Vaughan, 'Hanging Fragments: The Case of Turner's Oeuvre', in *Appearance, Opinion, Change: Evaluating the Look of Paintings*, London, 1990, pp. 85–7.

7 Ruskin, vol. 3, p. 92.

Cat. no. 57 (Hoff, pp. 203–4)

1 See C. R. Leslie, *Memoirs of the Life of John Constable, Esq., R.A., Composed Chiefly of His Letters* (1845), London, 1949, p. 25.

2 T. S. R. Boase, *English Art, 1800–1870*, Oxford, 1959, p. 112.

3 Joseph Farington, diary entry, 9 August 1808, in

J. Farington, *The Farington Diary*, ed. J. Grieg, vol. V, London, 1925, p. 94.

4 A. Cunningham, *The Lives of the Most Eminent British Painters, Sculptors and Architects*, vol. VI, London, 1833, p. 136.

5 See K. Garlick, *Sir Thomas Lawrence: A Complete Catalogue of the Oil Paintings*, Oxford, 1989, pl. 4.

6 David Wilkie, diary entry, 6 March 1808, cited in A. Cunningham, *The Life of Sir David Wilkie; with His Journals, Tours, and Critical Remarks on Works of Art; and a Selection from His Correspondence*, vol. I, London, 1843, p. 229.

Cat. no. 58 (Hoff, pp. 60–1)

1 See G. Reynolds, *The Later Paintings and Drawings of John Constable*, text vol., New Haven, 1984, pp. 4–5, no. 17.4; plate vol., pl. 6. See also L. Parris & I. Fleming-Williams, *Constable* (exh. cat.), Tate Gallery, London, 1991, cat. no. 79, repr.

2 John Constable, letter to Maria Bicknell, 21 August 1816, in *John Constable's Correspondence*, ed. R. B. Beckett, vol. II, Suffolk Records Society, Ipswich, 1964, p. 196. All quotations from Constable's correspondence retain the artist's original spelling and emphases.

3 See Beckett, vol. II, pp. 84–5, 196, 252; vol. VI, 1968, p. 47. For Constable's relationship with the Slater-Rebow family, see M. Rosenthal, *Constable: The Painter and His Landscape*, New Haven, 1983, pp. 14–16; M. Sommerlad, *Wivenhoe Park and John Constable*, Colchester, 1984.

4 Constable letter to Maria Bicknell, in Beckett, vol. II, p. 196.

5 See M. Girouard, 'Living in a Folly', *Country Life*, vol. CXXIV, 6 November 1958, p. 1040.

6 See J. Clark, *The Great Eighteenth Century Exhibition in the National Gallery of Victoria* (exh. cat.), National Gallery of Victoria, Melbourne, 1983, p. 85.

7 See P. Connor, *Oriental Architecture in the West*, London, 1979, pp. 68–73.

8 Girouard, p. 1041.

9 John Constable, *Various Subjects of Landscape, Characteristic of English Scenery* (1830), cited in I. Fleming-Williams, *Constable and His Drawings*, London, 1990, p. 111.

10 For a perceptive analysis of Constable's interest in the 'revealing and partial concealing' of the details of his compositions, see Fleming-Williams, p. 111.

11 Constable letter to Maria Bicknell, in Beckett, vol. II, p. 196.

12 See Beckett, vol. II, p. 199; M. Kitson, 'London: Constable at the Tate', *Burlington Magazine*, vol. CXXXIII, no. 1061, August 1991, pp. 559–60.

13 See G. Reynolds, *The Early Paintings and Drawings of John Constable*, plate vol., New Haven, 1996, pl. 1294.

Cat. no. 59 (Hoff, pp. 63–4)

1 John Constable, letter to John Dunthorne, 29 May 1802, in *John Constable's Correspondence*, ed. R. B. Beckett, vol. II, Suffolk Records Society, Ipswich, 1964, p. 32.

2 For the six works exhibited at the Royal Academy, see L. Parris & I. Fleming-Williams, *Constable* (exh. cat.), Tate Gallery, London, 1991, figs 65, 66; cat. nos 100, 101, 158, 162, reprs.

3   ibid., cat. no. 158, repr.
4   John Constable, letter to John Fisher, 23 October 1821, in Beckett, vol. VI, 1968, pp. 77–8.
5   See Parris & Fleming-Williams, cat. no. 160, repr.
6   See Hoff, p. 63.
7   G. Reynolds, *John Constable: The Natural Painter* (exh. cat.), Auckland City Art Gallery, Auckland, 1973, cat. no. 33. See also L. Parris, I. Fleming-Williams & C. Shields, *Constable: Paintings, Watercolours and Drawings* (exh. cat.), Tate Gallery, London, 1976, cat. no. 262; Hoff, p. 63.
8   Parris & Fleming-Williams, cat. no. 159.
9   ibid., cat. no. 157, repr.
10 See R. Dorment, *British Painting in the Philadelphia Museum of Art*, Philadelphia, 1986, p. 50.
11 See Hoff, p. 64.

Cat. no. 60 (Dean, p. 103)
1   T. Thoré, 'Open Letter to Théodore Rousseau' (1844), in *Art in Theory 1815–1900: An Anthology of Changing Ideas*, eds C. Harrison & P. Wood, Oxford, 1998, p. 221.

Cat. no. 61 (Dean, pp. 84–5)
1   See R. Herbert, in *Jean-François Millet* (exh. cat.), Hayward Gallery, London, 1976, cat. no. 16, repr.
2   See L. L. Meixner, Hunt entry, in *The Dictionary of Art*, ed. J. Turner, vol. 15, London, 1996, pp. 19–20.
3   J. Cartwright, *Jean François Millet: His Life and Letters*, rev. edn, London, 1910, pp. 134–5.
4   H. L. Hunt, letter, 5 November 1913, cited in Felton Papers, National Gallery of Victoria.

Cat. no. 62
1   See J. Christian, in *The Pre-Raphaelites* (exh. cat.), Tate Gallery, London, 1984, cat. no. 235.
2   See S. P. Casteras, 'Edward Burne-Jones and the Legend of Fair Rosamund', *Journal of Pre-Raphaelite and Aesthetic Studies*, vol. 1, no. 1 (part 2), Spring 1988, p. 36.
3   See S. P. Casteras, *English Pre-Raphaelitism and Its Reception in America in the Nineteenth Century*, London, 1990, p. 58.

Cat. no. 63
1   See M. H. Spielmann, *Millais and His Works*, Edinburgh, 1898, pp. 74–5; J. G. Millais, *The Life and Letters of Sir John Everett Millais*, vol. I, London, 1899, pp. 247–8.
2   John Everett Millais, quoted in Millais, vol. I, p. 248.
3   See A. Staley, in *Romantic Art in Britain: Paintings and Drawings 1760–1860* (exh. cat.), by A. Staley, F. Cummings & R. Rosenblum, Philadelphia Museum of Art, Philadelphia, 1968, cat. no. 227.
4   Millais, vol. I, pp. 250–1.
5   J. Ruskin, 'Academy Notes 1855', in *The Works of John Ruskin*, eds E. T. Cook & A. Wedderburn, vol. XIV, London, 1905, p. 22.
6   'Royal Academy', *Athenaeum*, no. 1437, 12 May 1855, p. 558.
7   ibid.
8   'Royal Academy', *Times*, 7 May 1855, p. 10.

9   M. H. Spielmann, 'In Memoriam Sir John Everett Millais P.R.A.', *Magazine of Art*, September 1906, p. xvi.
10 A. L. Baldry, *Sir John Everett Millais: His Art and Influence*, London, 1899, p. 34.
11 See Millais, vol. I, p. 253.

Cat. no. 64 (Hoff, p. 70)
1   Jean-Baptiste-Camille Corot, notebook entry, 1855, in *Art in Theory 1815–1900: An Anthology of Changing Ideas*, eds C. Harrison & P. Wood, Oxford, 1998, p. 535.

Cat. no. 65 (Dean, pp. 73–4)
1   E. Moreau-Nélaton, *Manet raconté par lui-même*, vol. 1, Paris, 1926, p. 51.
2   E. Zola, 'A New Style in Painting' (1867), in *Realism and Tradition in Art 1848–1900: Sources and Documents*, ed. L. Nochlin, Sources and Documents in the History of Art Series, ed. H. W. Janson, Englewood Cliffs, New Jersey, 1966, p. 74.

Cat. no. 66 (Dean, p. 76)
1   See R. Pickvance, *Manet* (exh. cat.), Fondation Pierre Gianadda, Martigny, 1996, fig. 18.
2   ibid., fig. 17.
3   S. Mallarmé, *Art Monthly Review* (1876), in *Modern Art and Modernism: A Critical Anthology*, eds F. Frascina & C. Harrison, London, 1984, p. 40.

Cat. no. 67 (Dean, pp. 43–4)
1   J. Janin, *L'Artiste* (1835), cited in H. Honour, *Romanticism*, London, 1981, p. 270.

Cat. no. 68 (Dean, pp. 21–2)
1   See M.-M. Aubrun, *Jules Bastien-Lepage 1848–1884*, Paris, 1985, pp. 132–5, no. 172, repr.
2   See W. S. Feldman, 'Jules Bastien-Lepage: A New Perspective', *Art Bulletin of Victoria*, no. 20, 1979, p. 6.
3   J. K. Huysmans, in *Le Voltaire* (1879), in *The Expanding World of Art, 1874–1902*, ed. E. Gilmore Holt, vol. I, New Haven, 1988, p. 215.
4   ibid.
5   ibid.

Cat. no. 69 (Dean, p. 90)
1   See D. Wildenstein, *Monet or the Triumph of Impressionism*, Cologne, 1996, p. 137.
2   See C. McNamara, 'Monet's Vétheuil Paintings: Site, Subject, and *Débâcles*', in *Monet at Vétheuil: The Turning Point* (exh. cat.), by A. Dixon, C. McNamara & C. Stuckey, University of Michigan Museum of Art, Ann Arbor, Michigan, 1998, pp. 74–5.
3   P. Sébillot, in *La Plume* (1879), cited in V. Spate, *The Colour of Time: Claude Monet*, London, 1992, p. 137.
4   Spate, p. 138.
5   T. Duret, 'Claude Monet' (1880), cited in S. Z. Levine, *Monet and His Critics*, New York, 1976, p. 44.

Cat. no. 70 (Dean, p. 89)
1   G. Sieberling, 'Monet's *Les Rochers à Pourville, marée basse*', *Porticus: The Journal of the Memorial Art Gallery of the University of Rochester*, vol. III, 1980, p. 44.
2   John Payne, examination report, 26 March 1993, National Gallery of Victoria (Conservation Department) files.
3   See R. L. Herbert, *Monet on the Normandy Coast: Tourism and Painting, 1867–1886*, New Haven, 1994, pp. 66, 82.
4   Payne examination report, 26 March 1993.
5   See C. F. Stuckey, *Claude Monet 1840–1926* (exh. cat.), Art Institute of Chicago, Chicago, 1995, p. 203.
6   Sidney Colvin, letter to Felton Bequests' Committee, 17 June 1913, Felton Papers, National Gallery of Victoria.

Cat. no. 71 (Dean, p. 38)
1   G. Moore, *Reminiscences of the Impressionist Painters* (1906), cited in J. Lindsay, *Cézanne: His Life and Art*, New York, 1972, p. 207.
2   Paul Cézanne, letter to Émile Zola, 24 September 1879, cited in J. Rewald (ed.), *Paul Cézanne Letters*, trans. M. Kay, 3rd edn, Oxford, 1946, p. 139.
3   See B. Schwarz, in *Cézanne: Finished – Unfinished* (exh. cat.), eds F. Baumann, E. Benesch, W. Feilchenfeldt & K. A. Schröder, trans. I. Feder, M. Thorson Hause, S. Lèbe, J. Rosenthal & C. Spinner, Kunstforum Wien, Vienna, 2000, cat. no. 72.

Cat. no. 72 (Dean, pp. 93–4)
1   Théodore Duret, letter to Camille Pissarro, 6 December 1873, cited in R. R. Brettell, *A Day in the Country* (exh. cat.), Los Angeles County Museum, Los Angeles, 1984, p. 180.
2   Sir D. Y. Cameron, cited in Dr Charles Bage, memorandum to Trustees of the National Gallery of Victoria, 2 March 1928, Trustees' minutes, National Gallery of Victoria.

Cat. no. 73 (Dean, pp. 94–5)
1   Camille Pissarro, letter to Lucien Pissarro, 8 February 1897, in J. Bailly-Herzberg (ed.), *Correspondance de Camille Pissarro*, vol. IV, Paris, 1989, p. 324 (my translation).
2   R. R. Brettell, 'Camille Pissarro and Urban View Painting: An Introduction', in *The Impressionist and the City: Pissarro's Series Paintings* (exh. cat.), by R. R. Brettell & J. Pissarro, Dallas Museum of Art, Dallas, 1993, p. xv.
3   Camille Pissarro, letter to Georges Pissarro, 13 February 1897, in Bailly-Herzberg, vol. IV, p. 325 (my translation).
4   See Bailly-Herzberg, vol. IV, p. 327.
5   ibid., p. 330.
6   ibid., p. 347.
7   Camille Pissarro, letter to Georges Pissarro, 17 April 1897, in Bailly-Herzberg, vol. IV, p. 348 (my translation).

Cat. no. 74
1   See G. Burne-Jones, *Memorials of Edward Burne-Jones* (1904), vol. I, London, 1993, p. 115.
2   ibid., vol. II, p. 174.
3   ibid., vol. I, p. 308.

4 J. Christian, in *Burne-Jones: The Paintings, Graphic and Decorative Work of Sir Edward Burne-Jones 1833–98* (exh. cat.), Hayward Gallery, London, 1975, cat. no. 156; J. Christian, in *Edward Burne-Jones: Victorian Artist-Dreamer* (exh. cat.), by S. Wildman & J. Christian, Metropolitan Museum of Art, New York, 1998, cat. no. 120.

5 See J. Ruskin, 'School of Mythic Painting', in *The Works of John Ruskin*, eds E. T. Cook & A. Wedderburn, vol. XXXIII, London, 1905, pp. 296–7.

6 See J. Boardman, *The Great God Pan: The Survival of an Image*, London, 1997.

7 'The Grosvenor Exhibition', *Athenaeum*, no. 3106, 7 May 1887, p. 613.

Cat. no. 75 (Dean, pp. 113–14)

1 Alfred Sisley, letter to Adolphe Tavernier, 1893, in *Artists on Art: From the XIV to the XX Century*, eds R. Goldwater & M. Treves, New York, 1945, p. 309.

2 Alfred Sisley, letter to Claude Monet, 31 August 1881, cited in S. Patin, 'Veneux-Nadon and Moret-sur-Loing: 1880–1899', in *Alfred Sisley* (exh. cat.), ed. M. Stevens, Royal Academy of Arts, London, 1992, p. 184.

3 See M. Stevens, 'La Celle-Saint-Cloud to Louveciennes: 1865–1875', in Stevens, pp. 78–82.

4 See F. Daulte, *Alfred Sisley: Catalogue raisonné de l'oeuvre peint*, Lausanne, 1959, nos 728–731, reprs.

5 ibid., no. 731, repr. (private collection, Elberfeld, in 1959).

6 Sisley letter to Adolphe Tavernier, in Goldwater & Treves, p. 309.

Cat. no. 76 (Dean, pp. 114–15)

1 See F. Daulte, *Alfred Sisley: Catalogue raisonné de l'oeuvre peint*, Lausanne, 1959, no. 771, repr.

2 Alfred Sisley, letter to Adolphe Tavernier, 1893, in *Artists on Art: From the XIV to the XX Century*, eds R. Goldwater & M. Treves, New York, 1945, p. 309.

Cat. no. 77

1 See R. Free, in *Victorian Olympians* (exh. cat.), Art Gallery of New South Wales, Sydney, 1975, cat. no. 39; for the vase, see M. Bonollo, 'J. W. Waterhouse's *Ulysses and the Sirens*: Breaking with Tradition and Revealing Fears', *Art Bulletin of Victoria*, no. 40, 1999, fig. 2.

2 See W. Smith (ed.), *A Classical Dictionary of Biography, Mythology and Geography*, 8th edn, London, 1866, p. 785, repr. (engraving).

3 J. Harrison, 'The Myth of Odysseus and the Sirens', *Magazine of Art*, vol. X, 1887, p. 135, pl. IV.

4 See F. Turner, *The Greek Heritage in Victorian Britain*, New Haven, 1981, p. 123.

5 Information kindly provided by Dr Elizabeth Pemberton, School of Fine Arts, Classical Studies and Archaeology, University of Melbourne.

6 E. Pemberton, cited in A. Inglis & J. Long, *Queens and Sirens: Archaeology in 19th Century Art and Design* (exh. cat.), Geelong Art Gallery, Geelong, Victoria, 1998, cat. no. 9.

7 See Bonollo, pp. 19–30.

8 H. Herkomer, in 'Selection of Pictures for the National Gallery: Important Statement by Professor Herkomer', *Argus*, 23 July 1892, p. 5.

Cat. no. 78 (Dean, pp. 98–9)

1 Pierre Puvis de Chavannes, quoted in A. Brown Price, *Pierre Puvis de Chavannes* (exh. cat.), Van Gogh Museum, Amsterdam, 1994, cat. no. 134.

2 See M.-C. Boucher-Regnault, 'Décoration du Salon à l'Hôtel de Ville de Paris', in *Puvis de Chavannes 1824–1898* (exh. cat.), Grand Palais, Paris, 1976, p. 214.

3 Frank Gibson, letter to Felton Bequests' Committee, 1910, Felton Papers, National Gallery of Victoria (Gibson is inaccurate, however, in suggesting that the Melbourne picture precedes the two murals at the Hôtel de Ville).

4 Bernard Hall, memorandum, 5 and 19 April 1910, Felton Papers, National Gallery of Victoria.

Cat. no. 79 (Dean, pp. 27–8)

1 F. Haskell & N. Penny, *Taste and the Antique: The Lure of Classical Sculpture 1500–1900*, New Haven, 1981, p. 235, repr.

2 For an interesting group of photographs taken by Bonnard of Marthe, showing her posing naked in their apartment and in the garden (some of which images can be directly related to compositions of this period), see F. Heilbrun & P. Néagu (eds), *Bonnard photographe* (exh. cat.), Musée d'Orsay, Paris, 1987.

3 See J. & H. Dauberville, *Bonnard: Catalogue raisonné de l'oeuvre peint*, vol. I, Paris, 1965, p. 235, no. 227.

4 See S. Whitfield, in *Bonnard* (exh. cat.), by S. Whitfield & J. Elderfield, Tate Gallery, London, 1998, cat. no. 15, repr.

5 S. M. Newman, 'Nudes and Landscapes', in *Pierre Bonnard: The Graphic Art* (exh. cat.), by C. Ives, H. Giambruni & S. M. Newman, Metropolitan Museum of Art, New York, 1989, pp. 145–72.

Cat. no. 80

1 See F. Spalding, Gertler entry, in *The Dictionary of Art*, ed. J. Turner, vol. 12, London, 1996, p. 493.

2 Luke Gertler, letter to Jennie Moloney, 1 July 2000, National Gallery of Victoria files.

3 P. G. Konody, in *Observer* (1912), cited in A. Dixon, '*The Apple Woman and Her Husband* and *Agapanthus*: Two Paintings by Gertler', *Gallery: Monthly Magazine of the National Gallery Society of Victoria*, July 1987, p. 9.

4 *Star* (1912), cited in Dixon, p. 9.

5 D. H. Lawrence, letter to Mark Gertler, 9 October 1916, in N. Carrington (ed.), *Mark Gertler: Selected Letters*, London, 1965, p. 130.

Cat. no. 81 (Dean, pp. 46–7)

1 R. Delaunay, in *Du cubisme à l'art abstrait*, ed. P. Francastel, Paris, 1957, p. 67.

2 R. Delaunay, 1915, cited in M. Hoog, *Robert Delaunay*, trans. A. Sachs, New York, 1976, p. 80.

Cat. no. 82 (Dean, pp. 86–7)

1 Jacques Lipchitz, *Amedeo Modigliani* (1952), cited in J. Modigliani, *Modigliani: Man and Myth*, trans. E. Rowland Clifford, New York, 1958, p. 81.

2 See *Amedeo Modigliani 1884–1920* (exh. cat.), Musée d'Art Moderne de la Ville de Paris, Paris, 1981, cat. no. 36, repr.

Cat. no. 83

1 René Magritte, cited in E. de Wilde, foreword to G. Ollinger-Zinque & F. Leen (eds), *Magritte 1898–1967* (exh. cat.), trans. T. Barnard Davidson, T. Alkins & M. Clarke, Royal Museums of Fine Arts of Belgium, Brussels, 1998, p. 11.

2 Lautréamont, *Les Chants de Maldoror* (1864), trans. G. Wernham, New York, 1946, p. 263.

3 A. Breton, *Manifestoes of Surrealism*, trans. R. Seaver & H. R. Lane, Ann Arbor, Michigan, 1969, p. 14.

Cat. no. 85

1 Paul Nash, quoted in R. Cardinal, *The Landscape Vision of Paul Nash*, London, 1989, p. 104.

2 Paul Nash, 'Picture History' (1943–45) (unpub.), cited in *Paul Nash: Paintings and Watercolours* (exh. cat.), Tate Gallery, London, 1975, cat. no. 202.

3 ibid.

4 See Cardinal, p. 117.

5 Paul Nash, quoted in J. Rothenstein, *Modern English Painters*, vol. 2, London, 1962, p. 53.

Cat. no. 86

1 Francis Bacon, in D. Sylvester, *Interviews with Francis Bacon 1962–1979*, London, 1980, p. 19.

2 ibid., p. 12.

3 See *Francis Bacon* (exh. cat.), Centre National d'Art et de Culture, Georges Pompidou, Paris, 1996, cat. no. 9, repr.

4 Francis Bacon, in Sylvester, *Interviews*, p. 12.

5 D. Sylvester, *Francis Bacon: The Human Body* (exh. cat.), Hayward Gallery, London, 1998, p. 14.

6 Francis Bacon, in Sylvester, *Interviews*, p. 66.

Cat. no. 87

1 See V. Monnier, *Balthus: Catalogue raisonné de l'oeuvre complet*, Paris, 1999, p. 157, no. P201, repr.

2 ibid., p. 163, no. P221, repr.

3 ibid., p. 153, no. P182, repr. p. 152.

4 ibid., p. 253, no. D648, repr.

Cat. no. 88

1 D. Hockney, *David Hockney by David Hockney*, ed. N. Stangos, London, 1976, p. 43.

2 R. Hughes, *Nothing If Not Critical: Selected Essays on Art and Artists*, London, 1990, p. 338.

3 See *David Hockney: A Retrospective* (exh. cat.), Los Angeles County Museum of Art, Los Angeles, 1988, cat. no. 12, repr.

4 M. Livingstone, *David Hockney*, London, 1981, p. 46.

5 Hockney, p. 92.

6 ibid., p. 89.

7 David Hockney, quoted in Hughes, p. 338.